# The environment and international relations

*The Environment and International Relations* examines the relevance of the theoretical approaches currently used in international relations to the study of the global environment. Rather than following the usual case-study approach, this book covers both theoretical issues and a range of key international processes.

The opening chapters deal with the neorealism–liberal institutionalism debate that has dominated the study of international environmental cooperation; they also bring a variety of other perspectives – from normative theory through gender studies to international political economy – to bear on such issues as environmental security and global environmental change. In the second part of the book, the emphasis shifts towards the organisations and processes involved in the formulation of global environmental policy. Here the contributors discuss the monitoring and implementation of environmental agreements, the relations between science, power and policy, and the role of trade interests and ideology in international negotiations on the environment.

The critical importance of environmental issues for international relations is now well established. This is a book that no student of international relations or environmental policy can afford to ignore.

**John Vogler** is Professor of International Relations at Liverpool John Moores University and convenor of the ESRC International Relations of Global Environmental Change group. **Mark F. Imber** is Lecturer in International Relations at the University of St Andrews.

D1166393

# GLOBAL ENVIRONMENTAL CHANGE SERIES

Edited by Michael Redclift, *Wye College, University of London*; Martin Parry, *University of Oxford*; Timothy O'Riordan, *University of East Anglia*; Robin Grove-White, *University of Lancaster*; and Brian Robson, *University of Manchester*.

The Global Environmental Change Series, published in association with the ESRC Global Environmental Change Programme, emphasizes the way that human aspirations, choices and everyday behaviour influence changes in the global environment. In the aftermath of UNCED and Agenda 21, this series helps crystallize the contribution of social science thinking to global change and explores the impact of global changes on the development of social sciences.

**Social theory and the global environment**
Edited by Michael Redclift and Ted Benton

**Global warming and emergy demand**
Edited by Terry Barker, Paul Ekins and Nick Johnstone

# The environment and international relations

Edited by John Vogler and Mark F. Imber

Global Environmental Change Programme

London and New York

*ftw*
*AKB1616*

First published 1996
by Routledge
11 New Fetter Lane, London EC4P 4EE

Simultaneously published in the USA and Canada
by Routledge
29 West 35th Street, New York, NY 10001

© 1996 John Vogler and Mark F. Imber

Typeset in Times by LaserScript, Mitcham, Surrey
Printed and bound in Great Britain by
Mackays of Chatham PLC, Chatham, Kent

*British Library Cataloguing in Publication Data*
A catalogue record for this book is available from the British Library.

*Library of Congress Cataloguing in Publication Data*
A catalogue record for this book has been requested.

ISBN 0–415–12214–7 (hbk)
ISBN 0–415–12215–5 (pbk)

To Our Parents

Catherine and Donald Vogler
Alan W. Imber and the memory of
Marjorie Imber (1921–1977)

# Contents

# Figures

# Contributors

**Sonja Boehmer-Christiansen** Reader at the School of Geography and Earth Resources, University of Hull

**Charlotte Bretherton** Senior Lecturer at the School of Social Studies, Liverpool John Moores University

**Hugh C. Dyer** Lecturer in International Studies at the Institute for International Studies, University of Leeds

**Owen Greene** Senior Lecturer in International Relations and Peace Studies, Department of Peace Studies, University of Bradford

**David Humphreys** Research Fellow in Global Environmental Change at the Open University

**Mark F. Imber** Lecturer in International Relations, Department of International Relations, University of St Andrews

**Roderick Ogley** Emeritus Reader in International Relations, University of Sussex

**Matthew Paterson** Lecturer in International Relations, at the University of Keele

**Julian Saurin** Lecturer in International Relations and ESRC-GEC Fellow, School of African and Asian Studies, University of Sussex

**John Vogler** School of Social Science, Liverpool John Moores University

**Peter Willetts** Reader in International Relations, Department of Systems Science, City University

**Marc Williams** Lecturer in International Relations, School of African and Asian Studies, University of Sussex

# Acknowledgements

The editors would like to record their gratitude to a number of institutions and individuals whose cooperation has been essential to the successful completion of this project: The British International Studies Association (BISA), which first provided financial support for the creation of the BISA-Environment Study Group; the Economic and Social Research Council (ESRC) GEC Programme, which thereafter provided travel funds over two years to enable the BISA group to hold a seminar series, 'The International Relations of Global Environmental Change', at which early drafts of the work contained herein were first subject to peer review. We are grateful to Peter Willetts and the Department of Systems Science at City University for hosting our meetings; to all the other members of the BISA-GEC groups whose comments were gratefully received on the earlier drafts of this work; and to Caroline Thomas who provided frank and decisive advice on the original publishing proposal.

We are also grateful to a number of staff in the secretarial and computing services at our two institutions. At Liverpool John Moores University: Phil Cubbin, Nicky Davies, Lynette Heppard, Elaine Hodkinson, Linda Pringle and Cathy Renton; and at the University of St Andrews: John Ball, Anne Cameron and Gina Wilson.

# 1 Introduction

The environment in International Relations:
legacies and contentions

*John Vogler*

The modern academic study of International Relations (IR) was a consequence of
the great inter-state conflicts of the first half of the twentieth century. Its problematic was war, endemic insecurity and the possibilities of peace through
international cooperation, and its focus was upon nation-state actors in an international system without centralised authority. In the dominant Realist conception, a Hobbesian anarchy prevailed in which order might only precariously be
maintained through a balance of power. Twentieth-century political Realism, as
most famously expounded by Carr (1939) and Morgenthau (1948), was in itself
a conscious reaction to political and military events of the 1930s and 1940s, and
in particular to the way in which they supposedly demonstrated the bankruptcy of
an earlier academic orthodoxy, liberal internationalism – or, as the Realists would
style it, Idealism or Utopianism. The latter flourished in the aftermath of the Great
War and brought an essentially optimistic and liberal approach to the project of
reforming the international system through the building of cooperative institutions and the development of international law.

The response of academic IR to the emergent problems of global environmental change (GEC) inevitably reflects this intellectual legacy. Just as modern
Realism was a reaction to the rise of Hitler, the collapse of the collective security
aspirations of the League of Nations and the onset of the Second World War, so
in lesser fashion the recent spate of interest in international environmental
politics is, with certain exceptions (Young 1977, 1982, 1989; Boardman 1981;
Kay and Jacobson 1983), a fairly direct reaction to political events. Others
(McCormick 1989; Thomas 1992; Brenton 1994) have charted the rise in salience
of GEC issues during the 1980s. 'Ozone diplomacy' led to the 1987 Montreal
Protocol, and climate change and even biodiversity became 'high politics' issues.
The culmination was the Rio 'Earth Summit' of 1992, or more properly the
United Nations Conference on Environment and Development (UNCED). The
latter was estimated to have been the largest diplomatic gathering ever held, and
it is, thus, small wonder that by the time of its inception in 1989 the environment
was beginning to attract the interest of IR specialists. The British International
Studies Association, whose GEC seminars supported by the Economic and Social
Research Council form the basis of this book, was itself created in 1990.[1]

It is fair to say that this surge of interest generally led to the incorporation of GEC issues into the existing IR paradigm. The introduction to an influential collection of articles makes the point clearly. The central problem for the IR scholar is seen as a variant of that which preoccupied earlier generations of Realists and liberal internationalists:

> Can a fragmented and often highly conflictual political system made up of over 170 sovereign states and numerous other actors achieve the high (and historically unprecedented) levels of co-operation and policy co-ordination needed to manage environmental problems on a global scale?
>
> (Hurrell and Kingsbury 1992: 1)

The connection between environmental matters and the abiding concerns of IR can be traced most explicitly in the current debate over whether traditional concepts of national security, involving armed threats, should be expanded to comprehend a 'new' range of environmental threats to human well-being. Yet, important as security concerns are, they have not been at the heart of the IR community's response to its discovery of GEC issues. Instead, much of the current work on GEC problems can be seen as an extension of long-standing concerns with international cooperation as a means to 'managing' the global economy. In this area, the dominant approach for the last twenty years has been that of regime analysis. Such work is often 'policy driven', involving attempts to solve the immediate problems of international environmental cooperation.

Although the contributors to this volume cannot divorce themselves entirely from questions of international cooperation, the debates that occurred within the Group nonetheless had a wider scope. No consensus view emerges from the chapters below, but they do reflect both an attempt to rethink and broaden the treatment of environmental change within International Relations and a parallel awareness that this process may have implications for the discipline itself. In this sense the present volume follows the course set by the first in the Global Environmental Change series where it is argued that, while environmental debate profits from the insights of social science (including in this case insights into the political and institutional bases of international cooperation), there is also a reciprocal benefit for the social sciences themselves. Two reasons are suggested for this. First, the environmental crisis exposes 'to critical examination some very basic "settled" assumptions of the "mainstream" traditions of the social sciences'. Second, environmental issues reflect 'several long-standing and unresolved disputes within social theory' (Redclift and Benton 1994: 2). In the experience of the Group, this is as true for international relations as it is for sociology and social theory.

## ENVIRONMENTAL ISSUES IN THE STUDY OF INTERNATIONAL RELATIONS

To say that the GEC problems were 'discovered' by IR scholars after they had already become matters of foreign policy concern suggests that there had been little or no previous interest in environmental matters. A reading of some current literature might well convey this impression, and it is, of course, true that the awareness of certain environmental problems (such as stratospheric ozone-layer depletion) and indeed the very concept of global-scale change are both of recent origin. Nonetheless, states have been concluding agreements about their mutual resource and environmental interests for more than a century (Carroll 1988: 17–18). Since 1945 – to judge from the number of agreements made, organisations created and conferences convened – there has been an exponential increase in international environmental concern. Much of the framework of current environmental regimes, in the areas of maritime pollution or trans-boundary air pollution, was in place well before the 1980s, but as an essentially technical and 'functional' activity received little public or, it has to be said, academic attention. Often, environmental matters were encountered as a subsidiary aspect of the extensive study of the law of the sea and the disposition of sea-bed mineral resources, or of the special demilitarised Antarctic Treaty regime.[2]

It is not the case that the natural environment has never been considered in IR writing, although in most analyses it was taken as either an implicit or explicit constant in human affairs. The way in which the term 'environment' has come, only recently, to connote the geo- and biosphere is significant. The etymology of the term can be traced to the Old French 'envirroner' ('to surround'), and the standard English meaning has generally been 'external conditions and surroundings'. It was in this way that the term was utilised by, for example, Sprout and Sprout (1968), who were responsible for several well-known discussions of 'man–milieu relations' in politics. The natural environment was only part of the milieu or 'operational environment' of decision-makers, and attention was focused upon the implications of technological change and the way in which, over time, geographic constants were reinterpreted. This approach was in response to older geopolitical debates (reflected in the works of Mahan (1890) and Mackinder (1904, 1919)) concerning the determinative role of 'physical reality' over the patterns of power and supremacy found in relations between nations. For Sprout and Sprout, physical conditions may have remained relatively stable, but their political significance was constantly altered by technological change (this was the era in which long-range rocketry transformed the spatial bases of strategy) and by shifts in the 'psychological environment' of foreign policy. This represents quite a sophisticated interpretation of relationships and resources which were seen by the dominant Realist school merely as constituents of national power capability. Indeed, the leading work in the Realist canon, by Morgenthau (1948: 109–12), devotes only three and a half of its 500 or more pages to natural resources. They are seen as a 'relatively stable' but important element of national power alongside others such as population, industrial capacity and national character and morale – the decisive factor being the 'quality of society and government' (ibid.: 132).

While sharing an overriding concern with the power relations between states, not all commentators regarded the physical environment as a constant. In a now-forgotten book published in 1915, Ellsworth Huntington advanced the thesis that there are long cycles of climate change, and (Huntington 1919) that a form of climatic geopolitics might be discerned in history. Shortly after the Second World War, Wheeler (1946) elaborated this view in ways which have surprising resonance today. The climate moved in 500-year rhythms, with the termination of the current cycle around 1980. Climate, culture and human activity were 'fluctuating back and forth in rhythmic fashion as a vast, complex but integrated whole' and there is 'no question but that nations or empires rise and fall on tides of climatic change' (Wheeler 1946: 346–7). In what might seem a premonition of the Intergovernmental Panel on Climate Change, the author advised world leaders to be cognisant of the fact that 'an intensive study of the climate of the past will ultimately lead to an accurate prediction of trends far ahead into the future' (ibid.: 349). However, this cyclical process would produce the same social and political effects as in the past, mainly through influencing the 'vitality' and 'energy level' of nations. Elsewhere, a form of global warming with more than cyclical effects was already being discussed which provided Russia, Scandinavia and Canada with their 'place in the sun' and showed a potential to melt the polar ice caps. A 1949 article in *Science* thus gave the following investment advice:

> anyone desiring to make use of this information for long term investment in northern real estate should buy high land, however, for the ocean level will rise roughly 150 feet as the ice caps disappear.
>
> (Mills 1949: 352)

Most prescient was John von Neumann, the co-founder of game theory. In the year before his death, he pondered whether 'we could survive technology' now that it threatened the finite resources of the earth by removing the geographical and political *lebensraum* that had, hitherto, served as a safety mechanism. Noting the likely impact of increasing carbon dioxide emissions on the world climate and the possibility of sea-level rises, he was mainly concerned with deliberate and possibly hostile human interventions to modify the natural environment. His conclusions foreshadow the concerns of a later generation:

> Extensive human intervention would deeply affect the atmosphere's general circulation, which depends on the earth's rotation and intensive solar heating of the tropics . . . . All this will merge each nation's affairs with those of every other, more thoroughly than the threat of nuclear war or any other war may already have done.
>
> (von Neumann 1955: 248)

It required a combination of circumstances in the early 1970s to focus political and academic attention on natural environmental and resource issues, and it is worth reiterating that in international relations they are usually inseparable. After decades of technological optimism, Malthusian 'limits to growth' were redis- covered in the controversial computer simulations published as a Club of Rome report under that name (Meadows *et al.* 1972, 1992). In terms of formal inter- national politics, the first UN Conference on the Human Environment (UNCHE) held at Stockholm in 1972 was a landmark in many ways. It was the starting point for much institutional activity centred upon the new United Nations Environment Programme (UNEP); and in the preparation and proceedings of the Conference itself, what was to become a persistent linkage between the environmental concerns of the North and the development demands of the South was already evident. The Conference enunciated twenty-six Principles and no less than 109 recommendations ranging from restrictions on the use of DDT to the call for a moratorium on commercial whaling. Stockholm excited a relatively brief flurry of interest within the IR community (Kay and Skolnikoff 1972). Although commentators frequently employed the metaphor of 'spaceship earth', the focus of this Conference was still upon 'point source pollution' and its transboundary effects. Its approach was best summed up in the wording of Principle 21, a piece of diplomatic craftsmanship that combined Southern demands for economic sovereignty with developed-world concern over responsibility for transboundary pollution. States had the

> sovereign right to exploit their own resources pursuant to their own environmental policies, and the responsibility to ensure that activities within their jurisdiction and control did not cause damage to the environment of other States or of other areas beyond the limits of national jurisdiction.[3]

In the next year, the Middle East war and the quadrupling of the price of crude oil by Arab producers were to have profound economic and political effects, and gave immediate point to the debates about resource scarcity and the limits to growth. The pressure created by the oil crisis was the indispensable basis for the development of the so-called North–South dialogue in which Northern governments, throughout the mid-1970s, listened to Southern demands for the reform of the international economy – demands articulated by the Group of 77 in the UN as the programme for a New International Economic Order.

The academic response to these events betrayed a shift away from the orthodox Realist analysis of power relations towards a new appreciation of the economic dimensions of international politics and above all of the complexities of interdependence. The oil crisis demonstrated the extent of the mutual vulnerability of societies. Keohane and Nye (1977) provided the most influential treatment of the new condition of 'complex interdependence' where societies were increasingly interconnected at various levels, where the priorities of foreign policy were reordered and where the use of force, at least between advanced countries, was of decreasing relevance. In this 'transformation' there was an abiding concern with a loss of control on the part of governments (Morse 1976), which mirrored an immediate concern with the diminished position of the USA. Although common vulnerability to environmental degradation could be regarded as the ultimate form of interdependence, this aspect did not become a focus of attention. In the hiatus between Stockholm and the preparations for UNCED in the late 1980s, international environmental relations remained the rather narrow preserve of a handful of specialists (Boardman 1981; Kay and Jacobson 1983; Caldwell 1984; Young 1977, 1982).

The dominating concern was with the management of international economic relations in the aftermath of the 1971 collapse of the Bretton Woods system of managed exchange rates and the recession induced by the oil-price 'shocks' of 1973 and 1979. It was hardly surprising that a great deal of academic effort was devoted to the problem of international economic cooperation and coordination in the 'management' of economic relations that seemed to be spinning out of control. The issues were conceptualised as an extension of the classic problem in international relations: how to provide some form of order and governance in an 'anarchic' system composed of sovereign nation states. An institutional approach involving the study of regimes – comprising systems of international principles, norms, rules and decision-making procedures – provided, and continues to provide, the dominant mode of analysis (Krasner 1983). Arguments about the origins, significance and fate of such regimes were clearly related to earlier debates about security between liberal internationalists and Realists (Strange 1982). The overwhelming concern until the end of the 1980s (and perhaps still) was with the institutions for global economic management.

Environmental degradation was inextricably related to the whole complex of economic, resource, population and North–South development issues, but it still did not occupy the centre of the stage. The Brandt Report (1980), which attempted to suggest management solutions to the twin problems of recession and underdevelopment, mentioned, but did not prioritise, environmental sustainability. In the interim between this Report and Brundtland (1987) – which can be seen as its successor – something clearly occurred which altered the salience of environmental questions, just at the time when the Second Cold War brought the old security and nuclear concerns back to the forefront of international attention, and when the resource anxieties of the 1970s, along with the North–South dialogue, appeared to recede. A convincing history of all of this has yet to be written, but what *is* evident is that by the late 1980s, and in the preparatory period prior to UNCED, there was a clear and measurable increase in the level of public and governmental environmental concern, which was now set in the context of fears about the scale of global change. The ESRC GEC programme itself and the current wave of IR research and writing were a direct consequence.

Why had there been so little previous interest? The simple answer, emerging from the preceding paragraphs, is that the discipline suffers from an excessively close association with policy questions and tends to respond, often rather belatedly, to the shifting international political agenda. In the main this is undoubtedly true. However, the continuing dominance of Realist thought has also been a hindrance. Initially leading to a consideration of natural resources and the environment from the perspective of geopolitics, the Realist analysis simply excludes or marginalises environmental concerns, even where they have profound (though less immediate) security implications. It took long enough for neorealism to come to terms with economic variables, and as a number of the contributing authors to this volume point out, even neorealism is intellectually incapable of embracing questions of ecological interdependence. Realism makes positivist claims to objective knowledge and explicitly excludes values not associated with national interest. It would not admit that universalistic values of the type associated with the preservation of the biosphere can have political relevance in a world of selfish and competing nation states. In parallel with the intellectual dominance of Realism there emerged the behavioural social-scientific approaches to IR which caused so much controversy in the 1960s and 1970s, and also militated against a full consideration of environmental issues. The behavioural approach was so focused on the observation and explanation of human beings, particularly as political and military decision-makers, that it was generally incapable of taking an ecologically holistic view of the human species. According to many critics, it shared with the Western scientific tradition, from which it was derived, a disastrously manipulative orientation towards the natural environment. In IR, this was coupled, as Vasquez (1983) has shown, with an implicit acceptance of the assumptions of state-centric Realism.

All this may help to explain why in the period after Stockholm environmental issues were regarded by most IR scholars as a technical specialism peripheral to their interests. However, this situation no longer pertains. It has already been argued that academic IR tends to echo 'real world' policy agendas, but there may well be something more profound at work in the awakening of interest in the environment. The key here may lie in the paradigmatic shift that was clearly evident in the interval between Stockholm and Rio. Simply stated, it involved the shift to an awareness of *global* rather than purely localised or transboundary phenomena. Stratospheric ozone-layer depletion and the projected climate change associated with the enhanced 'greenhouse effect' have a truly global scope. The extraordinary interconnection between the issues involved and the extraordinary range of interdependencies evident from even a cursory examination of global environmental change bear upon the fundamental concerns of students of international relations and international political economy. It was, therefore, no longer possible to *pigeonhole* environmental issues in International Relations as a narrow technical specialism.

## THE INSTITUTIONALIST MAINSTREAM

The response on the part of academic IR to the international environmental politics of the late 1980s and early 1990s was essentially in the liberal-institutionalist or – as Smith (1993) calls it – pluralist tradition. As reflected in works such as Young (1989), Mathews (1991), Porter and Brown (1991), Hurrell and Kingsbury (1992) and Haas, Keohane and Levy (1993), the discipline was resolutely 'problem-solving' rather than 'critical' in its approach.[4] The problematic was set from outside, by the Brundtland Report, by the Hague Declaration of 1989, by national funding agencies and by those involved in the UNCED process. All of them singled out international cooperation as a key determinant of sustainable development. In the words of the Chairman of UNCED:

> The need for international cooperation is inescapable and growing almost
> exponentially . . . the United Nations and its system of agencies, organizations
> and programs . . . provide the indispensable structure and fora on which
> international co-operation depends . . . . They represent not the precursors of
> world government but the basic framework for a world system of governance
> which is imperative to the effective functioning of global society.
>
> (Maurice Strong, cited in Haas, Keohane and Levy 1993: 6)

The problem was, once again, conceptualised as the management of interdependence in a system of sovereign states lacking the kind of central authorities
which are assumed (often quite erroneously) to be capable of providing order and
regulation within domestic societies. A contemporary formulation expresses this
in terms of 'governance without government' (Rosenau and Cziempel 1992).
Awareness of the close interconnections between an increasingly globalised
economic system and global-scale environmental change made the contrast with
a political system fragmented into rival sovereignties even more compelling. The
environment was thus added to a list of pressing issues confronting statesmen.
According to one widely cited analysis, environmental issues were:

> now established on the diplomatic agenda, but a degree of worldwide alarm
> and the resulting public pressure to act are still not felt in executive offices and
> legislatures.
>
> (Newsom 1988/9: 41)

The requirement was for cooperative international management, in much the same
way as ministers, bureaucrats and commentators fretted about their inability to exert
collective control over the footloose operations of deregulated financial markets.

The study of cooperation tends to assume the efficacy of international law and
organisation. In many cases it builds directly upon regime analysis, which, as we
have seen, was principally directed during the 1970s and 1980s towards
understanding international-level economic management. Now the focus is upon
'Institutions for the Earth' (Haas, Keohane and Levy 1993) or the 'Global
Commons' (Vogler 1995), or the reform of the United Nations system (Imber
1994). In line with a similar interest in the role of institutions elsewhere in the
social sciences (in economics, for example – see North 1990), this new approach
assumes institutions to be critical to the setting of agendas, to the coordination of
policy at the international level and most significantly to the environmentally
related behaviour of governments and other actors. The dominant school comprises what Paterson, in this volume, describes as neoliberal institutionalism,
heavily influenced by the theoretical assumptions of both microeconomic and
game theory. Above all, it assumes the efficacy and indeed necessity of international institutions in managing the behaviour responsible for environmental
degradation. Its neorealist counterpart, the main protagonist in debates about
international cooperation, is less convinced of the efficacy of institutions *per se*
and places great emphasis on the underlying power structure, and in particular the
requirement for hegemonic leadership.

Highly influential in any discussion of international cooperation and GEC, and often erroneously cited in discussions of climate change, is the regime for stratospheric ozone centred upon the 1987 Montreal Protocol. For environmental specialists, this has almost assumed a paradigmatic status equivalent to that once enjoyed in strategic studies circles by the Cuban Missile Crisis of 1962. It demonstrates both the need for, and effectiveness of, international-level rules (to maintain incentives to develop ozone-friendly technology) and, above all, the way in which policy can be rapidly developed in line with advancing scientific understanding (Benedick 1991).

Although the efficacy of regime institutions tends to be taken for granted in most of the mainstream writing, this assumption has always been subject to challenge. The most influential collection of essays on regime analysis made this abundantly clear more than a decade ago (Krasner 1983). It was only those occupying a broadly liberal or 'Grotian' position who were happy to assume the independent role of regimes in shaping state behaviour. On the other hand, Realist or Marxist commentators would treat them as mere 'epiphenomena', the product either of power (notably hegemonic) relationships or of the underlying material and class bases for the international political and legal system (see Williams, Paterson and Saurin in this volume).

Those of a liberal-internationalist persuasion proceed to investigate the ways in which the undoubted influence of institutions can be made more effective. Effective regimes do not 'supersede or overshadow states' but instead, according to Haas, Keohane and Levy (1993: 24), 'create networks over, around and within states that generate the means and incentives for effective cooperation'. The task for the researcher is to 'try to ascertain the conditions under which they have been more or less effective in so doing'. This is a relatively restrained view. Others have perceived a global policy process (Soroos 1986), and even some governmental representatives in the Hague Declaration of 1989 spoke openly of the imperatives for a supranational global environmental authority (Porter and Brown 1991: 153). The legacy of internationalist and Idealist thinking is clear in the normative purpose of mainstream writing, much of which has a quite technical character, relating as it does to the specifics of negotiation (Sjostedt 1993; Susskind 1994) or the elaboration of international law (Sand 1991, 1992; see also Ogley in this volume).

This legacy is also evident in research on the role of 'epistemic communities' (Haas 1990, 1990a, 1992) which stresses the role of transnational expert groups in developing environmentally desirable agreements in the face of resistance from reluctant politicians. As Haas himself says, this research is to be seen as an adjunct to a broader institutionalist approach, yet it is also clearly descended from earlier functionalist thought, associated in the first instance with Mitrany and others who sought the means towards a 'working peace system' through de-politicised technical cooperation. The proponents of 'epistemic' communities emphasise another key defining characteristic of international environmental cooperation, namely the critical interface between science and policy. This is something relatively novel for statecraft and has attracted much attention at academic and policy levels, where foreign offices have had to contend with a range of scientific and technical interests. The problem is usually stated in terms of the difficulty of persuading short-sighted and narrowly self-interested national politicians to respond to enlightened scientific prediction in a timely way. Once again, the Montreal Protocol provides a model, and the ongoing work of the significantly named Intergovernmental Panel on Climate Change gives an example of the problems involved in, and prospects for, the generation of consensual scientific knowledge and its application to international policy-making (Boehmer-Christiansen mounts a critical investigation in this volume).

Smith (1993) has argued that what has been described here as the mainstream approach to the International Relations of GEC remains at the margin of the discipline as a whole. In his view, most exponents of the IR of global environmental change share an essentially uncontested pluralist viewpoint. For Smith this is doubly unfortunate because, on the one hand, such exponents can be consigned to irrelevance by the still-dominant Realist school of power politics, while, on the other hand, missing the opportunity to engage in a variety of critical, normative, post-structuralist and gender debates that have opened up elsewhere in the discipline.

The pluralist label is appropriate if it means that most existing work acknowledges an international system in which there are a plurality of issues and where actors do not, as in the cruder versions of Realism, exhibit a monomaniacal pursuit of power. However, it is one thing to use the rhetoric of plural interests and values and quite another to develop and utilise an operational model of the international system which effectively supplants state-centric approaches by positing a variety of significant actors and connections across national frontiers. While most commentators on international environmental politics stress the particular significance of non-governmental organisations (NGOs) and, in line with the liberal-internationalist tradition, 'the rising influence of international public opinion' (Mathews 1991: 32), their focus of analysis remains resolutely fixed upon the interaction between nation states. International cooperation is, in effect, regarded as inter-state or intergovernmental cooperation. This may reflect the judgement, of which most Realists would approve, that despite all the rhetoric of sovereignty's erosion, state governments remain the essential agents of environmental improvement. For those of a more liberal inclination, it may also relate to the parsimony associated with the microeconomic and game-theoretical analysis which has been a key feature in the development of theories concerning the creation, maintenance and significance of regimes.

Attempts have been made to invoke and even alter the Realist agenda in discussions of the redefinition of security (Buzan 1991, and the critique by Dyer in this volume). While often well intentioned, they run the risk, as Deudney (1990) and others have argued, of co-option, such that environmental questions are considered as an item somewhere near the bottom of a list of militarised national security priorities. In any case, environmental and orthodox national security concerns are usually regarded as being profoundly antithetical in almost every possible respect.

This leaves Smith's other major reason for marginalisation: the theoretical isolation in which, he claims, exponents of the International Relations of the environment exist. They tend to be 'a very closed group, nearly all of whom share the same theoretical assumptions . . . insiders who work within a theoretical tradition, rather than questioning the boundaries and assumptions of that tradition' (Smith 1993: 40). Opinions may differ as to the validity of this assertion, although a great deal of evidence in its favour can be derived from reading the standard technical literature on international environmental cooperation. Most of the participants in the GEC seminars would disagree with Smith's assertion as regards their own work, but the statement actually provides both a challenge and a justification for the present volume.

## CONTRIBUTIONS TO THIS VOLUME

The contributions collected here and the discussions that they inspired in the seminars are critical and theoretically diverse. They are rather arbitrarily divided into two sections. The first is avowedly theoretical and considers the 'boundaries and assumptions' of the existing tradition, such as it is, of the study of the international relations of the environment. Dyer writes from the standpoint of normative international relations theory, while Paterson views orthodox accounts of international cooperation from the perspective of 'critical theory'. Saurin provides a radical reinterpretation of the meaning of the environment in IR from a critical social-ecological perspective, while the chapter by Bretherton includes a feminist account of the various roles that have been ascribed to women in discussions of GEC. Willetts' contribution provides a contrast to the others in this section with its reassertion of positivist epistemology within a global politics model.

A wide-ranging account, which helps to place those that follow in context, is provided by Williams' essay on international political economy and GEC. Much contemporary work on international cooperation, including the debates between neorealist and neoliberal regime theorists scrutinised by Paterson, may be regarded as falling properly within the field of International Political Economy (IPE). Saurin's analysis of global capitalist accumulation and the environmental crisis is also located squarely within a different tradition of IPE.

Arguing that the engagement of orthodox IR in environmental issues has served to 'reproduce orthodoxy', Williams considers whether International Political Economy allows a more satisfactory perspective. IPE shares many of the theoretical assumptions of orthodox International Relations (of which it may be seen as a sub-field) but it has the further advantage of focusing upon those economic structures and processes which are directly responsible for environmental degradation. Unfortunately, the three main approaches to IPE, which are derived from realist, liberal and Marxist paradigms, are all burdened by techno- and anthropocentric assumptions serving to externalise environmental variables. Nonetheless, the 'expanded terrain' of IPE does have significant academic advantages especially if it proves possible to incorporate ecological rather than merely environmental economics.

The second part of the volume puts a more concrete focus on the organisations and processes that usually figure in treatments of global environmental issues. Most of the contributors in this section have themselves been actively involved in detailed and policy-related research on international organisation (Imber), scientific advice and policy (Boehmer-Christiansen), and the development and implementation of international agreements (Ogley, Humphreys and Greene). They provide a great deal of commentary on current environmental issues while at the same time attempting to adopt a reflective and critical stance towards their own work. Thus, the second part of this volume is determinedly not a survey of the post-Rio landscape of international environmental politics but instead a counterpart to the broader theoretical concerns raised in the first.

A key question for all participants (and indeed for the whole GEC series) is whether IR (or social science generally) should merely incorporate GEC as an issue amongst others or whether it must itself be fundamentally altered. If the British ESRC Global Environmental Change Programme has a slogan, it is 'to take GEC to the heart of the social sciences and the social sciences to the heart of GEC'. The debate within IR reflects the tension between these two objectives. On the one hand, scholars are naturally concerned to apply their existing knowledge of the workings of the international system to the new and complex problems of global environmental diplomacy. The obvious contribution to be made here, as we have seen, is in the study of international cooperation. An excellent example of the potential that this affords is provided by the coordination of arms-control experience with monitoring and verification procedures as a means to the implementation of international environmental agreements (see Greene in this volume). What it does mean is that GEC is treated as another issue on the agenda of international politics, to be handled through the normal channels with reference to existing precedents and conceptions found in IR. However, GEC may not simply be 'another issue', and 'taking it to the heart of the social sciences' may require the radical revision of those sciences. Saurin asserts that the 'processes of global environmental change are subversive of both the theory and practice of orthodox IR'. By regarding GEC as an external problem to be handled by state bureaucracies and international organisations, and 'by continuing to focus on those institutional practices of modernity which have caused the environmental problem in the first place, prevailing scholarship misses the opportunity to step outside the premises of its own entrapment'.

Beneath this overarching concern three sets of issues recur which can be characterised as critical responses to three cardinal assumptions found in much of the existing work in IR. The first assumes the primacy of national interests (whether in terms of relative power maximisation in Realist theory or in terms of absolute wealth maximisation in neoliberal accounts). This assumption neglects the normative dimension of politics, both in theory and in practice, which is essential to debates about environment and development and emerges strongly from the empirical study of political activism and change. The second assumption relates to the basic ontology of modern IR and its definition as the study of the relations between states. The argument here is that it may be impossible to comprehend the causes of environmental concern within a state-centric paradigm, and that the retention of this paradigm serves to avoid such questions in favour of the consideration of inter-state 'solutions'. There is a growing body of opinion which states that even the latter cannot be adequately theorised in terms of the orthodox inter-state assumptions, and that some form of global politics model is more appropriate. The third set of assumptions centres around ideas about science and epistemology. For some time, mainstream IR (involving both Realism and behavioural social science) embraced an essentially positivist epistemology involving the relative neglect of normative theorising (as noted above). The vigorous intellectual challenge to which this has been subjected is reflected in the contributions to this volume. The point has already been made that this challenge may make it easier than it was in the past to come to terms with environmental issues. There is also a wider debate about science and its 'privileged discourse' in environmental politics. At the immediate level this involves questions about the interface between scientific expertise and policy-making. At a deeper level, however, it provokes speculation about the underlying responsibility of Western rationalistic civilisation for the global environmental predicament. Discussions within the field of International Relations can hardly be immune from this.

## INTERESTS, VALUES AND NORMS

The starting point of Dyer's chapter is provided by the standard and essentially Realist conception of security. From the perspective of normative theory, he criticises attempts to encompass environmental issues within the existing national security agenda and proceeds to explore the implications of environmental security as a universal value. Normative theorising has had enormous historical significance in the development of the discipline, not least in the Realist–Idealist debates of the inter-war period, but it was eclipsed during the Cold War. Renewed interest in normative theory is particularly relevant to the international relations of GEC because of the stress that it places upon the dichotomy between communitarian and cosmopolitan traditions (Brown 1992; Hoffman 1994). It is exactly this tension, between citizen and national community on the one hand and a broader conception of human beings as a single species within the global biosphere on the other, which is at the heart of much of the discussion of GEC. For Dyer, environmental security and national security are alternative values arising in the context of alternative world-views.

The meaning of and relationship between interests and values are at the core of Dyer's discussion, which is animated by an awareness that GEC has 'brought the traditional meanings of political concepts into doubt and opened the way for changes in International Relations theory'. Universalistic cosmopolitan values involving the preservation of the wilderness, of different species and, at the highest level, of the planetary biosphere counterpose communitarian interests. There are complex normative questions here, involving trade-offs between existing concepts of justice, equity and development and the broader long-term requirement of the preservation of the bases of existence. They were paraded but left unresolved by UNCED. As Imber's chapter demonstrates, although 'sustainable development' may have been a necessary political compromise, the UN system in general and the Commission for Sustainable Development in particular continue to face enormous difficulties in providing an operational definition. The real politics of GEC issues may be represented as a complex *mélange* of national and particularistic interests, values and – as Greene reminds us – learning processes. However, Willetts argues that the whole values–interests distinction is misleading, and that we ought to refer simply to values. In his view, the really critical questions are those which concern the circumstances in which environmental values assume priority over security or material-wealth values.

This conception of the significance of the contention between values (or their programmatic assertion as ideologies) for international environmental politics forms the basis of a detailed discussion of the International Tropical Timber Organisation by Humphreys. In an analysis which owes something to Gramscian approaches to IPE, the nexus between the dominant neoliberal ideology, the countervailing ideas of a New International Economic Order (NIEO) and ecologism and environmentalism are examined. The objective is to trace their influence on the shifting norms of the International Tropical Timber Agreement between 1983 and 1994.

Hitherto, normative and other discussions in IR could be conducted without reference to gender (a characteristic often shared with discussion of environmental issues). In the last decade, feminist critics have at minimum ensured that 'the era of IR as (uncontested) masculinity is over' (Light and Halliday 1994: 52). In this volume Bretherton explores the ways in which gender relations figure in the politics of GEC. Gender analysis demonstrates how views of the natural world have had a masculine cast. Recently, however, unprecedented official attention has been paid to women–environment links in the context of sustainable development. Although women have been variously portrayed as part of the problem or as the principal victims, in recent UN activities and recent environmental theorising they have also been portrayed as the saviours of the planet. The close connections between women's productive and reproductive roles and environmental change (and the fact that they are everywhere more disadvantaged than men) should not result in their being assigned special responsibility for nurturing the earth in circumstances of disempowerment. It is these latter circumstances that are revealed by social gender analysis.

## INTERNATIONAL RELATIONS OR GLOBAL POLITICS?

The debate about the validity of state-centric models is an enduring one in International Relations. Calling into question the independent existence of the discipline, it can be regarded as the empirical version of the normative debate between communitarian and cosmopolitan thought. Orthodox IR is state-centric, and as we have seen, environmental change is usually presented in terms of global problems mismanaged by a fragmented international system. The majority of authors in this volume accept that some attempt needs to be made to break free from the legalistic straitjacket of the inter-state system and acknowledge the role of transnational forces and non-governmental agencies. One of the most significant challenges to the discipline posed by gender analysis is the reminder, as evidenced in Bretherton's chapter, that *people* must be incorporated in the study of IR.

There is, however, no underlying agreement concerning what has been described in various social sciences as the 'agent structure debate'. Should the focus of analysis be upon the actions of individuals, transnational actors and governments, and upon inter-state politics, or instead upon the determinative role of international institutions, or upon the totality of the global system – however construed? The answer will naturally depend upon the theoretical standpoint taken but it will, in a very important sense, also be determined by the kinds of questions that are asked.

If the question is about the socioeconomic causes of the world environmental predicament, then, as various authors in this volume observe, International Relations has had very little to say of any significance. This question, Saurin argues, relates to the 'processes whereby the environment is defined and comes to be known', which are highly political. Orthodox IR singularly fails to comprehend the historical dynamic of the global system of capital accumulation which has been integral to the production of environmental degradation. There is a 'radical disjuncture between the dynamics and processes of environmental change and the development of the territorially based authority of the state'. The state is inappropriate both as 'a basic causal unit of environmental change and as the most competent unit for the mediation of environmental change'. Williams agrees to the extent that 'Neo-Marxist analysis with its emphasis on the structural relationship between labour and capital and its location of environmental degradation in the political and economic structures of capitalist societies does appear to represent an advance.'

Saurin is clear that the focus on states and inter-state cooperation is also inappropriate if the questions being asked concern both political activism and attempts to contain or reverse environmental decline. Such a focus has been the main defining characteristic of the discipline's response to GEC. Since the inevitable depression that followed UNCED, disillusionment with international cooperation and the UN system has been a marked feature of radical environmental commentaries. They have called instead for action at the 'grass-roots' and communal levels, and have focused on the significance of a variegated host of non-governmental actors (Sachs 1993; Middleton, O'Keefe and Moyo 1993; *The Ecologist* 1993). Interestingly, the idea of a 'global civil society' has been advanced not just as a normative cosmopolitan construct but also as a focus of political activity and empirical study (Ekins 1992).

Willetts sketches out an alternative global politics model to accommodate the analysis of such phenomena (the unprecedented significance of non-governmental organisations in environmental politics is something that achieves near-universal academic agreement). The focus on inter-state relations is replaced by a pluralist conception of open but interconnected systems that emphasises transnational interaction and reminds us that in empirical and behavioural terms the state is a legal abstraction. Changes in the old international system that have occurred since 1945, amongst which has been the rise in environmental concerns, have left it unrecognisable, and this makes the traditional emphasis on a world of states lacking supranational authority misplaced. 'Governments are still the focus of policy-making, but the systems of interaction have fundamentally changed, not only in the values that are dominant but also structurally.'

Despite all the questioning of the relevance of statehood and of the utility of international organisation and institutions, the latter still provide a primary focus of interest for those who define themselves as students of IR. The dilemmas are well captured in Imber's essay on the environment and the United Nations. The UN is 'both the best and the worst place in which to conduct environmental diplomacy'. On the one hand, if some form of global regulation is required (many problems can be dealt with on a regional basis), the UN is unavoidable as the 'only global forum or arena in which norms and laws for the management of GEC can be negotiated'. On the other hand, however, the UN is 'the worst place' because it is an organisation of states acting in defence of their own narrow sovereign interests. Imber is also painfully aware of the sheer scale of the 'structural' inequalities and sources of degradation, embedded in the operation of the global economy, that underlie discussions at UNCED or at the Commission for Sustainable Development. In this context, the activities of a fragmented and 'feudal' UN system can be represented as an 'institutional bandage applied to a structural haemorrhage'. The only politically realistic path remains that of 'constant agitation for reform'.

The generation of norms for changing and governing behaviour is, as Imber notes, a crucial function of the UN system and cannot be dispensed with. This view is shared by those other contributors whose primary concern is with the development and maintenance of effective international environmental regimes. Norm generation has also been the practical objective of the many NGO activists who have been an increasingly evident and recognised presence in international negotiations. Ogley addresses the highly salient question of the 'supply side' of global norm generation. He provides both a close analysis of the negotiating circumstances and processes involved and an assessment of their relative importance in the light of some recent environmental agreements. Informing the discussion throughout is the experience of the Third Law of the Sea Conference, the broadest and most sustained attempt ever to reform and codify a set of global environmental norms. The 1982 Law of the Sea Convention was the product of a decade of the most complex multilateral negotiations, and it only entered into force, in somewhat truncated form, in November 1994. Described by the UN Secretary-General as one of the 'greatest achievements of this century', one of the most 'definitive contributions of our era' and 'one of our most enduring legacies',[5] it provides a range of precedents and often salutary lessons.

As Ogley concludes, the point of all this activity is that of 'changing human behaviour'. When the fundamental question of regime effectiveness is addressed, the disjuncture between the international dimension and the global system of commerce, investment, consumption and pollution becomes very evident. It is too often assumed that the conclusion of international agreements and formal 'compliance' by governments will have the desired environmental effects. The chapter by Greene reflects on the problem of implementation and on the complex national–international linkages which determine regime effectiveness. The actual implementation of agreements involves altering the behaviour of a whole range of transnational, corporate and even individual actors who may fall within state jurisdiction but not necessarily under governmental control. Implementation and learning strategies, therefore, have major policy implications for institutional design.

## SCIENCE AND EPISTEMOLOGY

The growing awareness of environmental issues in the late 1980s coincided with a period of theoretical flux and uncertainty in International Relations. This state of uncertainty was associated with the collapse of the ideological and political certainties that had characterised the Cold War, but it was also a small part of a wider unease that permeated the social sciences as a whole. The positivist epistemology of orthodox IR came under attack from a number of theoretical directions. Paterson's essay on the explanation of the Framework Convention on Climate Change reflects this critical approach. The focus is upon neorealism and neoliberalism. Paterson applies them to the case of the climate-change negotiations and concludes that neoliberal institutionalism provides the more adequate account. On the other hand, however, both have an oversimplified view of international as opposed to domestic phenomena, and share a flawed positivist epistemology. This is particularly serious because supposedly value-free, problem-solving theories do in effect 'privilege' certain positions and social groups, and this is evident in discussions of climate change.

Positivist epistemology remains a source of deep contention. Willetts, for example, sets out a forthright defence asserting the possibility of the objective study of values in environmental politics, while at the same time completely disassociating himself from the ontological assumptions of political Realism. Beyond epistemological introspection in IR, the social construction and politics of science are a central question for all those interested in global environmental change issues. At the deepest level, radical critics of modernity have linked global environmental degradation with the entire 'enlightenment project' whereby science, since Bacon and Descartes, has enshrined a manipulative division between human beings and nature. A striking example is provided by a recent study of the World Bank's environmental policy containing an interpretative chapter entitled 'From Descartes to Chico Mendes' in which the Bank is described as the 'quintessential institution of high mid-twentieth century modernity, a practical embodiment of the philosophical and historical project of the modern era that began with the Enlightenment' (Rich 1994: 239).

Such views are present within the IR community amongst 'postmodern' critics and in writings on gender (see Bretherton in this volume). However, in general, scholars have avoided theorising on this scale, being more concerned with the specific connections between scientific advice and policy. What Boehmer-Christiansen describes as the 'global research enterprise' represents a novel challenge for students of international politics. The Intergovernmental Panel on Climate Change (IPCC) represents the apex of this complex inter- and trans-national enterprise with its mission to provide consensual scientific advice to the framers of the climate-change regime. Boehmer-Christiansen's study of the IPCC sets out to demonstrate that the 'global research enterprise has not only become a significant political actor promoting the globalisation of information collection and "business as usual" research, but has also done so with reference to specific global environmental concerns that were exaggerated for this purpose'. These are important and controversial claims, directly relevant to functionalist thinking on international cooperation and the supposedly 'benign' influence of epistemic communities on the creation of international environmental regimes.

## CONCLUSION

Whereas, in the hiatus between Stockholm and Rio, the study of the international relations of the natural environment may have been the neglected preserve of the technical specialist removed from the main axes of contention in the discipline, this is clearly no longer the case, as the essays in this volume demonstrate. Many of the themes pursued and the theoretical disagreements are clearly part of a wider debate within the social sciences – as portrayed by Redclift and Benton (1994). Questions of structure and agency, or of holism or individualism, and the assault on positivist orthodoxy all figure, along with the politics of science.

The international relations of GEC is not isolated, but has it a specific contribution to make within the social sciences? Political and IR research is omitted from some schema that outline the convergence between the natural sciences and the disciplines of sociology, anthropology, economics and geography.[6] Like environmental economics, IR exhibits a close connection with policy. As argued in the first part of this chapter, much of the intellectual history of the discipline can be written in terms of responses to political events, and it is probably inevitable that its primary contribution will continue to be in the study of policy-making at the international level, and in the engineering of 'solutions'. This places a heavy emphasis on the second part of the volume. There was at one time a serious discussion amongst participants about the desirability of publishing two separate volumes of papers. The temptation to do this was resisted on the grounds that both theoretical argument and 'policy-relevant' empirical work ought to inform each other. Otherwise, there is a danger that the consideration of theoretical questions will become arid introspection and that policy-related work will be unable to rise above institutional politics and the intricacies of framework conventions and protocols. Beyond this there is also the point, made by a number of contributors, that the study of global environmental change has the potential to alter (or even subvert) the essential elements of IR as an academic pursuit.

## NOTES

1 The British International Studies Association Environment Working Group was founded in 1990 and received initial financial assistance from the Association. During 1992 and 1993, it received a grant from the ESRC Global Environmental Change Programme which allowed the presentation and discussion of the papers that now form the chapters of this volume. We continue to hold meetings, and we gratefully ack- nowledge the support of the ESRC and its GEC Programme, of which the Group forms a small part.

2 A survey of citations in the *International Political Science Abstracts* for the period 1985–90 yielded the following results. Even though the Third Law of the Sea Conference had ended in 1982 without ratification of the Convention, the literature was still dominated by maritime issues. Indeed, there were no less than forty citations. Political, economic and legal aspects of the Antarctic regime received fourteen citations, while the Arctic received eight. The emerging global environmental agenda, the Brundtland Report, stratospheric ozone and climate change merited only six citations. By the early 1990s, this situation would have changed dramatically.

3 The *United Nations Yearbook 1972* (New York: United Nations, pp. 318–23), provides the text of the twenty-six Principles and a concise report of the Conference issues and participants.

4 This well-known distinction, highlighted by critical theorists, derives from the work of Cox (1981).

5 Boutros Boutros-Ghali, speech to the inaugural session of the Seabed Authority, Kingston, Jamaica, 16 November 1994, UN Press Release SG/SM/94/196.

6 See Figure 1.1, 'Environmental research', in Redclift and Benton 1994, p. 12.

## BIBLIOGRAPHY

Benedick, R.E. (1991) *Ozone Diplomacy: New Directions in Safeguarding the Planet*, Cambridge, Mass.: Harvard U.P.

Boardman, R. (1981) *International Organisation and the Protection of Nature*, London: Macmillan.

Brandt, W. (1980) 'Independent commission on international development issues', *North–South: a Programme for Survival*, London: Pan.

Brenton, T. (1994) *The Greening of Machiavelli: the Evolution of International Environmental Politics*, London: RIIA/Earthscan.

Brown, C. (1992) *International Relations Theory: New Normative Approaches*, Hemel Hempstead: Harvester Wheatsheaf.

Brundtland, G. (1987) 'Report of the World Commission on Environment and Development', *Our Common Future*, Oxford: O.U.P.

Buzan, B. (1991) *People, States and Fear*, 2nd edn, Hemel Hempstead: Harvester Wheatsheaf.

Caldwell, L.K. (1984) *International Environmental Policy*, 1st edn, Durham and London: Duke U.P.

Carr, E.H. (1939) *The Twenty Years Crisis: 1919–39*, London: Macmillan.

Carroll, J.E. (ed.) (1988) *International Environmental Diplomacy*, Cambridge: C.U.P.

Cox, R.W. (1981) 'Social forces, states and world order', *Millennium: Journal of International Studies* 10(2): 126–53.

Deudney, D. (1990) 'The case against linking environmental degradation and national security', *Millennium: Journal of International Studies* 19(3): 461–76.

*The Ecologist* (1993) 'Whose common future? Reclaiming the commons', London: Earthscan.

Ekins, P. (1992) *A New World Order: Grassroots Movements for Global Change*, London: Routledge.

Groom, A.J.R. and Light, M. (eds) (1994) *Contemporary International Relations: a Guide to Theory*, London: Pinter.

Haas, P.M. (1990) *Saving the Mediterranean: the Politics of International Environmental Cooperation*, New York: Columbia U.P.

—— (1990a) 'Obtaining international environmental protection through epistemic communities', *Millennium: Journal of International Studies* 19(3): 347–64.

—— (1992) 'Introduction: epistemic communities and international policy coordination', *International Organization* 46(1): 1–36.

——, Keohane, R.O. and Levy, M.A. (1993) *Institutions for the Earth: Sources of Effective International Environmental Protection*, Cambridge, Mass.: MIT Press.

Hoffman, M. (1994) 'Normative international theory, approaches and issues', in Groom, A.J.R. and Light, M. (eds) *Contemporary International Relations: a Guide to Theory*, London: Pinter, pp. 27–44.

Huntington, E. (1915) *Civilization and Climate*, New Haven, Conn.: Yale U.P.

—— (1919) *World Power and Evolution*, New Haven, Conn.: Yale U.P.

Hurrell, A. and Kingsbury, B. (eds) (1992) *The International Politics of the Environment*, Oxford: Clarendon.

Imber, M.F. (1994) *Environment, Security and UN Reform*, Basingstoke: Macmillan.

Kay, D. and Jacobson, H.K. (eds) (1983) *Environmental Protection: the International Dimension*, New Jersey: Allanheld Osmun.

Kay, D. and Skolnikoff, E. (1972) *World Eco-Crisis: International Organizations in Response*, Madison: University of Wisconsin Press.

Keohane, R.O. and Nye, J.S. (1977) *Power and Interdependence: World Politics in Transition*, Boston: Little, Brown.

Krasner, S.D. (ed.) (1983) *International Regimes*, Ithaca, NY: Cornell U.P.

Light, M. and Halliday, F. (1994) 'Gender and international relations', in Groom, A.J.R. and Light, M. (eds) *Contemporary International Relations: a Guide to Theory*, London: Pinter, pp. 45–55.

McCormick, J. (1989) *The Global Environmental Movement: Reclaiming Paradise*, London: Belhaven.

Mackinder, H.J. (1904) 'The geographical pivot of history', *The Geographical Journal* XXIII: 421–44.

—— (1919) *Democratic Ideals and Reality*, New York: Holt & Co.

Mahan, A.T. (1890) *The Influence of Sea Power upon History 1660–1783*, 1965 edn, London: Methuen & Co. Ltd.

Mathews, J.T. (ed.) (1991) *Preserving the Global Environment: the Challenge of Shared Leadership*, New York: Norton.

Meadows, D.H. *et al.* (1972) *The Limits to Growth: a Report for the Club of Rome's Project on the Predicament of Mankind*, London: Pan.

—— (1992) *Beyond the Limits: Global Collapse and Sustainable Development*, London: Earthscan.

Middleton, N., O'Keefe, P. and Moyo, S. (1993) *Tears of the Crocodile: From Rio to Reality in the Developing World*, London: Pluto.

Mills, C.A. (1949) 'Temperature dominance over human life', *Science*, 16 September, reprinted in Sprout and Sprout (eds) (1962) *Foundations of International Politics*, New York: Van Nostrand Reinhold, pp. 350–3.

Mitrany, D. (1943) *A Working Peace System*, London: Royal Institute of International Affairs.

Morgenthau, H.J. (1948) *Politics Among Nations: the Struggle for Power and the Struggle for Peace*, 4th edn (1967), New York: Alfred A. Knopf.

Morse, E.L. (1976) *Modernization and the Transformation of International Relations*, New York: Free Press.

Newsom, D.D. (1988/9) 'The new diplomatic agenda: are governments ready?', *International Affairs* 65(1): 29–42.

North, D.C. (1990) *Institutions, Institutional Change and Economic Performance*, Cambridge: C.U.P.

Porter, G. and Brown, J.W. (1991) *Global Environmental Politics*, Boulder, Col.: Westview.

Redclift, M. and Benton, T. (eds) (1994) *Social Theory and the Global Environment*, London: Routledge.

Rich, B. (1994) *Mortgaging the Earth: the World Bank, Environmental Impoverishment and the Crisis of Development*, London: Earthscan.

Rosenau, J.N. and Cziempel, E.O. (eds) (1992) *Governance Without Government: Order and Change in World Politics*, Cambridge: C.U.P.

Sachs, W. (ed.) (1993) *Global Ecology: a New Arena of Global Conflict*, London and Atlantic Highlands, NJ: Zed Books.

Sand, P.H. (1991) 'International cooperation: the environmental experience', in Mathews, J.T. (ed.) (1991) *Preserving the Global Environment: the Challenge of Shared Leadership*, New York: Norton, pp. 236–79.

—— (ed.) (1992) *The Effectiveness of Environmental Agreements: a Survey of Existing Legal Instruments*, Cambridge: Grotius/UNCED.

Sjostedt, G. (ed.) (1993) *International Environmental Negotiation*, Newbury Park, Cal.: Sage/IIASA.

Smith, S. (1993) 'The environment on the periphery of international relations: an explanation', *Environmental Politics* 2(4): 28–45.

Soroos, M.S. (1986) *Beyond Sovereignty: the Challenge of Global Policy*, Columbia: University of South Carolina Press.

Sprout, H. and Sprout, M. (eds) (1962) *Foundations of International Politics*, New York: Van Nostrand Reinhold.

—— (1968) 'Environmental factors in the study of international relations', in Rosenau, J.N. (ed.) *International Politics and Foreign Policy: a Reader in Research and Theory*, New York: Free Press.

Strange, S. (1982) 'Cave! hic dragones: a critique of regime analysis', *International Organization* 36(2).

Susskind, L. (1994) *Environmental Diplomacy: Negotiating More Effective Global Agreements*, Oxford: O.U.P.

Thomas, C. (1992) *The Environment in International Relations*, London: RIIA.

Vasquez, J.A. (1983) *The Power of Power Politics*, New Brunswick, NJ: Rutgers U.P.

Vogler, J. (1995) *The Global Commons: a Regime Analysis*, Chichester: Wiley.

von Neumann, J. (1955) 'Can we survive technology?', *Fortune*, June, reprinted in Sprout and Sprout (eds) (1962) *Foundations of International Politics*, New York: Van Nostrand Reinhold, pp. 242–50.

Wheeler, R.H. (1946) 'Climate and human behavior', *The Encyclopaedia of Psychology*, New York Philosophical Library Inc., reprinted in Sprout and Sprout (eds) (1962) *Found- ations of International Politics*, New York: Van Nostrand Reinhold, pp. 347–9.

Young, O.R. (1977) *Resource Management at the International Level*, New York: Nichols.

—— (1982) *Resource Regimes: Natural Resources and Social Institutions*, Berkeley: University of California Press.

—— (1989) *International Cooperation: Building Regimes for Natural Resources and the Environment*, Ithaca, NY: Cornell U.P.

# 2 Environmental security as a universal value

## Implications for international theory[1]

*Hugh C. Dyer*

This chapter explores the theoretical implications of invoking environmental security as a universal value. It begins with a discussion of the concept of environmental security that draws on recent literature, proceeds to a treatment of the concept in terms of values and interests, and concludes with a consideration of the implications of an emerging global norm of environmental security for the theory of international relations.

In presenting environmental security as a norm, the intention is to make out the case for value-based theory (characterised here as normative theory) as opposed to interest-based theory. For present purposes, and in brief, values are taken to be an object of choice, while norms are taken to be socially constructed by consensus: that is, norms are social values. The society in this case is the broadest possible one, though we shall see that it matters whether this is understood as international society (a society of states) or cosmopolitan society (a global civil society). It may be argued that the influence of civil society and non-state actors in environmental politics parallels other processes of globalisation such as those found in international financial markets.

The problems attending the conceptualisation of environmental security will be shown to arise from the preoccupation of traditional international theory with the categories of state interests and state power. In contrast to values, interests are objectified, thus reducing the grounds for choice down to strictly rational assessments of rank priority within the objective structure. The reification of the state and its interests is the grounds for accumulating state power for state purposes. However, the state itself is a value choice, inasmuch as other forms of social organisation and mechanisms of authoritative allocation might be equally successful.

The security of the global environment stands against the state system as another, perhaps contradictory, value or set of values. This possibility is not readily admitted from the perspective of state-centric interest-based theory, but could be addressed from the perspective of a value-based theory. The dichotomy of state and environmental values underlies a contradiction between traditional definitions of security and environmental security.

## ENVIRONMENTAL SECURITY

The principal difficulty in discussing environmental security is the recalcitrance of traditional politico-military definitions of security. It has been argued that the traditional threat to security, organised violence, is not analytically comparable to environmental threats (Deudney 1990: 461). Organised violence is a traditional prerogative of nation states, being both a domestic monopoly and (in the Clausewitzian sense) a tool of foreign policy. However, the developing logic of international environmental relations points to global relations among regional and local actors rather than to traditional inter-state relations. Global relations can be seen as succeeding what was begun by the phenomenon of transnational relations by further conditioning, if not eliminating, the role of nation states. Even where the state remains a principal focus, the traditional notion of national security 'becomes profoundly confused' when there is internal instability or insecurity (as would be the case environmentally, since the environment does not recognise political or territorial boundaries), and 'the image of the state as a referent object for security fades' (Buzan 1991: 103).

These developments present an opportunity, as Pirages (1991: 8) says, for re-examining 'the meaning of security'. Indeed, the question of redefining security is the topic of a broad area of recent literature, much of which specifically addresses environmental security.[2]

Traditional security discourse is not well equipped to address the pressing global issues that a (new) definition of security must cope with. A continuing dependence on the troubled concepts of sovereignty, national interest and (state) foreign policy, which have historically provided the framework and rationale for military threats and actions, suggests that the notion of 'security' does not lend itself well to the project of conceptualising a response to emerging global changes – not least global environmental change. Military power is the traditional manifestation of state power, and is the locus of value investment for notions of security attaching to the state and (in these terms, by definition) to populations under its jurisdiction. These values are seldom in step with the human environment, but vast resources have been exhausted in their name.

It is worth considering the origins of traditional security definitions, in order to place definitions of environmental security in context. As Richard Ullman notes, 'the tendency of American political leaders to define security problems and their solutions in military terms is deeply ingrained', and we 'should not overestimate the achievements of . . . nongovernmental organizations in putting forward alternative conceptions of national security, such as those involving limiting population growth or enhancing environmental quality' (Ullman 1983: 152–3). This is not perhaps true to the same extent for all countries, but it is to be expected that any sea change in the world political order will require the acquiescence if not the lead of the USA, and its security agenda will continue to influence others. At the level of international security (where one might hope the concept of environmental security would find a natural home), the traditional agenda is merely an extension of national state preoccupations such that collective security, far from escaping the parochialism of state-centric security, remains a fundamentally conservative notion, viewed by Herz as 'an attempt to maintain, and render more secure, the "territoriality" or "impermeability" of states upon which their "sovereignty" and "independence" had rested since the beginning of the modern era' (Herz 1959: 76).

The idea of international security as an improvement on national defence has a long history which includes various and sundry proposals for world government, but perhaps most significantly the initiatives leading to the League of Nations and the United Nations, both of which include collective security provisions in their founding documents. However, collective security is time-bound, and Herz, writing in 1959, is concerned with the new conditions of the 'Atomic Age', which he characterises in a final chapter entitled 'Universalism as an alternative to the Power Dilemma' (instructively, the conditions are also true of global environmental change):

> Any discussion of the details of a more integrated world structure . . . must of necessity remain rather theoretical and detached from present realities . . . . Our task is more basic; it concerns the conclusions to be drawn from the unprecedented condition that has befallen mankind. And the first thing to realize is that the situation confronts for the first time the whole human race as one group.
>
> (Herz 1959: 303)

Yet this realisation has had little effect on policy in the intervening years, and it is the famous 'security dilemma' which continues to dominate conceptions of security for the 'units' in international relations:

> a feeling of insecurity, deriving from mutual suspicion and mutual fear, compels these units to compete for ever more power in order to find more security, an effort which proves self-defeating because complete security remains ultimately unobtainable.
>
> (ibid.: 231)

It is an open question whether or not concepts of environmental security will allow an escape from the essential structure of international relations, but to the extent that the present structure remains inadequate, this must surely be an aspiration. Peter F. Drucker, for example, notes that crucial environmental needs such as the protection of the atmosphere and of forests 'cannot be addressed as adversarial issues' (Drucker 1990: 110–11). Ken Conca has suggested that it is not clear whether the existing global structures (and their inequalities) will be changed or reinforced by the pursuit of environmental security (Conca 1992, 1993). If environmental or ecological security means insulation or isolation from that which cannot be nationally controlled, there will not be much progress beyond traditional forms of isolation based on national sovereignty. It is even conceivable that environmental security itself could become militarised, and the opportunity for fundamental change lost through the co-option of the environmental agenda by a traditional security agenda. This prospect is enhanced by the complexity and ambiguity of the concept of environmental security, its definition being tied to 'insecurity' as a social phenomenon with localised variations in perception and valuation as well as a global dimension.

There are a number of different approaches and perspectives in the literature, and the discourse about environmental security is consequently unclear, exhibiting sometimes contradictory mixed metaphors (Conca 1992). Not surprisingly, proposals range from attempts at the reform of traditional security conceptions to the radical overhaul of world politics. At one end of the spectrum are proposals which advocate adding selected parts of the environmental agenda to the list of things to be secured militarily – obviously a very conventional approach. At the other end of the spectrum are proposals for the restructuring of the entire political order in such a way as to allow an effective response to a perceived environmental crisis of immense proportions. Neither of these polar positions on the spectrum is very convincing. The former position is clearly inadequate or retrograde, and the latter position cannot justify panic on the existing fragmentary evidence about global environmental change (Broecker 1992: 6–14).

There are, however, a number of intermediary positions, some recognising the profound changes in recent international relations, some ignoring them. Certainly, it seems appropriate to acknowledge change, since it is this feature of international relations which has brought existing concepts into disarray, if not disrepute. Any proposal for addressing environmental security must surely take into account the challenges that arise from both changes in the global environment and changes in the international political system following the end of the Cold War. The question is not, then, about changes themselves but rather about what these changes mean for our conception of security.

In some respects, it is not even clear what is being secured: some view the environment as a potential source of danger or insecurity to the state, and some view the states themselves as the principal threat to the environment, with the emphasis on environmental aspects of traditional threats such as military activity, migration, famine and drought. If it is populations which are being secured, then what is at risk? Existence, says Rowlands (1992: 299); life, ideals, beliefs, territorial integrity and well-being, says Pirages (1991: 8). And against what are these being secured? War, revolution and civil strife, says Pirages (1991: 8); non-military threats, says Rowlands (1992: 299).

The definition of that which is secured, and of that *against which* it is secured, is of course dependent on the conception of security employed. The case to be made is for the broadest possible definition of security, and this should be broad enough to 'include' environmental security – indeed, environmental security, broadly understood, could be the only, or the overall, conception of security from which all other considerations flow. This is not because traditional security concerns have vanished, but because they can be better incorporated into a broad notion of environmental security than can environmental security be squeezed into rigid and outmoded traditional, largely militaristic conceptions of security.

The influence of traditional (largely Realist) theories of international relations has made it very difficult to escape the traditional conceptions of security.

Because the dominant discourse is Realist, the most common approach to environmental security is to couch proposals in terms of the Realist paradigm. Pirages notes this phenomenon in pointing to a dominant social paradigm, in the cognitive dimension of social evolution, which is characterised by an industrial culture, and is also reflected structurally in social institutions – namely, the industrial paradigm: 'While individual world-views may differ slightly, there is a general set of values, attitudes, beliefs, and perceptions that are shared by most members of industrial societies' (Pirages 1991: 9). Under these conditions it is not surprising that proposals and arguments concerning environmental security play to the existing dominant discourse of security in an uncritical way, attempting to build on it rather than transcend it. Hence there are proposals to 'encompass' within the notion of security: resource and environmental threats (Brown 1977, 1986; Mathews 1989; Renner 1989a, 1989b); and the conflict-generating risks of environmental change (Brown 1989; Homer-Dixon 1991; Myers 1989). These include ozone depletion and global warming (Rowlands 1991), and extend to include a further, wide array of threats from earthquakes to demographic dislocation (Ullman 1983).

Another approach is to incorporate the environment indirectly by hitching it to the economic threats to national security. Sorenson does this by indicating the environmental implications of sustainable economic development and economic recovery, in the context of US foreign-aid policy (Sorenson 1990). Buzan tends to link environmental issues to economic security, as a subset within the overall topic of security, and refers to Mathews (1989) in agreeing that there is room for the environment on the security agenda (Buzan 1991: 256–8). The Brundtland Commission employs (for good reason, given its mandate) the hybrid tactic of connecting environmental stress to conflict, and conflict to unsustainable development (Brundtland 1987: 290–304). Although Bruce Rich's discussion of environmental reform in the multilateral development banks suggests mixed results at best (Rich 1990: 307–29), any of these propositions and activities might serve to bring environmental security onto the international agenda. However, this 'add-on' approach to environmental security does little to reform the traditional security discourse.

Porter and Brown take a broad perspective on security which more directly incorporates the environment (even if as only one of several global concerns), arguing that the traditional politico-military international security system in fact constrains international cooperation: 'the new concept of security in terms of common global threats, including threats to the environment, now presents an alternative to the traditional definition' (Porter and Brown 1991: 141). The interaction of threats to human populations which are of environmental origin (as seen from the anthropocentric perspective) and threats to the environment which are of human origin (including industrialisation in general) suggests the obvious point, which was implied by the Brundtland Report (1987), that there must be a complete integration of environmental perspectives into our understanding of the economic, social and political condition of our species. The Brundtland Report, however, is more concerned with the 'redefinition of priorities, nationally and globally', and with 'broader forms of security assessment' (Brundtland 1987: 302–3), and argues that:

> The whole notion of security as traditionally understood – in terms of political and military threats to national sovereignty – must be expanded to include the growing impacts of environmental stress – locally, nationally, regionally, and globally. There are no military solutions to 'environmental security'.
>
> (ibid.: 19)

But arguably, this idea of 'expanding' the security agenda has more in common with 'add-on' proposals than it has with the idea of actually redefining the concept of security from the intellectual starting point of a global perspective.

The notion of 'common security' advocated by the Palme Commission (1982) ('Independent Commission on Disarmament and Security issues') goes some way towards capturing the essence of a global approach to security, but inevitably it too is caught up in the discourse of the modern state system – as all proposals must be if they hope to find a contemporary audience. The real challenge is to find sufficiently impelling points of reference in present circumstances to raise support for a longer-term perspective. Perhaps the speed of technological change and the growing awareness of environmental degradation, combined with models of globalisation offered by financial markets, the information and communication revolution and other transnational activities, will provide the necessary impetus for taking advantage of the opportunity afforded by the collapse of Cold War structures and mind-sets.

The concept of 'security' has been overstretched, and is in some respects *passé* (Sorenson 1990: 3), since in the traditional discourse of international security the notion of 'security' implies a threat or action coming from an assignable agent to which a response can be made. Such a threat, either to the security of a state or to international security, and the subsequent response generally involve the threat or use of armed force (Johnson 1991: 172). Environmental 'threats' may be assignable in some cases, but more to the point are those cases where assignability is problematic (in the way of public goods), and where 'securing' from such generalised states of affairs or 'natural' conditions is not possible or appropriate within the traditional meaning of the term 'security'.

The 'security dilemma' is traditionally managed through the maintenance of relative symmetry between the parties (agents) involved, with special characteristics attaching to asymmetrical relationships. Thus, a 'balance' is sought through meeting perceived threats and by closing gaps in capability – paradoxically leading to the potential for spiralling arms races (hence the dilemma). The case of asymmetry is reflected, for example, in interventions by the more powerful, which are often presented as the management of general international security interests (not a dilemma for *realpolitik*). Yet, in the case of threats to the environment, where the threat in a given instance is identifiable with a particular agent (e.g. another state or non-state actor), asymmetry is more common because for any particular given case of environmental degradation the threat will be non-reciprocal. Consider, for example, the vulnerability of a state which is dependent on river water originating in the territory of another state upstream: while the potential environmental threat cannot be reciprocated, a military action may be substituted, bringing traditional security concerns back in (Homer-Dixon 1994: 19). On the other hand, the environment as a whole is an ecosystem in which all parties are ultimately implicated, so in a sense asymmetry may only apply in the relative short run (or at least not in the long run) given that global change will have widespread consequences, either directly or indirectly. Of course, it is well to remember that the differential impacts of climate change mean that some groups, such as small island states, will be sensitive to their special vulnerability over the relatively long time scale of global change. Indeed, asymmetry in security relations is rather more commonplace than the simple balancing model of the security dilemma suggests. The point here is simply the familiar one that international security is of general interest, given the potential for 'spill-over' from any localised threat, and this is no less true of environmental threats. A new concept (perhaps 'assurance'?) is required to reflect the nuances of both a changing security discourse and the particular characteristics of environmental degradation which may define security threats. In contrast to the traditional concept of security which emphasises short-term military threats to national populations and territories, a concept of environmental security should take account of both the spatial (universal) and the temporal (intergenerational) scope of the threat.

Finally, the real significance of taking a broad approach to environmental security (the security of the human environment) is the potential for employing this term as the all-encompassing conception of security, such that all other terms are derivative.

## VALUES

Positing the universal value of environmental security does not suggest that the value necessarily manifests itself in the same form everywhere, or even that a global norm concerning the environment will be established (Buzan 1991: 172). However, the notion of environmental security as a universal value opens up the possibility of employing a central problematic factor in international relations as the basis of a case for transforming international theory, if it can be concluded that value-based theory provides a more appropriate explanation and under-standing of this aspect of international relations than does interest-based theory. Buzan suggests that environmental security is linked to other problematic focal points of security – military, political, economic and social: 'Environmental security concerns the maintenance of the local and the planetary biosphere as the essential support system on which all other human enterprises depend' (Buzan 1991: 19–20). The more inclusive the notion of environmental security is taken to be, the more persuasive the case for theory based on related values.

In order to build the case for a normative, value-based approach, it is necessary to consider some of the traditional grounds for marginalising values in favour of interests. The first of these is the perception that values are subjective while interests are, in some respect, objective – in Morgenthau, this objectivity is attained by defining interests in terms of power, which is pursued by all states (these being the principal international actors, in the Realist account). Values are thought to be relative to states and their societies, and this value-relativism marginalises the importance of values as an analytical category in the study of relations among states. Of course, this relativism is largely overcome by global conceptions of international relations which admit 'reciprocity' within a shared framework (Kegley 1992: 21–40), and it vanishes entirely under a fully cosmopolitan view. Values are only relative (in exactly the same way as interests) in the most uninteresting sense that they have a parochial manifestation, but otherwise they are a universal and readily observed feature of human life. The pursuit of power does little to add objectivity, since it may always be asked for what purpose (and at what cost) it is being pursued, and the answer will always betray parochial concerns. The interesting problem is in fact how values are individually selected, politically manipulated, and socially entrenched as norms.

It may be clarifying to refer to the semiotician Greimas, and to note a parallel between our problem of values in international relations and his examination of ethnic literature where he distinguishes between two different kinds of manipulation of values. The first is the 'circulation of constant values (or equivalent ones) between equal subjects in an isotopic and closed universe' (Greimas 1987: 85–6). We might consider this to be the case in domestic or national societies, where the values in circulation are culturally embedded and where alien values are not readily admitted. The second, following from the first, involves 'the problem of the introduction and removal of these immanent values to and from the given universe, and it presupposes the existence of a universe of *transcendent values* that encompasses and encloses the first in such a way that subjects who possess the *immanent values* appear as receivers vis-à-vis the subject-senders of the transcendent universe' (ibid.). We might view this latter kind, then, as the problem of value exchange in international (global) relations, where the prospect of a shared system of values depends on such a shared system being somehow related to the various distinct value structures of the (local) participating societies. This could possibly, but not necessarily, result in the familiar settlement on lowest common denominators, given the difficulty of aggregating conflicting values. An important caveat here is that transcendent belief systems (for example, those involving a deity) exceed the limits of normative political theory, so any universe of transcendent values for international society cannot be a universalised reflection of a particular value system. The same may be said of any simplistic conclusions about the universal acceptance of liberalism – or any other political creed for that matter. Thus, what is required for the adoption of environmental security as a universal value is not the imposition of global consensus but rather a collective understanding of international political life as that which 'encompasses and encloses' the particularities of national political life, and for which both local environments and the global environment are of salience.

Invoking environmental security as a universal value allows the theoretical possibility that less abstract manifestations of environmental security can be grounded in such a universal value or menu of such values. Particular subjective environmental values may be chosen from such a menu as part of the formation of social norms concerning the security of the environment – whether these norms are global or local in their influence. Whatever their grounding or influence, it could still be held that values are insubstantial, whereas interests can be empirically identified, and it has already been suggested that traditional International Relations theory denies the significance of values, relying instead on the identification of material interests. One aspect of this denial of values, Greimas suggests, is that 'there is a tendency to confuse the notions of *object* and *value*; the figurative form of the object guarantees its reality and at this level value becomes identified with the desired object' (Greimas 1987: 85–6).

An apposite example drawn from international relations is that of the value of security, which traditionally takes objective defence capability (e.g. weapons) as its figurative form. Thus, defence postures become a pretext for the hidden value of security, a value which can then remain undifferentiated or assumed since it appears to be less than substantial in comparison to a concrete interest in an array of weapons, even though its implications are quite broad: security may, for example, take constructive economic relations, democratic political structures or indeed a clean natural environment as its figurative form, rather than defence capability. Built into the notion of 'security' are a range of values, readily ignored in an empirical calculation of defence interests, but accounted for in a normative approach. In fact, the value connotations of security are defined, and thus limited, by the traditional discourse of international security.

## THEORETICAL IMPLICATIONS

The conceptual and normative tensions between the security of the environment and the security of states as defining values may be overemphasised, if the main features of international relations remain unchanged or only modified (Conca 1993). Yet the possibility of global social and political change accompanying global environmental change is significant enough to warrant a theoretical consideration of the implications. The implications for international theory have two aspects: general implications, on the one hand, and those bearing specifically on the international relations of the environment on the other. Clearly, they are connected. It may be said that the theories of inter-state relations (whether they involve state-centric Realism or liberal internationalism) are no longer tenable – at least for explaining environmental politics in particular, but perhaps also generally as well. If so, international theory must become the theory of global processes, incorporating multiple actors and considering global, regional and local relations as aspects of the whole. It is precisely this aspect of considering the world as a whole which characterises the global approach. Globalisation, as a central concept, indicates the relative autonomy and distinct logic of the global, as opposed to the national or international (Robertson 1990).

In this respect, a normative approach may prove useful, showing environmental security as a value developing into a socio-political norm in a global context, one which influences both behaviour (as in political regimes) and knowledge (as in theoretical paradigms). Environmental security arises in a changing international context where interdependence is already widely accepted as the baseline of international relations, and where shared values such as environmental security are more salient than the particularistic interests (such as national politico-military security) of the individual nation states. This transition coincides with the relative decline in the salience of nuclear deterrence and the increasing salience of environmental concerns. In this sense, the environment becomes the manifestation of new political values and norms as the detritus of the Cold War experience and the international system it bolstered is tossed out. Normative theory is clearly an appropriate theoretical approach to such changing values and emerging norms, in preference to traditional interest-based theories which maintain the categories of nationalism and militarism in their accounts of security. Furthermore, a normative theory is better able to address processes of globalisation.

The absence of secure and certain knowledge generally (such uncertainty being a notable characteristic of global environmental change), and of undisputed theoretical foundations for global political life in particular, leaves the possibility of a 'correct' world-view an open question. Naturally, when political action is necessary, the question cannot be left open. One route to closure, of course, is ideological commitment, but there is a distinction between ideology, with its twin characteristics of 'an image of society and a political programme' (Eccleshall 1984: 7), and the role of ideas. In its descriptive mode, a normative theoretical account of world-views addresses the formation of an image of society – in this case, of international society or the global political condition – and is not concerned with political programmes as such. In its prescriptive mode, normative theory may nevertheless properly provide guidance with respect to the formation of political programmes, since it is not possible to separate political choice from the analysis of political life: in separating the wheat from the chaff, it must be acknowledged that they first grew as parts of one whole – a whole, in this case, which defies the 'is–ought' distinction such that what 'is' (as discovered by analysis) results from previous choices made on the grounds of what 'ought to be' or what one 'ought to do' (as affirmed by commitment).

The task at hand, however, is to uncover the origins and foundations of our political conceptions, or world-views, as the starting point for claims about political knowledge and choice. Such choice clearly involves a form of security which reflects the gradual shift of emphasis from politico-military threats to the threat of environmental degradation. Specifically, the following discussion will address the theoretical implications of invoking, in policy formation, what are held to be objective interests as a means of determining 'correct' action. In examining interest-based theory and practice, underlying value assumptions will be exposed in order to assess the role of values in determining interests. It is argued here that values come prior to interests in theoretical significance, and that attempts to understand global environmental politics must take into consideration the value structures underlying world-views. It is these sructures that are the key to an understanding of what is superficially presented as objective reality, and that provide the grounds for rational action based on interest calculations.

Initially, the problem is the attitude of positivism to the apprehension of reality, or to a knowledge of 'what is', since this approach restricts the social sciences to falsifiable propositional statements concerning empirically observable facts. A logical-hermeneutic, or interpretive, approach to the same reality sees 'what is' as something more than simple empirical factuality. In brief, the difference is that between the assumption that there is some independent reality 'out there', to be discovered by experimentation, and the view that reality is socially constructed and can only be 'discovered' through an interpretation of its meaning for the participants:

> Social reality is *constructed* by means of presuppositions (global, all-inclusive conceptions of social reality of a religious, ethical, political etc. kind), assumptions (epistemological and ontological) and rules (constitutive and regulative) ... 'what ought to be' and 'what is' belong to the same order of reality.
>
> (di Bernardo 1988: 152)

Because traditional positivist views in epistemology, and non-cognitivist views in ethics, deny the possibility of knowing reality in this comprehensive way, there is naturally a predisposition to explain sociopolitical phenomena in terms of objective interests which can be empirically observed. When this 'reality' of the world is understood in terms of threats to nation states under conditions of anarchy, the observed objective interest is likely to be that of national security. Yet this view of knowledge clearly restricts 'the conditions of possibility for all understanding of the social world'. If the activity of politics is to be properly understood (and likewise political objectives like 'security'), it is 'important to emphasize the decisive importance of the action of the subject as the provider of contents which condition his interpretation of reality'. Actions are thus comprehensible in the context of a shared system of meaning, or language, which nevertheless expresses subjective contents:

> if we employ subjective categories such as intentions, ends, rules, values, norms ... [action] may be explained in terms of the contents of the consciousness of the agent which are linked with his vision of the world. The sense of his actions depends on these contents, and they contribute to the construction of the social world.
>
> (ibid.: 173)

It follows that perceptions or interpretations of the world may vary with these contents of consciousness, and that knowledge of reality derives not only from a sensory experience of it but also from general interpretations, or world-views. A further consequence is that values figure prominently in political understanding from both an internal and an external perspective, since both the observer and the observed are engaged in the valuation of experience. Finally, the significance of interests is reduced if these rest ultimately on valuations provided by a normative structure.

The definition of 'national interest' (where it is defined at all) is dependent on prevalent norms, whether these are strictly national or to some degree systemic. If these norms arise within the traditional idiom of security, it will be difficult to arrive at a global understanding of environmental security. If, on the other hand, the consciousness of political agents (individuals, leaders, groups) is oriented towards environmental problems (say by the efforts of non-governmental organisations (NGOs)), the social world need not be constructed in terms of traditional national security. The 'objective interest' may then instead be understood in terms of the global environment.

In the last of eight lectures given at Oxford in 1908, William James concludes with a discussion of the 'will to believe' and the 'faith-ladder' used in reaching decisions (in this case, about the relationship between pluralism and monism). He describes the latter process thus:

> A conception of the world arises in you somehow, no matter how. Is it true or not? you ask. It *might* be true somewhere, you say, for it is not self-contradictory.
>
> It *may* be true, you continue, even here and now. It is *fit* to be true, it would be *well if it were true*, it *ought* to be true, you presently feel. It *must* be true, something persuasive in you whispers next; and then – as a final result – it shall be *held to be true*, you decide; it *shall be* as if true, for *you*.
>
> And your acting thus may in certain special cases be a means of making it securely true in the end. Not one step in this process is logical, yet it is the way in which monists and pluralists alike espouse and hold fast to their visions. It is life exceeding logic, it is the practical reason for which the theoretic reason finds arguments after the conclusion is once there. In just this way do some of us hold to the unfinished pluralistic universe; in just this way do others hold to the timeless universe eternally complete.
>
> (James 1977: 148)

James' position seems a strong one, and the direction of his thought is suggestive of the importance of considering values as an integral part of practical reasoning. What is referred to here as a world-view encompasses both theoretical assumptions about the essential nature both of international relations and of politics more generally and, consequently, assumptions about the 'real world' as well. It is this 'real world' in which people, groups and organisations (including states) must act, and of which theories must provide an account. Perspectives on environmental security form part of any world-view, and the role this part plays in theoretical assumptions will determine understandings of environmental security in the 'real world' of political action.

Thus, for understanding what is presented here as a world-view, it is necessary to consider the range and character of those theoretical assumptions about international relations which form the basis of world-views. For example, Hidemi Suganami suggests that ideas about world order are 'clustered around five basic positions'. The first two are the legal school (internationalist, *not* cosmopolitan) and the diplomatic school, both of which support the idea of a system of sovereign states. The third, democratic confederalism, emphasises representation. Federalism, the fourth position, reflects a cosmopolitan view, and the fifth position, welfare internationalism, is functionalist. Each of these theoretical starting points gives rise to different conceptions of, and hence prescriptions for, world order (Suganami 1989).

Where there are different national perspectives at work giving rise to different institutionalised forms of political life, it will matter which world-view underwrites institutions. However, a global conception of world-views suggests multiple perspectives and thus multiple sources of institutional development (such as institutional approaches to the environment). For example, institutions may be viewed from an internal or external perspective, and it is only from the internal perspective (where the observer 'belongs' to the institution) that constitutive rules are both known and accepted, and therefore have prescriptive force. From the external perspective, rules may simply be known, being therefore only descriptive. The latter perspective may be said to have resonance in a specifically international view of the world as a states system, but the former (internal) perspective applies when all actors are implicated in global politics by a cosmopolitan view. In this case, any global value structure is prescriptive as well as descriptive, and must be reflected in policy (including environmental policy).

Where such a value structure can be said to exist, at least to the extent of providing grounds for communication, there may still be differences about the nature of the values concerned, which can be considered differences in world-views. Ideas are not always freely transferable in a world comprised of many different political systems and cultures.

To begin with, the experience of political association, and of the values so established, is no doubt generally more parochial than what is implied in speaking of international relations, yet it must be emphasised again that international relations is an integral part of political life as a whole, and that national and local politics are equally a part of international relations to the extent that they are a source of political values. Second, there may be considerable differences concerning human nature, giving rise to different aspirations for political community.

Nevertheless, talking about international relations at all requires some universal claims, whether moral or epistemological (note the close relation between these two), and hence a central difficulty is that of contending with the relativism implied above – which is undeniable in some respects – while at the same time locating and characterising those features of global political life which are universal. Presumably, the value of a secure environment counts as one such universal feature.

It is argued here that such universals lie in the common objective of human betterment, which may be pursued by diverse means (for example, by enhancing the quality of the human environment). There is a similarity of form with respect to ends, which is represented by the assumption of values (such as the value of environmental security) in the face of ultimate indeterminacy, but a diversity of means, which is represented by contingent expressions of value in political life and in the pursuit of particular interests. As L.T. Hobhouse says: 'We consider laws, customs and institutions in respect of their functions not merely in maintaining any sort of social life, but in maintaining or promoting a harmonious life' (Hobhouse 1958: 27). We all live in different realities, holding different views of our world. If there were perfectly shared perceptions of social, political and economic reality, the coordinating functions of communication would be redundant, and we would enjoy a common world-view. However, even in the simplest (interpersonal) relations, variations in experience make such perfect sharing impossible, and communication essential. In international relations, communication is the principal feature, with other cooperative and coordinated forms of activity still less commonplace here than they are in intra-national relations, in spite of increasing interdependence among nation states (and other actors). Communication, if effective, may lead to shared perceptions (or at least an awareness of differences), but perfect communication, perfect sharing, cannot be achieved. Consider, for example, the argument that translation (or rather interpretation) is always possible between human languages, but that an understanding of the cultural context, the nuances and hidden assumptions of another language requires direct experience. The consequence of this argument is that different world-views become endemic, and that interactions both positive and negative revolve around these different global perspectives. Positive interactions may involve coming to terms with differences, while negative interactions may involve conflicts as one or another world-view is imposed in order to resolve differences.

To a large degree, conventional or traditional theories of international relations (principally, versions of realism) assume a shared world-view in the form of a power-oriented, interest-based, rational technical system susceptible to political management – including the management of conflict, in the event of opposing interests, by means of the rational application of technical sources of power. In the absence of value considerations, the possibility of incommensurable world-views is not entertained, unless this can be readily translated into conflicts of interest (which would allow power to settle the issue). The assumption of a unitary reality in which interests are the key factor does not allow the contemplation of alternative world-views, nor of political options which might arise from such contemplation. Thus are excluded both a global world-view drawing on universal values, and the possibility of globally based environmental security.

In this way, the governing assumptions of Western political thought – which suggest that politics is to do with power, and that power is to do with mastery – tend to dictate a particular kind of world-view which then limits the range of possible interpretations of international political life:

> Supreme political power thus comes to be viewed – very much in the manner of Max Weber – as a capacity to deploy a monopoly of legitimate violence.
>
> (Skinner 1981: 36)

The attending conception of security, then, is bound to considerations of military power, whether in terms of an 'external' threat or in terms of 'internal' capability.

The normative significance of this image of political life is generally lost among the deeply imbedded assumptions of traditional theory.

> This is not – in spite of what we sometimes like to think – because we analyze our political arrangements in such a hardheaded fashion that the element of imagery never intrudes at all. On the contrary, the terms in which we habitually talk about the powers of the state are densely metaphorical in texture. The point is rather that the metaphors we favor all tend to support the idea of politics as a realm of domination, subordination, and the exercise of force.
>
> (Skinner 1981: 36)

None of these conceptions lend themselves to the global perspective demanded by the problem of environmental security. As Weston argues, there are insoluble philosophical problems (universals, infinitude, etc.) which are nevertheless solved for practical purposes, through politics and culture, in every successful society (Weston 1978). Yet it is a common political conceit to universalise practical solutions, as a result of an inablity to acknowledge their subjectivity from the sheltered position of a given political culture, and such universalisation leads to alienation when the grounds for political action require justification from without the relevant political culture.

In international relations, the global political system (however conceived) provides an objectifying framework in which the intersubjectivity of particular political cultures may be recognised, but it also presents the problem of relativistic definitions, not simply of politics in a given society, but also of the global political system itself. And here lies the significance of world-views as regards explanations or understandings in International Relations. In the absence of agreed solutions to insoluble philosophical problems, in the absence of a properly developed global political culture, the traditional solution has been a pseudo-scientific claim to the empirical reality of power relations; that this conception of international politics provides no overall framework of meaning has not troubled those who continue to discuss the protection of national interests and the maintainance of a stable (imposed) international order. No doubt this provides justification for the activities of some state actors, but it does not provide a theory of international relations. To pretend either that there is an objective political reality (which is revealed by Realist theory), or that there is a universally relevant culture (a Western culture of rationality, for example) that provides a locus for the resolution of insolubles, is simply to evade the most interesting and important political questions – questions which are brought to life in international relations precisely because they have no cultural solution there.

Hence, the problem in international politics is not simply the location of objective interests – these are indeterminate. The problem is also that of locating those political values that can ascribe meaning to global political life, and can provide grounds for selecting practical solutions to insoluble philosophical problems. In locating these values, however, contrasting or contradictory national cultures may stand in the way of agreed solutions. However, asserting cultural relativism is no answer to this problem, nor does it close the debate: this problem of clashing views and opposing wishes is the apogee of all *political* problems, and requires nothing more nor less than a *political* solution. To abrogate political responsibilities just because the traditional boundaries of political organisation have been exceeded is to abandon our collective fate to the vagaries of historical accident; a dangerous weakness in view of the globalising forces of modernity. The place that values hold in political understanding is, nevertheless, often ignored since the location of values remains problematic – particularly so in International Relations. Because intellectual tastes have tended to favour the analysis of quantifiable utilities, the analysis of values has been marginalised in social science. However, this situation has changed somewhat in recent years, with greater attention given to a values-centred approach to public-policy analysis (Aaron, Mann and Taylor 1994: viii, 2), and a growing interest in normative International Relations theory (Hoffman 1994; Brown 1992; Smith 1992; Dyer 1989; Frost 1986).

On such an account, values are the underlying substance of political systems and structures, and the appropriate objects of study. Any comprehension of interests or tangible assets in politics depends on a comprehension of the values at play, for it is they which endow political meaning. The International Relations of global environmental change have brought the traditional meanings of political concepts into doubt, and the challenge of making new sense of them has opened the way for changes in International Relations theory. This is particularly true for the suspicious concept of 'environmental security'.

Environmental security and national security are alternative values, arising in the context of alternative world-views. If the case is made out for adopting a global perspective, environmental security could stand as a universal value on which more localised environmental policy could be properly founded. If traditional inter-state perspectives hold sway, there is little chance of environmental security becoming any more than an addendum to the traditional politico-military security agenda.

## NOTES

1 The research leading to this article was supported by the Economic and Social Research Council (ESRC) through a Research Fellowship in the Global Environmental Change Programme (Grant No. L320 27 3071). I am also grateful to the members of the British International Studies Association Environment Group, which is also supported by the ESRC, for their helpful comments on an earlier draft.
2 For literature which specifically addresses environmental security, see: Bennett 1991; Brown 1977, 1986; Brown 1989; Dalby 1992a, 1992b; Homer-Dixon 1991, 1994; Lowi 1993; Mathews 1989; Myers 1989; Pirages 1991; Renner 1989a, 1989b; Rowlands 1991; Sorenson 1990; Tickner 1989, 1992; Ullman 1983; Vogler 1993.

## BIBLIOGRAPHY

Aaron, H.J., Mann, T.E and Taylor, T. (eds) (1994) *Values and Public Policy*, Washington, DC: The Brookings Institution.

Bennett, O. (1991) *Greenwar: Environment and Conflict*, London: Panos.

Brenton, T. (1994) *The Greening of Machiavelli*, London: Earthscan/RIIA.

Broecker, W.S. (1992) 'Global warming on trial', *Natural History*, April: 6–14.

Brown, C. (1992) *International Relations Theory: New Normative Approaches*, Hemel Hempstead: Harvester Wheatsheaf.

Brown, L.R. (1977) 'Redefining national security', Worldwatch Institute Paper No. 14, Washington, DC: Worldwatch Institute.

—— (1986) 'Redefining national security', in Brown, L.R. *et al.*, *State of the World 1986*, a Worldwatch Institute Report on Progress Toward a Sustainable Society, New York: Norton.

Brown, N. (1989) 'Climate, ecology and international security', *Survival* 31(6): 519–32.

Brundtland, G. (1987) 'Report of the World Commission on Environment and Development', *Our Common Future*, Oxford: O.U.P.

Butterfield, H. (1951) *History and Human Relations*, London: Collins.

Buzan, B. (1991) *People, States and Fear*, 2nd edn, Hemel Hempstead: Harvester Wheatsheaf.

Conca, K. (1992) 'Peace studies and the multiple meanings of the global environment', paper presented at the 33rd Annual Convention of the International Studies Association, Atlanta, 4 April 1992.

—— (1993) 'Environmental change and the deep structure of world politics', in Lipschutz, R.D. and Conca, K. (eds) (1993) *The State and Social Power in Global Environmental Politics*, New York: Columbia U.P.

Dalby, S. (1992a) 'Modernity, ecology and the dilemmas of security', paper presented at the 33rd Annual Convention of the International Studies Association, Atlanta, 4 April 1992.

—— (1992b) 'Security, modernity, ecology: the dilemmas of post-Cold War security discourse', *Alternatives* 17: 1.

Deudney, D. (1990) 'The case against linking environmental degradation and national security', *Millennium: Journal of International Studies* 19(3): 461–76.

—— (1991) 'Environmental security: muddled thinking', *Bulletin of the Atomic Scientists*, April, pp. 22–8.

di Bernardo, G. (ed.) (1988) *Normative Structures of the Social World*, Amsterdam: Editions Rodopi.

Drucker, P.F. (1990) *The New Realities*, London: Mandarin.

Dyer, H.C. (1989) 'Normative theory and International Relations', in Dyer, H.C. and Mangasarian, L. (eds) *The Study of International Relations: the State of the Art*, London: Macmillan.

Eccleshall, R., Geoghagen, V., Jay, R. and Wilford, R. (1984) *Political Ideologies: an Introduction*, London: Hutchinson.

*Environmental Security Network Newsletter*, 1991, 1(1).

Frost, M. (1986) *Towards a Normative Theory of International Relations*, Cambridge: C.U.P.

Geertz, C. (1981) *Negara: the Theatre State in Nineteenth-Century Bali*, Princeton, NJ: Princeton U.P.

Gleick, P. (1993) 'Water and conflict: fresh water resources and international security', *International Security* 18(1): 79–112.

Greimas, A.J. (1987) *On Meaning: Selected Writings in Semiology*, London: Pinter.

Herz, J.H. (1959) *International Politics in the Atomic Age*, New York and London: Columbia U.P.

Hobhouse, L.T. (1922, 1958) *Elements of Social Justice*, London: George Allen & Unwin.

Hoffman, M. (1994) 'Normative international theory: approaches and issues', in Groom, A.J.R. and Light, M. (eds) *Contemporary International Relations: a Guide to Theory*, London: Pinter.

Homer-Dixon, T.F. (1991) 'On the threshold: environmental changes as causes of acute conflict', *International Security* 16(2): 76–116.

—— (1994) 'Environmental scarcities and violent conflict: evidence from cases', *International Security* 19(1): 5–40.

James, W. (1977) *A Pluralistic Universe*, Cambridge, Mass. and London: Harvard U.P.

Jervis, R. (1976) *Perception and Misperception in International Politics*, Princeton, NJ: Princeton U.P.

Johnson, T.P. (1991) 'Writing for International Security: a contributors' guide', *International Security* 16(2): 172.

Kegley, C.W. (1992) 'The new global order: the power of principle in a pluralistic world', *Ethics and International Affairs* 6: 21–40.

Lipschutz, R.D. and Conca, K. (eds) (1993) *The State and Social Power in Global Environmental Politics*, New York: Columbia U.P.

Lowi, M. (1993) 'Bridging the divide: transboundary resource disputes and the case of West Bank Water', *International Security* 18(1): 113–38.

Lukes, S. (1974) *Power: a Radical View*, London: Macmillan.

Mathews, J.T. (1989) 'Redefining security', *Foreign Affairs* 68(2): 162–77.

Morgenthau, H.J. (1978) *Politics Among Nations*, 5th edn (revised), New York: Alfred A. Knopf.

Myers, N. (1989) 'Environment and security', *Foreign Policy* 74: 23–41.

Palme, O. (1982) 'Independent commission on disarmament and security issues', *Common Security: a Programme for Disarmament*, London: Pan.

Pirages, D. (1991) 'Environmental security and social evolution', *International Studies Notes* 16(1): 8–13.

Porter, G. and Brown, J.W. (1991) *Global Environmental Politics*, Boulder, Col.: Westview.

Renner, M. (1989a) 'Enhancing global security', in Brown, L.R. *et al.*, *State of the World 1989*, a Worldwatch Institute Report on Progress Toward a Sustainable Society, New York: Norton.

—— (1989b) 'National security: the economic and environmental dimensions', Worldwatch Institute Paper No. 89, Washington, DC: Worldwatch Institute.

Rich, B. (1990) 'The emperor's new clothes: the World Bank and environmental reform', *World Policy Journal* 7(2): 307–29.

Robertson, R. (1990) 'Mapping the global condition: globalization as the central concept', in Featherstone, M. (ed.) *Global Culture: Nationalism, Globalization and Modernity*, London: Sage.

Rowlands, I.H. (1991) 'The security challenges of global environmental change', *Washington Quarterly* 14(1): 99–114.

—— (1992) 'Environmental issues in world politics', in Rengger, N.J. and Baylis, J. (eds) (1992) *Dilemmas of World Politics: International Issues in a Changing World*, Oxford: O.U.P.

Skinner, Q. (1981) 'The world as a stage', *The New York Review*, 16 April.

Smith, S. (1992) 'The forty years' detour: the resurgence of normative theory in International Relations', *Millennium: Journal of International Studies* 21(3): 489–506.

Sorenson, T.C. (1990) 'Rethinking national security', *Foreign Affairs* 69(3): 1–18.

Suganami, H. (1989) *The Domestic Analogy and World Order Proposals*, Cambridge: C.U.P.

Tickner, A. (1989) 'Redefining security: a feminist perspective', unpublished paper.

—— (1992) *Gender in International Relations: Feminist Perspectives on Achieving Global Security*, New York: Columbia U.P.

Ullman, R.H. (1983) 'Redefining security', *International Security* 8(1): 129–53.

Vogler, J. (1993) 'Security and global environmental change', *Conflict Processes* 1(2): 1–13.

Weston, D.E. (1978) 'Realism, language and social theories: studies in the relation of the epistemology of science and politics', unpublished PhD thesis (1978), University of Lund, Sweden.

# 3 International political economy and global environmental change

*Marc Williams*

One of the most notable features of world politics in the 1990s is the emphasis given to the environment. The recent upsurge of interest in global environmental issues reflects changes in world politics; an increasing awareness of environmental degradation; the global nature of many environmental problems; and changing attitudes to the relationship between humans and the natural world. In the contemporary global system, the nature and dimensions of the ecological crisis have become an unavoidable issue for governments, business corporations and civic groups. Recently, students of international relations have begun to analyse the dynamics of global environmental change. This chapter is an attempt to examine the ways in which one particular type of international theory has addressed the issue of global environmental change. It will provide a critical introduction to international political economy (IPE) analyses of global environmental change. This task is necessarily complicated because it is impossible to specify a single approach to international political economy. A central task of this chapter, therefore, will be to develop an argument which recognises both the unity and the diversity of IPE as a discipline. In doing so it will assess the contribution of the different perceptions of and responses to the ecological crisis which arise from the differing approaches to IPE.

International political economy (IPE) as a distinct sub-field of international relations is keen to differentiate itself from its parent discipline (Boyle 1994: 351). Specifically, IPE theorists accuse International Relations scholars of state-centrism and a failure to recognise the interconnectedness of politics and economics (Underhill 1994: 17–44). It can be argued that IPE approaches are more appropriate because they are sensitive to questions of values and for the most part begin not with the state but with a range of actors in their analyses of world politics. The first part of this chapter will therefore provide a brief introduction to, and a critique of, the way in which global environmental change has been studied in international relations. Given the need to identify the contours of international political economy, the second part of this chapter will explore IPE as an academic practice. It will distinguish between competing conceptions of IPE in terms of their core assumptions and research strategies. The third section of the chapter will note those implications for the study of global environmental change which arise from these competing IPE perspectives. I will demonstrate that although

IPE is presented as a critique of conventional international relations theory, and to some degree does extend and improve the analytical power of conventional accounts of global politics, orthodox IPE, nevertheless, replicates many of the key assumptions and values of conventional international relations theory. The conclusion considers briefly the reformulation of IPE in such a way that analyses of global environmental change might be made more central to the discipline.

## INTERNATIONAL RELATIONS AND GLOBAL ENVIRONMENTAL CHANGE

IPE sets itself up *against* orthodox IR theory. In examining IPE contributions to a subject area, it is therefore helpful to recapitulate the tenets of traditional theory and to ask two key questions. First, what are the limitations of traditional theorising in this field? And second, how distinctive are the various IPE approaches? It is the contention of this chapter that the engagement of the discipline of international relations in the issue of global environmental change has served to reproduce orthodoxy in the discipline. The 'failure' of international relations theory to provide adequate explanations of global environmental change thus opens up the possibility that IPE approaches, on the other hand, will be more fruitful. But it can also be argued that the close connection between IPE and conventional international relations theory prevents IPE from fulfilling this promise.

In this section I will briefly survey the manner in which the discipline of international relations has responded to the urgent international environmental crisis. In doing so I am centrally concerned with the ways in which the 'new' field of global environmental politics has been incorporated into the discourse of international relations. I will be arguing that the theorisation and conceptualisation of global environmental politics proceed not from an appreciation of the distinctive nature of the subject matter but from the abstractions of a framework informed by neorealism and liberal institutionalism. Moreover, it will be my contention that this incorporation of environmentalism into orthodox international relations theory fails to provide an adequate understanding of global environmental degradation. It is widely agreed that three paradigms or perspectives can be discerned in international relations theory. The realist (and neorealist) paradigm, the dominant approach, is challenged by the respective pluralist (liberal-institutionalist) and radical, or structuralist, perspectives. I am not, of course, suggesting that three clearly demarcated perspectives exist such that, for example, it is an uncontentious exercise to see into which perspective the work of a given writer can be placed. Moreover, each perspective is a complex body of thought with specific historical variants. Nevertheless, International Relations is widely perceived to be riven by competing perspectives informed by competing beliefs, by contrasting sets of values and assumptions about the nature of the discipline, and by a focus on different core actors and relationships (Cox 1992: 166).

Before the 1980s, international relations scholars paid minimal attention to environmental issues. The recent reconciliation of international relations theory with global environmental change has taken as its starting point the recognition of a wholly new issue, and as a result, the reasons for the previous exclusion of the environment have not been investigated. Instead, the failure of international theory – along with theory in other branches of the social sciences – to theorise the environment is accepted as a *fait accompli*. The misrecognition of environmental concerns is now remedied through an approach which attempts to bring the environment into international relations. Such an approach is inherently limited, however, because it fails to account for the previous exclusion. Studying the political economy of the environment necessitates an attempt to understand why environmental issues had been hitherto neglected. That is, a past failure to include environmental concerns in the discipline cannot simply be regarded as a fact with no implications for the theorisation of the global system. Accelerated environmental degradation raises crucial questions concerning humanity's relationship with the natural world, and with other species. Analyses of the global ecological crisis therefore require a rethinking of fundamental concepts and assumptions. Unless international relations theory sets out explicitly to tackle the set of questions which arise from the interaction between the economy and the ecosystem, it will instead merely find itself co-opting environmental analysis and accommodating 'green' issues within the prevailing conception of international relations. It is not in fact the case that international relations theory had previously ignored environmental issues altogether, but rather that (like all social sciences) by internalising environmental issues, it had rendered them invisible. International relations theory had traditionally removed from critical view the ways in which, historically, environmental issues had been silenced.

The crucial question now becomes: how is the new-found visibility to be articulated? And it is important, indeed, to recognise which approaches will provide the best starting point for assessing the politics and economics of global environmental degradation. Before examining the contribution of IPE, it is necessary to look at the manner in which conventional international-relations theory has approached this task of assessment.

Although I do not wish to contest the claim that, in the 1990s, studies of global environmental change have developed predominantly from a pluralist perspective (Smith 1993: 32), nevertheless, it is not the case that realist premises are entirely absent from current accounts of international environmental politics. Traditional international relations theory, in its approach to environmental issues, has made three crucial assumptions. The first concerns the reasons for renewed interest in the environment. In this view, global environmental problems only became issues of high politics in the 1980s, largely through the end of superpower competition with the collapse of the Cold War (Porter and Brown 1991: 1). It should be stressed that two claims are implied here. First, the movement from 'low politics' to 'high politics' is presented as an objective and external event. A series of changes in the global system, it is argued, produced a changing conception of the role of environmental issues in world society. Global environmental change is here conceived as a *given*, as just one more issue on the agenda of states. What should be noted here, however, is that our response to environmental degradation is invariably conditioned by a given ideologically structured conception of the environment. The notion of an environmental crisis is not self-evident. It is open to contestation, and any discussion of global environmental change must be recognised as a reflection both of sets of interests and values and of patterns of power distribution which need to be radically interrogated. Second, this view claims that issues are only worthy of attention in the discipline when they are of consequence to state actors. The privileged position accorded to states is thus doubly reinforced.

In responding to the rise of global environmental politics, international-relations theory has thus continued to privilege the state, and this indeed is its second key assumption. Accounts of global environmental politics focus on the activities of states and pose questions from the perspectives of states (Hurrell and Kingsbury 1992: 1). The problem of environmentalism, in this view, arises from the difficulty of regulating independent political actors in the context of an anarchical international system. States are the key players in this system, engaged in zero-sum, relative-gain power games and required to defend their interests against each other. Non-state actors can be included, but their role by definition is restricted to that of supporting players. One consequence of the state-centric focus of international relations theorising is that although attention *is* given to the role of non-governmental organisations (NGOs) in studies of environmental diplomacy, 'The nature and extent of NGO influence on international environmental policy has not received comprehensive or detailed study' (Caldwell 1988: 24). When NGO influence is noted, it is seen merely as an additional factor which has to be taken into account, and in the end, analysts tend to the conclusion that 'State actors are still primary determinants of issue outcomes in global environmental politics' (Porter and Brown 1991: 68).

The third main assumption in the literature of traditional international relations theory is that of a narrow concept of environmental security. In line with traditional security studies, security is defined as the absence or containment of a threat. Although the national security problem has been redefined to take account of threats arising from environmental degradation (Westing 1991), and although various studies have tried to show how environmental threats can be accommodated within the existing security paradigm, the debate nonetheless fails either to ask whose security is at stake or to question whether traditional security approaches give adequate responses to the problems posed by environmental degradation.

Realism's fixation with state power and the possible use of force, its failure to recognise the role of NGOs in regime building, and the inadequacy of its response to a problem which, in its manifestation, presents a challenge to sovereignty have all made it less helpful as an approach to global environmental politics than the pluralist approach, which starts from a recognition of transnationalism and interdependence. In a continued dialogue with realism, liberal-institutionalist and pluralist accounts of global environmental change contest the state-centric biases of realist explanations and insist instead on the importance of international institutions, international organisations and NGOs in the search for solutions to the global environmental crisis. In a similar vein to realism, pluralist approaches stress environmental management and problem-solving solutions. But within the contemporary interrogation of the ecological crisis, pluralist analysts focus instead on the importance of regimes in structuring expectations and behaviour in the international system. The liberal-institutionalist perspective, which recognises both the importance of knowledge and ideas and the role played by transnational actors, appears to be the more apposite one, given the fact that the ecological crisis arises from increased interdependence and increasing globalisation. The complexity of the issues which arise from global environmental change demands international responses that are sensitive to a complex web of cultural, social, political and economic processes. Consequently, any approach fixated on an unreconstructed concept of the state will be increasingly unable to provide an adequate analysis of the international dimension of the environmental crisis. The limitations of state-centrism and the necessity to examine the environmental impact of other kinds of actors are both explicitly recognised in the pluralist literature.

> Institutionalized sovereignty does not imply that states are the only (or necessarily the most important) agents or institutions responsible for transforming (depleting or degrading) social and natural environments . . . . Many, if not most, of the more powerful human impacts on the natural environment are exerted by private firms, corporations, and comparable organisations and institutions.
>
> (Choucri 1993: 14–15)

A number of studies have looked more closely at the role of international institutions. In this literature, 'institutions' is given two different meanings. Some authors use institutions synonymously with organisations. For example, the collection edited by Peter Haas, Robert Keohane and Marc Levy (1993) assesses the impact and potential contribution of international organisations (institutions) in the promotion of international environmental cooperation. Oran Young (1994), on the other hand, analyses the role of social institutions in terms of the protection of the environment.

Whether the focus is on formal organisations or on informal institutions, liberal-institutionalist analyses challenge the state-centrism of neorealism and provide a less rigid approach to the study of global environmental change. However, a number of criticisms can be levelled at liberal-institutionalist analyses of global environmental politics. First, regime theory can be criticised for its tendency to assume that international cooperation is the result of rational behaviour on the part of self-interested units, for its propensity to treat regimes as if they had an independent and autonomous existence, and for the largely ahistorical and static nature of its analysis (Williams 1994: 37). Second, these approaches are inherently problem-solving, and as such they reduce politics to a mere technical discourse and fail to question existing structures.

To what extent does IPE provide a better starting point for analyses of global environmental change? Before we can examine IPE approaches to global environmental change, it is necessary to look at IPE as an academic discipline. This is because IPE is an arena of competing and contrasting theoretical positions. An understanding of the historical development of IPE and of the conceptual map of the terrain will be helpful in understanding the contemporary applications of IPE to the study of global environmental change.

## INTERNATIONAL POLITICAL ECONOMY

Political economy as a tradition in social and political thought has a long history. The term political economy first emerged in the eighteenth century and signalled an increasing focus upon the role of the state in the economy (Caporaso and Levine 1992: 1). International political economy, while clearly influenced by the history of speculation on the interrelationship between politics and economics, did not emerge as a self-defined field of study until the 1970s. Contemporary IPE has to be understood in the context of the history of political economy, the emergence of IPE within the disciplinary matrix of international relations, and the material conditions surrounding the growth of the study of international political economy.

The absence of consensus on the definition or conceptualisation of IPE is a direct result of the intellectual antecedents of the IPE approach. The history of political economy is one of contrasting theories of politics and economics, and contending views on the central questions of political economy. Agreement may exist on the assumption that political economy is expressly concerned with authority and market relations, but no agreement exists on how the intersections of power and wealth are to be studied. International political economy, then, has to be seen as a site of contention. Indeed, most analysts perceive IPE as a field in which three distinct perspectives or ideologies are battling for control. The specific name given to these ideologies may vary, but the crucial distinction made is that between realist, liberal and Marxist perspectives (Gilpin 1987: 25–64). Contemporary IPE can thus be seen as a contest between competing perspectives, and one in which the protagonists acknowledge the existence of different perspectives.

It follows from the above that no single precise definition of IPE as a distinct discipline is possible (Higgott 1994: 156). IPE has indeed been variously defined, with some definitions stressing the subject matter of the discipline (Keohane 1984: 21; Strange 1988: 18; Stiles and Akaha 1991: xi), some focusing on the sets of questions posed (Gilpin 1987: 9), and others concentrating on an interdisciplinary approach (Gill and Law, 1988: xviii). Given the existing plethora of definitions, it is perhaps unwise to add to the list. Nevertheless, for the purposes of this chapter I will define international political economy as the analysis of the exchange of goods and services across national boundaries, the institutional arrangements which govern these transactions, the policies taken by governments and other actors concerning these flows and institutional arrangements, and the sets of questions posed by the existence of global production, distribution and consumption.

IPE developed within the discipline of international relations at a time when the postwar liberal international economic order was under severe strain (Choucri

1980: 103; Jones 1983: 3–4). The 1970s witnessed a period of increased turbu-lence and uncertainty in the international political economy, brought on by a number of developments. These included the end of the long postwar boom period of economic expansion; the collapse of the Bretton Woods system of fixed exchange rates; a rise in protectionism; a (temporary) rise in the economic power of the developing countries through the influence exerted by the Organisation of Petroleum Exporting Countries (OPEC); the strident clamour of the developing countries (through the Group of 77) for a reform of the liberal order of world trade and payments, and for greater participation in global economic management; the relative decline of American power; and the consequent increased importance of the European Community and Japan as centres of economic power.

Furthermore, the theoretical separation between politics and economics was becoming increasingly untenable in the light of events in the world. In eco-nomics, the dominant neoclassical perspective separated politics from economics on the basis of the assumption that the operation of the market existed outside the political realm. The market, and market relations, could in this view be analysed adequately without recourse to politics. Likewise, in international relations, realism, the dominant paradigm, separated economics from politics. Inter-state relations were analysed largely in terms of power, understood for the most part as military power. The recognition of the limitations of traditional theories of international relations led to the establishment of a theoretical space in which international politics and international economics were enjoined (Strange 1970: 304–15). But the three perspectives that were now delineated were not wholly divorced from conventional international relations theory. In fact, the three IPE perspectives have served to replay and replicate the three paradigms found in international relations.

These three strands of orthodox IPE have not achieved equal prominence in the discipline. Neorealism, the dominant paradigm in the study of IPE, is based, naturally enough, on the central conceptions and categories of realism, and enjoys a superiority which has arisen from the supremacy of realist analyses in the discipline of international relations. As a result, the Marxist or radical paradigm, which offers an alternative analysis of IPE through its concentration on the historical expansion of the capitalist mode of production, has been marginalised in favour of the realist, and the liberal, approaches.

Given the cross-fertilisation of methods and ideas in the contemporary study of IPE, clear distinctions between the various perspectives are not always pos-sible (Crane and Amawi 1991: 3–33) – especially regarding the realist and liberal perspectives. Although the debate between the three perspectives continues to dominate much scholarship, a number of writers, including Strange (1988, 1991), and Gill and Law (1988), have attempted to produce an eclectic or integrated approach which uses insights from all three perspectives. Thus, contemporary research in IPE continues to reflect the diversity within each perspective while also producing analyses which *merge* the three schools of thought.

## ORTHODOX INTERNATIONAL POLITICAL ECONOMY AND GLOBAL ENVIRONMENTAL CHANGE

In this section I will examine the ways in which traditional IPE theories have approached the problem of global environmental degradation. It can be argued that all three perspectives have tended to silence, marginalise and neglect environmental concerns. In so far as this argument is accepted, it is clear that this tendency is not accidental but inscribed in the underlying philosophies of these approaches. The peripheralisation of the environment from the central concerns of orthodox IPE echoes, for example, the exclusion of gender from IPE theories. Environmental concerns are rendered invisible in IPE because the liberal, realist and Marxist paradigms treat the environment as an external factor. The environment merely provides resources for the economic process, rather than being important in its own right.

Underlying the realist, liberal and Marxist perspectives is a technocentric and anthropocentric approach to natural resource use (Eckersley 1992: 21–6). Both liberalism and Marxism share a belief in material growth and technological optimism. And realism, with its emphasis on state interests, is wedded to industrialisation in the contemporary international political economy. It is of course evident that in perspectives with such long histories and internal diversity, not all writers will share these underlying assumptions in their totality. Indeed, in both liberalism and Marxism, one can find theorists who have introduced qualifications to the prevailing technocentrism and anthropocentrism (Eckersley 1992: 23; Dobson 1990: 175–92). Nevertheless, it is possible to argue that the intellectual heritage of international political economy bequeaths it a view in which economic systems should be designed to satisfy the unlimited wants of human beings. The sustainable use of resources was not an important consideration in traditional approaches to the economy. Political philosophy supplied the principles behind such approaches: 'From Hobbes and Locke through to Marx, the notion of human self-realisation through the domination and transformation of nature persisted as an unquestioned axiom of political enquiry' (Eckersley 1992: 25). Recent concern about the threat to both the ecosystem and the future of humanity if unfettered economic growth is not curbed has led to attempts to modify the conventional paradigms. For example, in Marxist analysis there have been attempts to make environmental concerns central to an understanding of international political economy – this will be evident in the discussion of the radical perspective below. In a similar vein, environmental economics uses the tools of neoclassical economics to assess the economic consequences of environmental degradation (Dorfman and Dorfman 1993; Turner, Pearce and Bateman 1994).

Notwithstanding this history of neglect, the contemporary social, economic and political impact of global environmental change is so extensive that IPE cannot ignore environmental concerns. There are two principal aspects to the integration of environmental concerns into IPE. First, a number of environmental problems have an impact on the global political economy, and some form of international agreement is necessary to cope with these problems. As Hurrell and Kingsbury argue: 'international co-operation is required both to manage global environmental problems and to deal with domestic environmental problems in ways that do not place individual states at a political or competitive disadvantage' (Hurrell and Kingsbury 1992: 5). This intersection of environmental concerns and the international political economy can be termed the problem of international or global governance. In the context of international governance, Oran Young identifies four environmental problem sets: '(international) commons, shared natural resources, transboundary externalities, and linked issues' (Young 1994: 19). Problems such as ozone depletion, the management of regional seas, acid rain and sustainable development may arise in different environmental problem sets, but they all require action by international actors.

Second, global environmental change is intimately linked to national and international systems of production, distribution and consumption: 'The . . . most important aspect of increased globalisation derives from the complex but close relationship between the generation of environmental problems and the workings of the effectively globalised world economy' (Hurrell and Kingsbury 1992: 3). This can be characterised as the problem of sustainability. The historical process of capital accumulation and the pursuit of economic growth have both contributed to current environmental degradation. Key issues concerning growth and development strategies, industrialisation, international trade and North–South relations, for example, all require re-examination in the current historical conjuncture. In this context, it can be argued that modern global environmental challenges are characterised by three main features: uncertainty, irreversibility and uniqueness (non-substitutability) (Pearce 1990: 366). Uncertainty arises from the fact that there is no guarantee that sometime in the future, a finite natural resource will be replaceable by technology. Irreversibility can clearly be seen in, for example, the extinction of species, but it also pertains to a wider class of natural assets which, once destroyed, cannot be replaced. And uniqueness is the result of the non-substitutability of some environmental assets by human-made assets.

## GLOBAL GOVERNANCE

IPE approaches to the environment have concentrated on identifying the conditions under which international cooperation will result in the creation of stable institutions which promote environmental sustainability. It is not surprising that the problem of international cooperation has figured so prominently in IPE analyses of global environmental change. Central to both neorealist and neoliberal IPE theories has been the issue of the management of the international economy. Such management is constructed around the necessity to provide international public goods, the creation and maintenance of international regimes to facilitate international order, and the role of leadership in the provision of public goods. The research agenda of IPE has been dominated in the last decade by hegemonic stability theory and regime theory. Both neorealists and liberal institutionalists focus attention on the creation and maintenance of international order through formal international organisations and informal institutionalised practices.

It is possible to discern the outlines of a realist IPE critique of global environmental change. Central to the realist and neorealist project are two assumptions. First, that states are likely to be constrained from cooperation by the anarchic nature of international society. Second, that the state's formal apparatus and enduring interests are what shape and transform economic processes. International cooperation, from this perspective, only arises in so far as it supports the political interests of the state. Within the realist paradigm, with its focus on states and its concern for the accretion of state power, any resource use which increases the influence of states is held to be valid. Realist analysis stresses the difficulty of establishing cooperation on the environment. In this respect, the environment is seen as no different from other international 'issue-areas'. Realism, in its concentration on states and state power, marginalises the role of international organisations. The neorealist version of hegemonic stability theory argues that a necessary condition for international cooperation is the existence of a dominant or hegemonic state. Regimes are created, in this view, only when a dominant state has both the resources for and an interest in providing the necessary leadership to foster international cooperation. This realist tendency to assume that international cooperation is the result of rational behaviour on the part of self-interested states is echoed by economic analyses of international environmental cooperation. Richard Blackhurst and Arvind Subramanian (1992) use game theory to examine the scope for multilateral cooperation on the environment. In a similar vein, Scott Barrett (1993) constructs a formal model to explain why countries will cooperate in the face of the free-rider problem. The limitations of these assumptions are well known and need not be rehearsed here. A number of studies have shown that regimes can be created and maintained in the absence of a hegemon (Keohane 1984; Axelrod and Keohane 1985; Young 1989). The postulate of rational action is very limiting, and a focus on states misrepresents the complex interplay of actors in global environmental politics. And in a complex and changing world, the ahistorical approach of neorealist IPE fails to capture the underlying causes of environmental degradation, which are 'fundamentally rooted in the process of globalisation which has effectively rendered the territorial state incapable of fulfilling its traditional functions' (Thomas 1993: 3).

The liberal-institutionalist approach extends the neorealist analysis on a number of levels, and provides different answers to questions concerning the definition of the international system. World politics, in this view, cannot be encapsulated through a focus on the most powerful states. The international system is perceived as a series of networks and transactions which involve a number of actors, and as one in which cooperation is more than just a coincidence of short-term interests. In other words, states are enmeshed in a network of transactions and interdependencies which limit and constrain their authority. In the liberal-institutionalist approach to IPE, institutions are crucial determinants of behaviour (Young 1994: 1–8; Haas, Keohane and Levy 1993).

From the perspective of liberal IPE, ecological degradation arises from the interconnectedness of national societies. Environmental degradation is therefore one result of the growth of interdependence. Since global environmental change does not respect national borders, multilateral cooperation and the identification of common or shared interests across territorial units are required if it is to be successfully addressed. Regimes may reflect the preponderant power of *one* state actor, but they need not do so. As already established, regimes are sometimes formed in the absence of a hegemonic state and can continue to function when leadership is absent. Collective action in pursuit of environmental stability and environmental sustainability is thus seen as involving a number of different actors, and the state-centric focus of realist IPE is thus relaxed to allow for the contribution of non-state actors. Klinger, in an analysis of debt-for-nature swaps, argues that 'the anarchy of international politics is not always incompatible with cooperation, but that cooperation will not always come from the efforts of states' (Klinger 1994: 243). Developing the transnational relations perspective of IPE, Klinger demonstrates that the diffusion of science and technology, and the activities of NGOs are crucial determinants of international cooperation on behalf of the environment. Extending further this argument concerning the diffusion of science and technology, Peter Haas (1990a, 1990b) argues that significant international environmental cooperation is the result of the influence of ecological epistemic communities. Epistemic communities are defined as 'transnational networks of knowledge based communities that are both politically empowered through their claims to exercise authoritative knowledge and motivated by shared causal and principled beliefs' (Haas 1990a: 349). These studies focus on elite dynamics, and thus tend to have little to say about non-elite social movements. However, the role of transnational social movements in the analysis of global environmental politics cannot be reduced to the activities of elite groups (Laferrière 1994). And moreover, although liberal IPE examines power relations in the context of the institutions it describes, it neglects the role of power in shaping those institutions in the first place. In other words, considerations of structural inequalities are not given sufficient prominence.

The radical approach to international governance begins from a critique of realist and liberal approaches. Radicals argue that environmental degradation arises from the capitalist mode of development. In contrast to liberal theories, the radical approach does not regard environmental degradation as an accidental outcome of development which can be easily rectified through market-led or command and control solutions. On the contrary, environmental degradation is seen as the direct result of the processes of accumulation, production and reproduction central to capitalism. In discussing the problems of global governance, radical analyses urge a shift in focus from the deliberations of multilateral organisations and their outcomes to a concentration on the underlying structural conditions which give rise to environmental degradation (Woodhouse 1992). Global environmental management as exemplified by the UNCED process is likely to fail. Far from tackling the root causes of the ecological crisis, such multilateral management organisations merely reinforce existing power structures

(Doran 1993: 61; Chatterjee and Finger 1994). Furthermore, radical and neo-Marxist writers tend to argue that in a hierarchical international power structure, the developed countries of the North dominate international decision-making. The exploitation of the Third World countries, established in colonial times and continued through a variety of neocolonialist practices, will be replicated, it is claimed, in the debates on international environmental issues (Haas 1990b: 47–52). International organisations are not, however, mere epiphenomena with a negligible impact on international relations, and in underestimating the salience of institutional bargaining, radical writers present a static picture of the dynamics of the international political economy. Their depiction of the countries of the South as mere pawns of the North both misrepresents the exercise of power and is politically disabling.

## ENVIRONMENTAL SUSTAINABILITY

In this section, the differing approaches of the liberal and radical perspectives only will be considered. This is not because realist writers have nothing to say on these issues but rather because, in terms of economic analysis, any distinctively realist approach will share a similar foundation to that of the liberal paradigm. (The major difference, however, lies in the role given to the state and to state interests. Whereas liberals emphasise the role of individual actors and the potential harmony of interests, realists stress the importance of the state and the possibility of conflict.) In what follows, a realist argument can be extrapolated from the economic analysis of liberal economics.

Within contemporary IPE, the politics of sustainability generates a debate on various issues. Conflicts arising from international trade, pollution control, the preservation of biodiversity and sustainable development have all figured prominently on the international agenda. Of the many issues debated in the field of the political economy of global environmental change, sustainable development is perhaps the most urgent. Sustainable development has become, within a very short time, a term to which all subscribe, but to which all attach different meanings. The Brundtland Commission's definition of sustainable development as 'development that meets the needs of the present without compromising the ability of future generations to meet their own needs' ('World Commission on Environment and Development' 1987: 43) has become, if not the standard definition, the point from which other contestations flow. A number of common themes emerge in the debate on sustainable development. First, there is general agreement on the principle of intergenerational equity. In other words, sustainable development policies should ensure that the welfare of future generations is no lower than our own. Second, proponents of sustainable development focus on efficiency of resource use. After a closer look at the use of natural resources, and at the pollution created as a result of economic production, efficiency is defined in such a way that the full social costs of goods and services are reflected in the price of production inputs and consumer goods. Third, the literature on sustainable development has been concerned with the inter-country and intra-country effects of changes in economic policies. In the context of the global political economy, North–South relations are a prime site for discussions of equity. The advanced industrial states achieved their current living standards through a process of industrialisation which resulted in untold environmental degradation. This industrialisation option is now closed to the developing countries. However, the adoption of sustainable policies will be costly, and unless the advanced industrial countries are willing to effect major transfers of resources, the necessary policies are unlikely to be implemented.

Liberal theorists locate the problem of sustainability within the context of a global economy of mutually interdependent actors. They regard nature as a commodity which can be subject to property rights, and believe that market mechanisms create the most efficient use of resources. Sustainable development policies can be pursued through the creation of economic incentives to retard, stop or reverse the processes of environmental degradation. In this analysis, economic growth *per se* is not challenged. Indeed, economic development, here seen principally as growth-oriented, is regarded as a vital component of a sound environmental strategy. In this context it is argued that a symbiotic relationship exists between development and environmental protection. Far from being oppositional, development and environmental protection are, in this view, compatible. The crucial link between environmental sustainability and economic development arises from the interactions between poverty and environmental management. Economic growth is necessary for poverty reduction, but such growth can also cause serious environmental degradation. On the other hand, poverty, too, is a significant contributor to environmental damage. It is only through the possibilities of alternative policies introduced by sustained growth that sound environmental policies can be instituted. Sustainable development is therefore both a desirable goal and a feasible outcome. Economic growth can cause environmental degradation, and it is only through the more efficient use of resources and through technological innovation that sound environmental protection will be guaranteed. In the words of the World Bank:

> rising incomes combined with sound environmental policies and institutions can form the basis for tackling both environmental and development problems. The key to growing sustainably is not to produce less but to produce differently.
>
> (World Bank 1992: 36)

One of the key areas of conflict in the debate over sustainable development concerns the merits of free trade. Liberal theorists argue that no inherent conflict exists between trade liberalisation and sustainable development. Indeed, increased protectionism to safeguard the environment will, according to this perspective, lead to a reduction in welfare (Williams 1993: 88–90). The case for free trade is based on the view that where external costs exist, they are better dealt with by non-trade policy instruments. Developing the argument further, liberal theorists stress the additional benefits of maintaining an open trading environment (World Bank 1992: 67). Doing so, they argue, would contribute to conflict resolution, because in the contemporary international economic system of mutually interdependent actors, the failure on the part of the developing countries to implement environmentally friendly technologies will eventually result in adverse impacts on Northern lifestyles. And therefore, the developed countries will come to recognise their own self-interest in providing substantial assistance to the developing countries so that the latter can afford the new technologies necessary for sustainable development.

Radical approaches to sustainability locate environmental degradation in the dynamics of capitalist industrialisation and development. As Carolyn Merchant argues, 'The patterns of uneven development and their differential economic and ecological effects are the products of a global market economy that has been emerging since the sixteenth century' (Merchant 1992: 23). The quest for sustainable development consequently has to confront the values, interests and power behind the capitalist international division of labour. The ecological crisis is the result of a specific pattern of economic growth, i.e. capitalism, and embodies the contradictions inherent in that economic and social system. Unsustainable development in the South is a direct consequence of the incorporation of developing countries into an asymmetrical international division-of-labour system. Southern dependence and unsustainable agricultural and industrial policies are maintained through the prevalent patterns of trade, finance and investment, and unless these structures are overturned, sustainable development will remain an aspiration rather than a practical goal (Ekins 1993: 91–103). Moreover, radical critics allege that a contradiction exists between the goals of sustainability, on the one hand, and development as defined in the conventional paradigm on the other. The relationship between economic growth, development and sustainability is complex and problematic. Redclift argues that 'The concentration on "growth" has served to obscure the fact that resource depletion and unsustainable development are a direct consequence of growth itself' (Redclift 1987: 56). Sustainable development will only be achieved through a radical rethinking of both the postwar concept of development and the traditional resource use paradigm. It will be impossible to implement the desired changes under existing structures of political and economic power.

The liberal case for free trade is rejected by radical writers, who argue that international trade is a major mechanism in the creation and maintenance of environmental degradation. Lang and Hines assert: 'To free trade further now would be to add insult to environmental injury. Trade already directly damages the environment and further deregulation would be an incentive to greater harm' (Lang and Hines 1993: 61). The case for environmental protection rests on a number of claims. First, it is alleged that international trade reinforces inequality and thereby results in environmental damage. Producing raw materials for export rather than growing food for internal consumption is one mechanism whereby existing inequalities within a country are reinforced through participation in international trade (Ropke 1994). Second, specialisation through trade, it is argued, can result in reduced incomes and environmental degradation for primary producers. Trade liberalisation and existing patterns of North–South specialisation maintain the South's impoverished position. Falling terms of trade lead to declining export receipts and to patterns of land use which exacerbate environmental degradation (Arden-Clarke 1992). Third, some writers claim that the liberal trade regime encourages transnational corporations to transplant pollution-intensive industries from the industrialised countries, where environmental regulations are strict, to the developing world where environmental controls are relatively lax (El-Hinnawi and Hashmi 1982: 10–11).

The debate between the liberal and radical views will remain unresolved, given the competing methodologies and value preferences of the various writers. Neither perspective provides convincing explanations of the international political economy of global environmental change. Liberal theories are deficient because they fail to deal adequately with power and power relations – specifically, they are unable to represent structural forms of power. Neo-Marxist analysis, with its emphasis on the structural relationship between labour and capital, and its location of environmental degradation in the political and economic structures of capitalist societies, does appear to represent an advance. However, the historical evidence clearly shows that both capitalist and socialist regimes have failed to protect the environment. The failure to implicate socialist development strategies in environmental degradation arises from a continued attachment to economic growth and a failure to recognise the ecological limits to growth.

## CONCLUSION

Given the extensive nature of the social, economic and political impact of environmental degradation, ecological concerns should form a central role in IPE. The connections between economics and the environment, combined with the necessity of collective action to counter common resource problems, place contemporary environmental concerns at the centre of international relations. To date, however, global ecology has been only of marginal concern to IPE. The continued marginalisation of the environment in IPE reflects the close connection between the production of knowledge in international relations and the production of knowledge in IPE.

The causes of environmental degradation are complex and require a careful understanding of the ways in which economic systems interact with the ecosystem. The expanded terrain of IPE provides at first sight a more appropriate starting point for the analysis of global environmental change than conventional international relations theory. However, although IPE analyses of global environmental change include the activities of transnational corporations and international organisations, the roles of social movements, the influence of ideas and ideology, and the impact of debt and trading patterns in structuring outcomes, to date, these analyses have failed to provide convincing explanations of the political economy of global environmental change.

The constraints of space prohibit an extended critique of the limitations of orthodox IPE. Contemporary analyses of the political economy of global environmental change can be challenged on two broad grounds. First, much of the current theorising is constructed within a positivist epistemology (Murphy and Tooze

1991). This commitment to positivism and empiricism limits the explanatory power of orthodox IPE. Positivism separates subject from object, 'facts' from values, and presents a view of knowledge constructed around the concept of a knowable and objective external reality. But 'facts' do not exist independently of the observer. Positivist approaches prohibit critical self-reflexive theory. Analysis of the complex interplay between social theory and social practice is an interpretative process, and it is impossible to produce critical theory without a recognition of the subjectivity of knowledge production. The so-called new IPE (Murphy and Tooze 1991), involving a critique of the epistemological and methodological bases of orthodox IPE, provides a departure point for analyses of globalisation and environmental change. The linkages between globalisation and ecological degradation are more usefully addressed through an approach which explores the interactions between transnational ideologies, transnational social movements and states. The neo-Gramscian analysis of historical blocs and social forces (Cox 1981) provides a useful site from which to analyse the problem of governance in global environmental politics, since a reformulated version of IPE will need to develop a complex understanding of the linkages between knowledge, power and interests. We need to assess those structures of the global political economy which gave rise to environmental degradation. This will only be possible through a critical self-reflexive approach.

The second main challenge to conventional IPE is that it has failed to incorporate the ecological perspective on political economy, a perspective which starts from the assumption that economics and the environment are inseparable. Ecological economics is based on the premiss that a reciprocal and dynamic process exists wherein the economy is in continuous exchange with the environment. The economy alters the environment, and the environment in turn affects the economy (Georgescu-Roegen 1976: 4). The environment is part of the economy because the biosphere performs three key functions for economic systems: it provides both renewable and non-renewable resources for the production process; it assimilates the resulting waste products; and it provides amenities and life-support mechanisms for consumption (Jacobs 1991: 3–5). Similarly, the economy is also part of the environment: 'It is constrained by the same physical laws and its processes mirror those of the biosphere' (Jacobs 1991: 15). Ecological economics stands in sharp contrast to environmental economics which believes that no insoluble conflict exists between economic growth and environmental conservation. Ecological economics is based on the premiss that the earth has natural limitations which restrict an unbridled growth in productive and technological capacities. It starts from the assumption that economic activity is subject both to the constraints of the biosphere and to the laws of thermodynamics (Daly and Cobb 1990). These constraints limit the growth of production and consumption – in other words, the carrying capacity of the earth represents a barrier to the pursuit of unlimited growth in GNP. IPE should explore the prevailing assumptions concerning the relationship between humans and the natural world. This critical task will not be accomplished if ecological economics remains invisible in IPE.

# BIBLIOGRAPHY

Arden-Clarke, C. (1992) 'South–North terms of trade, environmental protection and sustainable development', *World Wide Fund for Nature Discussion Paper*.

Axelrod, R. and Keohane, R.O. (1985) 'Achieving cooperation under anarchy: strategies and institutions', *World Politics* 38(1): 226–54.

Barrett, S. (1993) 'International cooperation for environmental protection', in Dorfman, R. and Dorfman, N.S. (eds) (1993) *Economics of the Environment*, 3rd edn, New York: Norton, pp. 445–63.

Blackhurst, R. and Subramanian, A. (1992) 'Promoting multilateral cooperation on the environment', in Blackhurst, R. and Anderson, K. (eds) *The Greening of World Trade Issues*, Hemel Hempstead: Harvester Wheatsheaf, pp. 247–68.

Boyle, C. (1994) 'Imagining the world market: IPE and the task of social theory', *Millennium: Journal of International Studies* 23(2): 351–63.

Caldwell, L.K. (1988) 'Beyond environmental diplomacy: the changing institutional structure of international cooperation', in Carroll, J.E. (ed.) (1988) *International Environmental Diplomacy*, Cambridge: C.U.P., pp. 13–27.

Caporaso, J.A. and Levine, D.P. (1992), *Theories of Political Economy*, Cambridge: C.U.P.

Chatterjee, P. and Finger, M. (1994) *The Earth Brokers*, London: Routledge.

Choucri, N. (1980) 'International political economy: a theoretical perspective', in Holsti, O.R., Silverson, R.M. and George, A.L. (eds) *Change in the International System*, Boulder, Col.: Westview, pp. 103–29.

—— (1993) 'Introduction: theoretical, empirical, and policy perspectives', in Choucri, N. (ed.) *Global Accord: Environmental Challenges and International Response*, Cambridge, Mass.: MIT Press, pp. 1–40.

Cox, R.W. (1981) 'Social forces, states and world orders: beyond international relations theory', *Millennium: Journal of International Studies* 12(2): 126–55.

—— (1992) 'Multilateralism and world order', *Review of International Studies* 18(2): 161–80.

Crane, G.T. and Amawi, A. (1991) 'Theories of international political economy', in Crane, G.T. and Awami, A. (eds) *The Theoretical Evolution of International Political Economy*, New York: O.U.P., pp. 3–33.

Daly, H.E. and Cobb, J.B. (1990) *For the Common Good*, London: Green Print.

Dobson, A. (1990) *Green Political Thought*, London: Routledge.

Doran, P. (1993) 'The Earth Summit (UNCED): ecology as spectacle', *Paradigms* 7(1): 55–65.

Dorfman, R. and Dorfman, N.S. (eds) (1993) *Economics of the Environment*, 3rd edn, New York: Norton.

Eckersley, R. (1992) *Environmentalism and Political Theory*, London: UCL Press.

Ekins, P. (1993) 'Making development sustainable', in Sachs, W. (ed.) (1993) *Global Ecology*, London: Zed Books, pp. 91–103.

El-Hinnawi, E. and Hashmi, M.H. (1982) *Global Environmental Issues*, Dublin: Tycooly International Publishing Ltd.

Georgescu-Roegen, N. (1976) *Energy and Economic Myths*, New York: Pergamon.

Gill, S. and Law, D. (1988) *The Global Political Economy*, Hemel Hempstead: Harvester Wheatsheaf.

Gilpin, R. (1987) *The Political Economy of International Relations*, Princeton, NJ: Princeton U.P.

Haas, P.M. (1990a) 'Obtaining international environmental protection through epistemic consensus', *Millennium: Journal of International Studies* 19(3): pp. 347–63.

—— (1990b) *Saving the Mediterranean*, New York: Columbia U.P.

——, Keohane, R.O. and Levy, M.A. (eds) (1993) *Institutions for the Earth*, Cambridge, Mass.: MIT Press.

Higgott, R. (1994) 'International political economy', in Groom, A.J.R. and Light, M. (eds) *Contemporary International Relations: a Guide to Theory*, London: Pinter, pp. 156–69.

Hurrell, A. and Kingsbury, B. (1992) 'The international politics of the environment: an introduction', in Hurrell, A. and Kingsbury, B. (eds) (1992) *The International Politics of the Environment*, Oxford: Clarendon, pp. 1–47.

Jacobs, M. (1991) *The Green Economy*, London: Pluto.

Jones, R.J.B. (1983) 'Political economy: contrasts, criteria and contribution', in Jones, R.J.B. (ed.) *Perspectives on Political Economy*, London: Pinter, pp. 3–13.

Keohane, R.O. (1984) *After Hegemony*, Princeton, NJ: Princeton U.P.

Klinger, J. (1994), 'Debt-for-nature swaps and the limits to international cooperation on behalf of the environment', *Environmental Politics* 3(2): 229–46.

Laferrière, E. (1994) 'Environmentalism and the global divide', *Environmental Politics* 3(1): 91–113.

Lang, T. and Hines, C. (1993) *The New Protectionism*, London: Earthscan.

Merchant, C. (1992) *Radical Ecology*, New York: Routledge.

Murphy, C.N. and Tooze, R. (1991) 'Getting beyond the "common sense" of the IPE orthodoxy', in Murphy, C.N. and Tooze, R. (eds) *The New International Political Economy*, Boulder, Col.: Lynne Riener, pp. 11–32.

Pearce, D. (1990) 'Economics and the global environmental challenge', *Millennium: Journal of International Studies* 19(3): 365–87.

Porter, G. and Brown, J.W. (1991) *Global Environmental Politics*, Boulder, Col.: Westview.

Redclift, M. (1987) *Sustainable Development*, London: Routledge.

Ropke, I. (1994) 'Trade, development and sustainability: a critical assessment of the "free trade" dogma', *Ecological Economics* 9(1): pp. 13–22.

Smith, S. (1993) 'The environment on the periphery of international relations: an explanation', *Environmental Politics* 2(4): 28–45.

Stiles, K.W. and Akaha, T. (1991) 'Preface', in Kendall W.S. and Akaha, T. (eds) *International Political Economy: a Reader*, pp. ix–xiv.

Strange, S. (1970) 'International economics and international relations: a case of mutual neglect', *International Affairs* 46(2): 304–15.

—— (1988) *States and Markets*, London: Pinter.

—— (1991) 'An eclectic approach', in Murphy, C.N. and Tooze, R. (eds) (1991) *The New International Political Economy*, Boulder, Col.: Lynne Reiner, pp. 33–49.

Thomas, C. (1993) 'Beyond UNCED: an introduction', *Environmental Politics* 2(4): 1–27.

Turner, R.K., Pearce, D. and Bateman, I. (1994) *Environmental Economics*, Hemel Hempstead: Harvester Wheatsheaf.

Underhill, R.G.D. (1994) 'Introduction: conceptualising the changing global order', in Stubbs, R. and Underhill, R.G.D. (eds) *Political Economy and the Changing Global Order*, Basingstoke: Macmillan, pp. 17–44.

Westing, A.H. (1991) 'Environmental security and its relation to Ethiopia and Sudan', *Ambio*, August: 168–71.

Williams, M. (1993) 'International trade and the environment: issues, perspectives and challenges', *Environmental Politics* 2(4): 80–97.

—— (1994) *International Economic Organisations and the Third World*, Hemel Hempstead: Harvester Wheatsheaf.

Woodhouse, P. (1992) 'Environmental degradation and sustainability', in Allen, T. and Thomas, A. (eds) *Poverty and Development in the 1990s*, Oxford: O.U.P., pp. 97–115.

World Bank (1992) *World Development Report 1992*, New York: O.U.P.

'World Commission on Environment and Development' (the Brundtland Report) (1987) *Our Common Future*, Oxford: O.U.P.

Young, O. (1989) 'The politics of regime formation: managing global resources and the environment', *International Organization*, Summer: 349–77.

—— (1994) *International Governance*, Ithaca, NY: Cornell U.P.

# 4 IR theory

## Neorealism, neoinstitutionalism and the Climate Change Convention[1]

*Matthew Paterson*

This chapter is the product of an investigation on the one hand into some strands of IR theory,[2] and on the other into the process of international cooperation on global warming that led up to the signing of the framework convention in June 1992. It engages in the (possibly overambitious) task of simultaneously trying to say something both about the politics of global warming and about international relations theory.

The chapter takes as a background two developments. First are the developments during the 1980s within IR theory. During this period, IR theory could be characterised as having involved a 'great' debate between neorealism and neo-liberal institutionalism. Certainly, with regard to the phenomenon of international cooperation, this debate has been prominent, with both schools offering differing accounts of the phenomenon of cooperation and the likelihood of its endurance. However, the 1980s, particularly the later part of that decade, also witnessed a rise in theories which came from thoroughly different traditions from those underlying the essentially neopositivist approaches of both neorealism and neo-liberal institutionalism. Critical theory, Gramscian thought, post-structuralist theories and feminism all started to generate a literature, specifically on international relations, which focused on a critique of the epistemological presumptions of much mainstream IR theory, and called into question many of the latter's central assumptions.

The second development is the emergence of environmental issues, and more specifically of global warming, as focuses of international attention. A brief account is given below of international cooperation on global warming as achieved through the Intergovernmental Panel on Climate Change (IPCC) and then the Intergovernmental Negotiating Committee for a Framework Convention on Climate Change (INC) and the Framework Convention.[3] This development remains severely undertheorised. Most of the literature on the international politics of global warming either simply makes prescriptions for international action in one form or another, or, where theoretical material *is* used, rather crudely presses such material into service in order to support one or another normative position. There remains an analytical gap in the understanding of processes of international cooperation with regard to the issue of global warming. Most of the literature which has expressed the problem in either of the above two ways has assumed that international cooperation is a phenomenon which can be theorised in the abstract, and therefore that 'truths' learned, say, over arms-control agreements can also be applied to global warming. For example, Sebenius (1991) simply applies existing theory normatively to global warming, assuming both that the model holds for other areas of international cooperation (without demonstrating this belief) and that 'lessons' learnt in other areas of international politics can be applied to global warming.

These prescriptive uses of IR theory fail to recognise the specificity of climate change as a political phenomenon. It seems plausible, after all, that specific areas of international politics will exhibit different patterns and processes of cooperation, since they will have different underlying problem structures. Some may have a very highly technical component; others may not. Some may be about securing the physical territory of a state; others about securing collective goods. Some may require the compliance of recalcitrant states; others may exist in a situation of relative harmony. Thus, it is justifiable to study IR theory, in the light of international cooperation over global warming, more deeply before pronouncing judgement with respect to prescriptions. The aim then of this chapter is to try to see how the differing theoretical approaches to international relations would account for the process of cooperation on global warming; to evaluate the adequacy of these accounts; and to offer some thoughts on what this says both about IR theory and about the international politics of global warming.[4]

## CLIMATE CHANGE AND INTERNATIONAL POLITICS

Climate change hit the international political agenda in 1988. There were a number of reasons for this. In the background was the development of a scientific consensus that some warming was likely if current trends in emissions of the gases involved (primarily carbon dioxide ($CO_2$), methane, chlorofluorocarbons (CFCs) and nitrous oxide) continued. Second, climate change arrived on the back of a series of other environmental issues which rose onto the political agenda in the West during the 1980s, such as acid rain, ozone depletion and tropical deforestation. Third, it also arrived during an economic boom in most Western countries, meaning that the usual economic objections to action on environmental issues were not at the forefront of public consciousness. And fourth, there was a series of freak weather conditions, of which the most important politically were the US drought in 1988 and the empirical observation that the 1980s provided the six hottest years on record. These four main factors combined to make claims by scientists about climate change increasingly plausible both to the general public and to policy-makers.[5]

In response to this rise in public and scientific concern, politicians instituted three main initiatives. First was the establishment of the Intergovernmental Panel on Climate Change (IPCC) in late 1988, to provide a full report for policy-makers about the state of the scientific consensus about climate change and its possible impacts, as well as ideas about possible response strategies (see Boehmer-Christiansen, this volume). Second was a series of international conferences at which high-level politicians made pronouncements on desirable responses. And third was a series of unilateral targets which states set in 1988–91 to limit their emissions of $CO_2$, the main greenhouse gas.[6] Most of these latter targets committed the state concerned to stabilising its $CO_2$ emissions at 1990 levels by the year 2000, although some (such as Germany's) involved commitments to actual reductions in emissions.

These three responses kept climate change on the political agenda, so that by 1990, the momentum had built up sufficiently to lead to international negotiations towards an international convention on the subject. Negotiations towards this end started in February 1991 in Chantilly, near Washington, DC, within the Inter-governmental Negotiating Committee (INC). They were intended to lead to the signing of a treaty at the United Nations Conference on Environment and Development (UNCED) in 1992.

The negotiations in question can be characterised by two main conflicts. The first of these was between the USA and other industrialised countries concerning the nature of their commitments to limit greenhouse gas emissions. The USA, informed by a scepticism about the nature of the scientific knowledge on climate change, and more than aware of the economic costs of action, refused to set a quantified target. The European countries and Japan tried repeatedly to persuade the USA of the necessity of such an approach, suggesting an agreement based on the wording they had already set out in their unilateral targets. Occasionally, they made implicit threats to the effect that they would go ahead with a Convention without the USA if the USA did not agree to such approach, but in the end, however, they were not prepared to carry these through. Eventually, a compromise wording was reached which included mention of dates but was sufficiently ambiguous to make claims that it was a binding commitment implausible (United Nations 1992: Article 4.2 (a) and (b)).

The second conflict was a North–South one. This primarily concerned the resources which industrialised countries would commit themselves to giving in order to enable developing countries to meet any commitments they would have under the Convention. The argument for these transfers was that since it was the industrialised countries that were primarily responsible for causing climate change, and since it was they who had the financial and technological resources to enable developing countries to limit the growth of their own emissions in the future, such transfers should be organised by the North. However, while in principle industrialised countries accepted this (more or less), they committed few resources, and as a result the commitments undertaken by developing countries in the Convention were correspondingly minimal (limited to compiling inventories of their greenhouse-gas sources and sinks).[7]

The Convention was signed in 1992, as anticipated, and came into force in March 1994, following the required 50 signatures.[8] However, although the negotiations continued beyond UNCED, extending up to the first Conference of the Parties in Spring 1995 in Berlin, political pressure for action on climate change waned in the West in the early 1990s, and the pace of negotiations correspondingly declined.

## NEOREALISM AND NEOLIBERAL INSTITUTIONALISM

However contested by the recent development of critical approaches, mainstream contemporary IR theory is still dominated by the neorealism associated with Waltz and Gilpin, and with the neoliberal institutionalism associated with Keohane, Young and most 'regime analysts'. These writers generally share a particular conception of what it involves to engage in theorising. Specifically, they share a neopositivist epistemology, with Waltz appealing to 'philosophy of science' values (apparently unaware of the divergences between various philosophies of science) and Keohane relying heavily on Lakatos (c.f. Keohane 1983). The role of theory in this schema is to generate hypotheses which can be tested, and even if (as in Waltz) it is suggested that strict falsification tests cannot be applied, or that generalisations are necessarily conditional and limited in scope (as in Keohane), the intention is nonetheless to be able to infer validity for the theory according roughly to the standards of the natural sciences.

The problems involved with this form of epistemological position are well known. Of particular note here are two factors. One is the 'theory-ladenness of fact' problem; that the theory will generate hypotheses which, instead of simply being applied to pre-existing 'facts', will themselves generate lines of enquiry which produce and at least partially constitute the 'facts' to be used in analysis.

Another problem with this position is that by creating a strict distinction between facts and values, it creates an equivalent distinction between analytical, or empirical, theory and normative theory. Not only this, but it also explicitly privileges the analytical, 'value-free' theory. Thus, one ends up trying to theorise either about the way the world is or about how the world ought to be, and these activities are held to be irredeemably separate (see Dyer in this volume).[9]

The point of this discussion of epistemological questions is that it affects the discussion of some of the substantive analytical points made by both neorealists and neoliberal institutionalists. Many of the critiques of those theories made elsewhere (e.g. Ashley 1986; Der Derian and Shapiro 1989) and below are grounded in objections to the epistemological position of these writers, and in particular to their insistence on a strict fact–value, or analytical–normative distinction. This point will be followed up below.

What follows is a brief account of the neorealist and neoliberal-institutionalist theories. The following section will involve a description of how they could account for the international politics of global warming. Neorealism is a school of thought largely associated with Kenneth Waltz, Robert Gilpin and Joseph Grieco. While some (including Grieco and Gilpin themselves) would object to this group being separated off from 'classical' Realists, Keohane gives a useful account of how they differ; particularly through neorealism's emphasis on the importance of the structure of anarchy (Keohane 1983: especially 38–44).[10] Neorealism, essentially an ontological account, embodies a set of basic theoretical assumptions which it suggests give a reasonably accurate account of the way the world is. First, the world is composed primarily of sovereign states, which can be treated as unitary actors. Second, these states exist in a condition of anarchy; that is, there is no government holding power over them. Third, as a consequence of this anarchy, the states must always be on guard against their neighbours since they are always in potential danger of invasion. And fourth, as a consequence of this, states behave in such a way as to maximise their power relative to others.[11] Thus, neorealism's account of how outcomes in international politics are produced is simply that they are generated by the distribution of power capabilities in the system.

Neorealism came to draw on another theory which had grown across various areas of the social sciences during the previous ten to twenty years, namely game theory. Some of the insights of game-theoretical constructs, particularly those of non-cooperative games such as Prisoner's Dilemma (PD) and Chicken, were seen to be applicable to various areas of international politics, in order to explain, for example, arms races. Frequently, they were held to uphold central Realist assessments of the conflictual nature of international politics.

What in fact was the case, however, was that theoretical developments within game theory tended to *undermine* these realist assessments. In particular, Taylor (1976) and Axelrod (1984) showed how when games such as PD are iterated, there is no necessary reason why non-cooperative outcomes will prevail. Thus, on the basis of game theory, which relied on an essentially Realist account of the nature of international politics (Axelrod 1984: 190–1), a theory developed which suggested how enduring cooperation could emerge which would alter the nature of international politics.[12]

This theoretical development was mainly responsible for generating the theoretical position largely associated with Keohane, which he (following Grieco's original (1988) characterisation) termed neoliberal institutionalism (Keohane 1989). Only one different assumption is then necessary to turn neorealism into neoliberal institutionalism. That is the assumption about state rationality and motivation. Neorealists assume, as stated above, that states act in order to maximise their relative gains. Neoliberals, on the other hand, assume that states act merely in order to maximise their *absolute* gains; they do not care about the gains of other states except in so far as these gains interact (or interfere) with their own. This assumption relies on the assumption that for most international interactions, 'states' margins of survival' are not small; i.e. states can act in most areas of international relations without worrying whether a particular outcome is going to increase the likelihood of their being invaded. As a further consequence of this, the gains states are assumed to be maximising have not necessarily to do with power, but are more reliant on an economic measure of welfare. And within a game-theoretic framework, absolute-gains-maximising behaviour makes cooperation even more likely, since each actor is not concerned to 'win' each play of the game.[13]

Thus, neoliberal institutionalism posits the following central assumptions, counter to those of neorealism. Although states remain the primary actors in international relations, and remain treated as *unitary* actors, it is assumed now that they merely act to maximise absolute gains rather than relative gains. Thus, it is cooperation that becomes a more endemic feature of international relations.

This leads to what are called institutions, defined as 'persistent sets of rules (formal and informal) that prescribe behavioral roles, constrain activity, and shape expectations' (Keohane 1989: 3), and regarded as a prevalent and important feature of international political life, influencing and constraining, and even generating, state behaviour. It is clear from this definition that institutions are understood as much more than organisations. As Oran Young puts it, in contrast to institutions (of which he gives a definition similar to Keohane's given above), organisations are 'material entities possessing physical locations (or seats), offices, personnel, equipment, and budgets' as well as a 'legal personality' (Young 1989: 32).

## NEOREALISM, NEOLIBERAL INSTITUTIONALISM AND GLOBAL WARMING

Of these basic perspectives on world politics, neoliberal institutionalism produces the more satisfactory explanatory account of the international politics of global warming. The account of neorealism, that outcomes are generated as a product of the distribution of power capabilities, is simply inadequate, as shown below. Neoliberal institutionalism's focus on institutions allows us more space to explain many of the developments which ultimately produced the framework convention.

Before developing this argument, it seems worth elaborating on two distinct processes that need to be examined in order to explain the 'outcome' in this case. One is the formal inter-state negotiations which occurred between February 1991 and May 1992. What forces drove these negotiations? And with regard to neorealism in particular, were the most powerful states able to get their own way? But there is a second process which was very important for global warming: the development of global warming as first a scientific and then a political issue. In order to explain the final outcome, it seems inadequate to take the situation in early 1991 as a given, as if no politics had occurred before then. Neorealism would indeed preclude such a prior interest almost by definition, by treating states' interests as given.

As outlined above, neoliberal institutionalism takes a broad conception of what a social institution is. While some of its analysis follows this through logically, many of its analyses conflate this usage of institutions with international organisations, presumably because it is simpler to investigate the latter than the former. We can illustrate the importance of institutions through investigating both these forms of analysis.

Looking at the role of international organisations, we can see that they were crucial in the period up until the start of negotiations, after which they became relatively unimportant (except in the sense of the UN providing a forum for negotiation – which probably speeded up the process). Their role can be described in terms of two factors: cognitive development and agenda-setting.[14]

The role of international organisations in the cognitive development of the global-warming issue can be traced primarily through the role of the World Meteorological Organisation (WMO), previously the International Meteorological

Organization (IMO). The IMO was established in 1873, and, even early on, engaged in some coordination of research projects, notably the International Polar Year of 1882–3. A general importance can be ascribed to this coordination of meteorological research, since it provided the cognitive base on which later, more climatic-change-oriented research developed. However, in addition to this general function, the WMO (after it became a world organisation following the establishment of the UN) was involved directly in many important events and developments. Of note in these is the International Geophysical Year (1957–8), which among other things produced the first continuous measurements of atmospheric $CO_2$. The WMO was later highly involved in organising the collection of data on, for example, $CO_2$, temperature changes, etc., specifically in the light of the greenhouse theory.

The WMO also actively fostered a scientific consensus on climate change throughout the 1970s and 1980s. Of note here were the Stockholm Conference of 1974 (on climate modelling), the Norwich meeting in 1975 which ended speculation about possible global cooling because of other industrial pollutants, the World Climate Conference of 1979, the establishment of the World Climate Programme in 1979 – which itself led to the Villach Conference which proved to be the turning point in the politicisation of climate change as an issue – and finally the establishment of the above-mentioned IPCC, which consolidated the consensus originally reached at Villach.[15]

The fact that the IPCC was heavily politicised (see Boehmer-Christiansen in this volume) illustrates how successful the international organisations and the international climatological community had been in setting a political agenda, and it demonstrates, moreover, that global warming was a potentially severe problem which states needed to address. An initially organisational role, in coordinating research, etc., led directly to the setting of a political agenda. What is potentially politically more important is that they were able to set this agenda in such a way that certain political solutions became ideologically privileged. The presentation of scientific and technical information is never purely that: it always has a political character also. Thus, while the IPCC consolidated the scientific consensus on global warming and set an agenda for policy-makers, they were also framing the problem in a specific political mould.

In particular, the political prescription put out by those organisations came largely from a perspective which explicitly dealt with problems of North–South inequality, and which delegitimised any potential Northern attempts to construct the problem differently. Many Northern states, for example, refused to organise significant North–South transfers. However, they were prevented from being able to frame the problem as one where all states had equal obligations, which some of them clearly would have liked to have done. This would have produced significantly different negotiating conditions, had they been able to do this.

The international organisations (in particular the scientists within Working Group I of the IPCC) were crucial in this process, in their role as agenda-setters. They were in a position to influence strongly the way in which information was presented. In particular, they highlighted the disparities in *per capita* emissions across countries, and they took sides explicitly in the debates over 'eco-imperialism' which raged throughout that period.[16] Examinations of the IPCC's Policy-makers Summaries, or of the Scientific and Technical Declaration of the Second World Climate Conference (SWCC), amply illustrate the political nature of those statements (Houghton, Jenkins and Ephraums 1990; McTegart, Sheldon and Griffith 1990; IPCC 1990; SWCC 1990; see also Boehmer-Christiansen in this volume). For example, the SWCC Declaration stated that 'In order to stabilize atmospheric concentrations of greenhouse gases *while allowing for growth in emissions from developing countries*, industrialized countries must implement reductions even greater than those required, on average, for the globe as a whole' (SWCC 1990: 501; italics mine), and added that 'industrialized countries and developing countries have a common but differentiated responsibility for dealing with the problems of climate change. The problem is largely the consequence of past patterns of economic growth in the industrial countries' (ibid.: 502).

Thus, international institutions, even when defined merely as organisations, can be shown to have had an important role in climate politics. Neoliberal institutionalists have the capacity here, however, to undermine the criticism, levelled against them by the neorealists, that they ignore the influence of anarchy. As shown above, institutionalists have demonstrated how institutions can become important even when the background condition is one of anarchy. Cooperation does not become easy to achieve, but institutions help facilitate it.

Most institutionalists would seek, however, to define institutions in a broader manner, as outlined above. One process involved in the international politics of global warming can be identified as the development of such institutions, and that indeed is the norm-generating process which occurred in the case of the global-warming issue during 1988–91 through the spate of unilateral declarations of targets to limit emissions by industrialised countries. It seems plausible to claim that in this 'unilateral targets' process, an international institution (in the sense given by Young above) was emerging. This institution developed around the 'easily recognized roles' of the industrialised states involved, and took as its primary rule the adoption of a target – along the lines of 'stabilisation at 1990 levels by the year 2000'.[17]

This 'unilateral targets' process is difficult, on the other hand, to explain in Realist terms. A Realist could argue for one of two positions (at least). First of all, he or she could argue that states were simply behaving in bad faith; and that the targets were established purely for ideological reasons, and were ones either that the states had no intention of meeting or that were in reality very easy to meet. There is a certain amount of plausibility in this approach, especially in the latter claim, since the history of energy-forecasting clearly shows a tendency to overproject energy demand (and hence $CO_2$ emissions) for political purposes (Baumgartner and Midttun 1987).

The second line of argument a Realist could use is that states were 'testing the waters' (Ward 1989); engaging in a tit-for-tat strategy, cooperating in order to elicit cooperation in turn. However, this remains a problematic interpretation in the face of persistent 'defection' by the USA throughout 1991–2, since, if this interpretation were correct, other industrialised states ought to have reneged on their commitments.[18] Such a Realist interpretation leads us into an institutionalist conclusion, namely that what institutions could have done (and to an extent, however imperfectly, *did* do) was create 'stable expectations' about what precisely constituted cooperation and defection.

However, this conclusion seems at the same time to undermine any game-theoretic-institutionalist accounts. These accounts could interpret the 1988–91 'unilateral targets' process in the same way as does Keohane, in his discussion of reciprocity (Keohane 1989a). But such analyses assume a *predefined* notion of what constitutes cooperation and defection – notions which clearly didn't exist for $CO_2$ targets in that period. It is a misleading interpretation to say that the states which set targets were cooperating *in order* to elicit cooperation, since those states which refused (e.g. the USA) cannot properly be called defectors (or, in terms of collective-goods provision, free-riders).[19] States still had to negotiate and define what precisely was involved in cooperating and defecting, as well as the nature of the collective good they would be trying to provide. This version of institutionalist theory relies on being able to interpret behaviour as involving cooperation or defection in the context of a political process which is essentially about the very definition of what constitutes cooperation and defection.

It seems more plausible to interpret this 'unilateral targets' process in the following way: instead of engaging in strategies to meet a predefined end ($CO_2$ abatement), states were (are) in a process of *redefining* that end (i.e. redefining $CO_2$ abatement as a collective good). The establishment of targets is then seen less as a strategy for eliciting like behaviour from other actors, and more as a signal to other actors as to what initial steps are involved in acting on the new norm. This interpretation is more in line with Young's suggestion that states act more as role-players than as utility maximisers (Young 1989: 209–13), or with the analyses of what Keohane refers to as the 'reflective school' (Keohane 1989b).

## CRITIQUES

This discussion of the international politics of global warming in the light of dominant strands of IR theory leads to several conclusions, critical of those strands. These are not ones uniquely drawn from an examination of global warming – they have been made elsewhere – but global warming can be used to highlight them. Four particular lines of objection are pursued here. The first of these is the commonly made point about the false division between international and domestic politics, a point amply illustrated by global warming; the second focuses on the opposition between structuralist and historicist theoretical positions; the third looks at the ontological bases of the positions adopted particularly by neorealists; and the last looks at the question of what (and whom) theory is for.

## The domestic–international split

An often-made criticism of much international thought (not only, but most commonly, of Realist thought) is that it erroneously tries to draw a clear dividing line between the domestic and the international. Waltz's position is most explicit in his attempt to construct international political theory as a 'bounded subject-matter', and in his rejection of looking at the internal characteristics of states in terms of 'unit-level theory' or 'reductionism' (Waltz 1979). This tendency is widespread and general. Within both neorealist and neoliberal-institutionalist theory, it expresses itself through the state-as-(unitary)-actor assumption, which precludes any consideration of domestic politics.

An analysis of the politics of global warming reveals the poverty of this position. Domestic politics clearly intrudes importantly into the picture. A simple look at its effect in one country – the USA – is sufficient to illustrate the point. Internal politics in the USA, through the politically important 1988 drought, was crucial in making the Toronto Conference of that year an important political event which spurred on the global-warming debate at the international level. The exceptional influence of the coal and oil lobbies in the USA, combined both with Bush's having an oil background and with the scientific hostility of his Chief of Staff, served to produce the intransigent position of the USA in international negotiations. More broadly, the influence of the world recession on the political feasibility of aggressive abatement programmes has helped the development of many countries' climate strategies to stagnate since 1990 (Paterson 1993; Tanzer 1992).

These interactions between domestic and international politics can be put into two categories. The first is that of the general historically constituted structural situations which influence states' positions. In relation to climate politics, useful categories could be divisions over wealth–poverty (the North–South split), over dependence on fossil fuels (either on exports or on large indigenous supplies), over vulnerability to potential climate-change impacts, and over historically generated attitudes to the state of uncertainty associated with environmental problems more generally (see Paterson and Grubb 1992 for an elaboration of these groupings). The other category concerns those specific developments within domestic politics which interact with and influence international political possibilities, of which Clinton's election is the most obvious example. Others, however, could also be cited; for example, even though those who saw the departure of John Sununu in December 1991 as a likely precursor to a change in the US position were largely wrong, that episode still revealed how specific domestic political events could be important in influencing international outcomes.

## Structure vs history

Lines of analysis from two differing positions have grown during the 1980s which draw a distinction between historicist and structuralist theories.[20] These arguments have come in the main from the Gramscian analyses associated with

Robert Cox and Stephen Gill in particular (Gill 1993), and from the post-structuralist writers, of whom those who focus on this question include Rob Walker and Richard Ashley (Walker 1993: Ch. 4; Ashley 1986). While there are significant divergences between these positions, for the purpose of this section they provide similar critiques.

The focus of these critiques is on how structuralist theories tend to reify the status quo and provide static accounts of social life. Gill (1993) suggests that structuralist accounts are more adequate in times of relative stability, since these situations are more amenable both to its assumptions about the stable preferences of actors and to an analysis of events in terms of limited numbers of variables which can be (more or less) isolated and 'controlled for'. But he and others insist that historically based accounts are in fact able to give more convincing and adequate accounts of events than structuralist ones even in these times, since they give an account of the emergence of those preferences which structuralist writers (at least of the neorealist variety) would treat as given. And he suggests that in times of rapid change, structuralist theories give us no ability to account for such change. This is because, in Ashley's words, structuralist theories 'tend to accentuate the one-way dependence of diachrony (dynamics) upon synchrony (statics)', thus producing a model of change which presumes that the structure itself is somehow immutable (Ashley 1986: 265–6). As these writers point out, this is to engage in a reification of the status quo (Walker 1993: 116; Griffiths 1992: Ch. 6).

The weaknesses of a static, structural model can be seen in the working-through of the implications of the neoliberal institutionalist account of global warming given above. While such an account arguably provides a more adequate explanation of developments to date on global warming than the theory of neorealism, it can also be seen to undermine some of the rationalistic assumptions of that theory. A rationalistic theory in this context would begin by evaluating the preferences of the relevant actors and relating these, along with assessments of both the power of each actor and the underlying structure of the situation, to the various outcomes. It is an essentially static way of looking at the world, which it views as a sequence of isolatable snapshots. However, in order to demonstrate the importance of institutional arrangements in international affairs, it is necessary to engage in an essentially historical enquiry into the origins of the institutions concerned and their evolution over time, in such a way as to preclude (or at the very least severely limit the usefulness of) such a 'snapshot' approach. The politics of global warming can only be adequately understood in terms of (among other things) the historical development of scientific knowledge, international institutional development, the politics of environmental problems in general in 'advanced' capitalist states during the 1980s, and the interaction between these factors, all of which require a historicist analytical approach.

## Ontology

As suggested at the start of this chapter, the assumptions used by neorealists and neoliberal institutionalists are best understood as ontological positions; that is, as basic understandings about the way the world is which guide and are constitutive of their analyses. Thus, any evaluation of the contribution these theories can make to our understanding of world politics must take their ontological character into account; our critique cannot simply be based on an evaluation of the 'facts' out there, since the ontological positions of these theories at least partly *constitute* those facts.[21]

On the one hand, this line of enquiry can lead us to question the positions of those theories, either by laying them bare as ontologies and evaluating them as such, or by reflecting on whether they provide adequate accounts of the world.[22] Neither of these theories, we find, provide such an account. On the other hand, it can lead to an investigation as to why particular positions have historically been privileged over others; for example, why has Realism been traditionally privileged over Idealism? Moreover, the very naming of each as such reveals the depth of the privileging process. This privileging must be understood not simply in terms of the 'failure' of the application of the analyses of Idealism in the inter-war years, but also in terms both of the way in which the Realist assessment of the implications of anarchy logically privileges assumptions both that the world will not be a very cooperative place and that prudential, if not aggressive, foreign policies will therefore be desirable, and of the use of these assumptions by foreign policy and military elites in the 1930s, 1940s and early 1980s (see, for example, Gill 1993: 46). Such privileged ontologies can be criticised on a number of grounds, from the game-theoretic à la Axelrod to the feminist critiques of the heavily gendered nature of the assumptions Realists derive about human motivation and behaviour from, among others, Hobbes (see, for example, Grant 1991; also, Bretherton in this volume). But it remains the case that they have for a variety of reasons remained privileged within policy-making circles.

### Who is theory for?

This question leads into a discussion of the purpose of theory. This is so since if different theories are clearly of use to different social groups, and if the possibility of 'value-free' theory is denied, then the question of who is privileged by a theory becomes an integral part of the theory's formulation. Two competing accounts (at least) of this problem are present within the critical literature. On the one hand, Cox makes a distinction between 'problem-solving' and 'critical' theory. The former category involves the solution of problems within the context of given political arrangements; it corresponds to the 'management of international affairs' referred to in Waltz's last chapter of *Theory of International Politics*, and it is one which Waltz explicitly accepts (Waltz 1986). This would fall into the positivist mode of trying to generate 'If A then B'-type statements. The latter category of theory is designed to analyse existing situations with an explicit view towards the transformation of the existing system. Cox's account, however, is in conflict with Gill's account (1993: 21) which describes social science as investigating a 'second order' reality, pre-ordered by its investigators, in contrast to natural science which analyses a 'first order reality'.[23] According to this view, indeed, problem-solving would become an impossible activity. All theory is imbued with the value systems and ontologies of the theorist, as a result, and the question of who the theory privileges becomes all the more important.

With regard to global warming, and many other environmental problems, our accounts of the prospects for, and the forms of, cooperation at the international level will thus have to include a consideration of who gains and loses from such accounts of social life. For instance, with regard to global warming, neorealist theory would, in its applications, lead to an underplaying of any cooperative potential, and to the extent that it informs policy-makers, this theory would necessarily benefit the already powerful.

An example of how the Realist assumption of the non-cooperative nature of international politics could be argued to have influenced the US position on global warming and benefited the already powerful can be seen in the following. The USA frequently made the argument, during the negotiations and in other fora, that it would be irrelevant for it to take substantial action on global warming if developing countries would not also undertake commitments to reduce the rate of growth of their emissions. Developing countries claimed they were willing to undertake these commitments provided they would be financed by the North. The US argument (as well as being based on the political unfeasibility of facilitating North–South transfers at that point) was clearly based on assumptions about potential 'free-riding' on the provision of a collective good such as (relative) climate stability. The USA was unprepared to cooperate unless it had cast-iron guarantees that other countries would also cooperate, and it assumed (being historically informed by realists) that such a level of cooperation would not be forthcoming. The theory thus becomes self-fulfilling. The discussion on the game-theoretic aspects of neorealism and neoliberal institutionalism above showed, however, that such a situation is non-determinate. Mutual cooperation cannot be presumed, but it certainly cannot theoretically be precluded. Thus, since the USA is likely to be hit less severely by the potential impacts of global warming (if only because it has the financial resources to cope with adaptation) than, for example, Bangladesh or most of the Small Island States, Realism (if only unintentionally) here benefits the already privileged by giving them theoretically reasonable grounds for *not* cooperating.

## CONCLUSIONS

This chapter has tried to illustrate how differing strands of IR theory might account for the international politics of global warming that led up to the signing of the Framework Convention. It has suggested that the neoliberal institutionalism of Keohane and others provides a more adequate account than does the neorealism of Waltz or Gilpin, but that an analysis of global warming on the former's terms reveals weaknesses in both theories. These weaknesses have to do on the one hand with their epistemological positions, which assume simple subject–object and fact–value distinctions which cannot be strictly maintained, and which privilege stasis and structure over change, and on the other hand with their ontological positions, which preclude a discussion of significant portions of relevant material (e.g. domestic politics). It has not tried significantly to build these critiques into an alternative account; such a task is one for the future.

This chapter has ended up saying more about IR theory than about the politics of global warming, but hopefully some implications are reasonably clear. One obvious one is that the present analysis would support claims that have been made, by many writing on UNCED, about the importance of institutions (e.g. Gardner 1992; Imber 1993; French 1992). However, much of the policy debate on these institutions has tended to associate institutions with organisations *per se*, and is still concerned with 'strength' of the Commission on Sustainable Development (CSD). The institutionalist analysis above, and that outlined by Keohane, Young and others, suggests a different conclusion with regard to institutions. In this analysis, what matters is the way in which institutions are inserted into, and relate to, those states that will be implementing any agreements – the way in which they confer roles onto states.

Three points are worth making by way of conclusion. First, institutions serve to stabilise expectations about others' actions so that all involved know that their cooperation will be reciprocated. This stabilisation process involves both building ongoing negotiations to develop trust and mutual learning, and a carrying-out of monitoring or 'verification' functions (on this, see Greene and Salt 1992; see also, Greene in this volume). Second, ongoing scientific and technoeconomic consensus processes will be crucial in developing the cognitive base for future negotiations. Third, and possibly most important, the above analysis highlights how important the informal development, and the intersubjective development, of norms will be (see Dyer in this volume). States will not enact policies or sign up to commitments without greater mutual understandings of why it is they are acting, and without those norms being internalised by the decision-makers. With respect to these conclusions, the bodies set up by the Climate Convention are likely to be of significantly greater importance than the CSD.

## NOTES

1 I am grateful to John Barry, Mark Imber, Mick Smith, John Vogler and Hugh Ward for reading earlier versions of this paper and commenting on them, as well as to members of the British International Studies Association Environment Group who were at a meeting where this paper was presented.
2 This follows to an extent a distinction made by James Der Derian between international relations theory and international theory. The former he associates with contemporary North American theory, which he suggests is less speculative, less philosophical and less historical than the former, which he associates with the British tradition identified with Wight and Bull. The focus here is largely on the former of these two groupings (see Der Derian 1993: 12, Note 1).
3 For fuller accounts, see Paterson (1992, 1993), or Bodansky (1993). The fullest, but unpublished, account is in Paterson (1994: Chs 2, 3 and 4).
4 Since it is reasonable to assume on a priori grounds – and we know it is in fact the case – that inter-state negotiations, and politics more generally, will continue in the foreseeable future on global warming, it is also reasonable to try to draw some of these

conclusions. However, hopefully, what follows is a more thorough treatment of theoretical assumptions and positions than many of those already offered.

5 See Paterson (1994: Ch. 4), for details on these.

6 See the IEA (1992) on the details of these.

7 For an extended analysis of this weakness in the Convention, see Paterson (1992a).

8 For commentaries on the Convention focusing on its adequacy, see for example Berreen and Meyer (1992); Bodansky (1993); Grubb (1992); Pachauri (1992); and Paterson (1992a).

9 This can be seen most clearly with Keohane. He accepts explicitly that the reasons for which he studies world politics are normative ones, but operates as if the only effect this has is to guide what questions he asks of some reality 'out there' (see Keohane 1989c).

10 Previous Realists, such as Morgenthau, did make some mention of anarchy, but much more emphasis was placed on the power-maximising behaviour of humans and states, derived from an account of human nature rather than from the logic of anarchy. Thus, in this earlier view, power-maximising becomes an absolute activity – there is no theoretical limit to power – whereas with neorealism, states are satisfied simply with enough power to survive.

11 This is what is variously called, in neorealist terminology, 'status-maximising' behaviour, 'relative-gains-maximising' behaviour or behaviour based on the motivation of 'interest defined as power', although the latter formulation comes strictly from Morgenthau.

12 Keohane was influenced by other literatures related to game theory, such as microeconomics and public choice theory (see especially Keohane 1984). However, the game-theoretic logic is sufficient to account for how neorealism became neoliberal institutionalism.

13 Axelrod's computer tournament for iterated PD games showed that, against a range of strategies, the one which ended up with the best score overall ('Tit for Tat') never beat any other individual strategy. It simply worked well by eliciting cooperation from the other strategies. See, throughout, Axelrod (1984).

14 It is the function of cognitive development which is clearly involved in the resolution of most environmental issues, and which has led to Peter Haas's 'epistemic communities' theory (Haas 1989). However, this theory should properly be regarded as a subset of a broader institutionalist theory, with a focus on cognitive factors as generators of institutional influence. The point which needs emphasising here is that the epistemic networks rely on international organisations in order to operate, and that many of these organisations already existed prior to the establishment of such networks. Thus, while in a narrow sense it was climate scientists who developed knowledge about climate change, it was the organisations, importantly, that provided the framework within which research operated and was disseminated (both to other scientists and to policy-makers), and that, in some cases, directed the research questions which scientists asked. A convergence of Haas's views with neoliberal institutionalism can be seen in the recent joint Keohane–Haas (with Marc Levy) book (Haas, Keohane and Levy 1993).

15 See Lunde (1991) on many of these meetings.

16 For a discussion of the acrimonious debate over the World Resources Institute's 'Greenhouse Index', see Agarwal and Narain 1990; and the World Resources Institute 1991.

17 Note again that this is a use of the term institution which does not explicitly involve any formal organisations (see also Imber in this volume).

18 This remains so whether the presumed game structure is that of iterated Prisoner's Dilemma or that of Assurance (Stag Hunt). It would not be the case if the structure were that of Chicken, which Ward (1993) suggests *is* the game structure for global warming.

19 Some might object here that those states which refuse, for example, to accept limits on their $CO_2$ emissions while other states *do* acccept these limits are free-riding on the climatic benefits provided by others' actions. However, it is not possible to call something like 'climatic benefits' a collective good (on the provision of which one actor could 'free-ride') until states have intersubjectively agreed that it is a collective good. Public goods do not objectively exist; they are constructed through discourse. I am grateful for the objection by Roderick Ogley which clarified this point in my own mind.

20 The terminological distinction is difficult to make clear here, since the different writers use these two terms in differing, and overlapping, fashions. The use of structuralism here, as in Gill (1993), is one which Popper associated with historicism, and which is taken up by Ashley (1986: 289). In broad terms, structuralism is used here to connote theories which frame their analyses in terms of those general sets of structures (linguistic, economic, political) which constitute social life and which determine events, outcomes, identities and even human agency – theories of which neorealism is a prime example. Historicist theories, on the other hand, are ones which place emphasis on the historical formation of structures, and thus on human agency, when considering the potential for their transformation. In addition to Gill and Ashley, see Walker (1993: Chs 4 and 5); Conca (1993), for an elaboration with respect to environmental problems; and Wendt (1987), from a structurationist position.

21 As an aside, it may be interesting to note that, to date, post-structuralist writers on international relations have tended, in my view, to reify that Realist ontological position which regards the problematical war–peace state of affairs as fundamentally constitutive of the subject matter of IR. For example, James Der Derian, in his excellent book *Antidiplomacy* (1993), criticises a traditional security studies analyst (Stephen Walt) for denying the utility of broadening the concept of security to include global environmental problems (Der Derian 1993: 11). But his critique nonetheless reinforces the notion that the war–peace security question is constitutive of IR, and that therefore its analyses (although Der Derian posits a greatly different form for these than Walt) can be applied across the field. Walt's point is, in fact, important in that it implicitly precludes the notion of one fixed vision of reality, and at least in principle denies the privileging of military–security relations within IR, which Der Derian reifies. Other books, in this vein, which in my view engage in a similar reification include Der Derian and Shapiro (1989) and Walker (1993). This is not to deny that these writings are intensely useful, but simply to point out that these writers seem to share a limited concept of what is involved in IR in much the same way as do the neorealists.

22 It is important to note that this need not necessarily imply relativism. It is not necessary to hold the position (although some post-structuralists would) that since the 'facts out there' are constituted in various discourses and theories, these discourses are incommensurable and cannot be compared or evaluated. Even though reality is constituted through discourse, different theories may still constitute overlapping versions of reality, and there is therefore a potential for the evaluation of these respective theories through debate. Were this not the case, the evaluation made above of neorealism and neoliberal institutionalism with regard to explaining the politics of global warming would have been impossible.

23 Much of this criticism would be shared by post-structuralists and many feminists (e.g. Harding 1986). However, they would in general go further and deny the 'first order' reality status to the natural sciences also.

## BIBLIOGRAPHY

Agarwal, A. and Narain, S. (1990) *Global Warming in an Unequal World: a Case of Environmental Colonialism*, New Delhi: Centre for Science and Environment.

Ashley, R. (1986) 'The poverty of neorealism', in Keohane, R.O. (ed.) *Neorealism and Its Critics*, New York: Columbus U.P., pp. 255–300.

Axelrod, R. (1984) *The Evolution of Cooperation*, New York: Basic Books.

Baumgartner, T. and Midttun, A. (1987) *The Politics of Energy Forecasting*, Oxford: Clarendon.

Berreen, J. and Meyer, A. (1992) 'A package marked "Return to Sender": some problems with the Climate Convention', *Network 92* 18: 6–7.

Bodansky, D. (1993) 'The United Nations Framework Convention on Climate Change: a commentary', *Yale Journal of International Law* 18(2): 451–558.

Bull, H. (1977) *The Anarchical Society*, London: Macmillan.

Conca, K. (1993) 'Environmental change and the deep structure of world politics', in Lipschutz, R.D. and Conca, K. (eds) (1993) *The State and Social Power in Global Environmental Politics*, New York: Columbia U.P.

Cox, R. (1987) *Production, Power and World Order*, New York: Columbia U.P.

Der Derian, J. (1993) *Antidiplomacy: Spies, Terror, Speed, and War*, Cambridge, Mass.: Blackwell.

—— and Shapiro, M.J. (1989) *International/Intertextual Relations: Postmodern Readings of World Politics*, New York: Lexington.

French, H. (1992) *After the Earth Summit: the Future of Environmental Governance*, Washington, DC: Worldwatch Institute.

Gardner, R.N. (1992) *Negotiating Survival: Four Priorities After Rio*, New York: Council on Foreign Relations Press.

Gill, S. (ed.) (1993) *Gramsci, Historical Materialism and International Relations*, Cambridge: C.U.P.

Gilpin, R. (1987) *The Political Economy of International Relations*, Princeton, NJ: Princeton U.P.

Grant, R. (1991) 'The sources of gender bias in international relations theory', in Grant, R. and Newland, K. (eds) (1991) *Gender and International Relations*, Milton Keynes: Open University Press.

Greene, O. and Salt, J. (1992) 'Verification and information exchange in the development of an effective climate change convention: the agenda after UNCED', paper presented to the IRNES Conference on Perspectives on the Environment: Research and Action in the 1990s, Leeds University, September 14–15.

Grieco, J.M. (1988) 'Anarchy and the limits of cooperation: a realist critique of the newest liberal institutionalism', *International Organization* 42(3): 485–507.

Griffiths, M. (1992) *Realism, Idealism and International Politics: a Reinterpretation*, London: Routledge.

Grubb, M. (1992) 'The heat is on', *The Higher*, 5 June: 16.

Haas, P.M. (1989) 'Do regimes matter? Epistemic communities and Mediterranean pollution control', *International Organization* 43(3): 377–403.

——, Keohane, R.O. and Levy, M.A. (1993) *Institutions for the Earth: Sources of Effective Environmental Protection*, Cambridge, Mass.: MIT Press.

Harding, S. (1986) *The Science Question in Feminism*, Milton Keynes: Open University Press.

Houghton, J.T., Jenkins, G.J. and Ephraums, J.J. (1990) *Climate Change: the IPCC Scientific Assessment*, Cambridge: C.U.P.

IEA (1992) *Climate Change Policy Initiatives*, Paris: International Energy Agency.

Imber, M. (1993) 'Too many cooks? The post-Rio reform of the UN', *International Affairs* 69(1): 55–70.

IPCC (1990) *Climate Change: the IPCC Response Strategies*, Geneva: World Meteorological Organization.

Jäger, J. and Ferguson, H.L. (1991) *Climate Change: Science, Impacts and Policy – Proceedings of the Second World Climate Conference*, Cambridge: C.U.P.

Keohane, R.O. (1983) 'Theory of world politics: structural realism and beyond', in Keohane (1989), pp. 35–73.

—— (1984) *After Hegemony: Cooperation and Discord in the World Political Economy*, Princeton, NJ: Princeton U.P.

—— (ed.) (1986) *Neorealism and Its Critics*, New York: Columbia U.P.

—— (1989) *International Institutions and State Power: Essays in International Relations Theory*, Boulder, Col.: Westview.

—— (1989a) 'Reciprocity in international relations', in Keohane (1989), pp. 132–57.

—— (1989b) 'International institutions: two approaches', in Keohane (1989), pp. 158–79.

—— (1989c) 'A personal intellectual history', in Keohane (1989), pp. 21–32.

Lunde, L. (1991) *Science or Politics in the Global Greenhouse? A Study of the Development towards Scientific Consensus on Climate Change*, Oslo: Fridtjof Nansen Institute.

McTegart, W.J., Sheldon, G.W. and Griffith, D.C. (eds) (1990) *Climate Change: the IPCC Impacts Assessment*, Canberra: Australian Government Publishing Service.

Morgenthau, H. (1978) *Politics Among Nations*, 5th edn (revised), New York: Alfred A. Knopf.

Pachauri, R.K. (1992) 'The Climate Change Convention . . . what it may mean for the poor', *Network 92* 19: 14–15.

Paterson, M. (1992) 'Global warming', in Thomas, C. *The Environment in International Relations*, London: Royal Institute of International Affairs, pp. 155–95.

—— (1992a) 'The Convention on Climate Change agreed at the Rio Conference', *Environmental Politics* 1(4): 267–72.

—— (1993) 'The politics of global warming after the Earth Summit', *Environmental Politics* 2(4): 174–90.

—— (1994) 'Explaining the Climate Change Convention: International Relations theory and Global Warming', PhD thesis, Essex University.

—— and Grubb, M. (1992) 'The international politics of climate change', *International Affairs* 68(2): 293–310.

Sebenius, J.K. (1991) 'Negotiating a regime to control global warming', in Benedick, R. *et al.* (1991) *Greenhouse Warming: Negotiating a Global Regime*, Washington, DC: World Resources Institute.

SWCC (1990) 'Declaration of the Scientific and Technical Sessions of the Second World Climate Conference', in Jäger, J. and Ferguson, H.L. (1991) *Climate Change: Science, Impact and Policy – Proceedings of the Second World Climate Conference*, Cambridge: C.U.P.

Tanzer, M. (1992) 'After Rio', *Monthly Review*, November: 1–11.

Taylor, M. (1976) *Anarchy and Cooperation*, New York: Wiley.

United Nations (1992) *Framework Convention on Climate Change*, New York: United Nations.

Walker, R.B.J. (1993) *Inside/Outside: International Relations as Political Theory*, Cambridge: C.U.P.

Waltz, K. (1979) *Theory of International Politics*, Reading, Mass.: Addison-Wesley.

—— (1986) 'A reply to my critics', in Keohane, R. (ed.) *Neorealism and its Critics*, New York: Columbia U.P.

Ward, H. (1989) 'Testing the waters: taking risks to gain reassurance in public goods games', *Journal of Conflict Resolution* 33(2): 274–308.

—— (1993) 'Game theory and the politics of the global commons', *Journal of Conflict Resolution* 37(2): 203–35.

Wendt, A. (1987) 'The agent-structure problem in International Relations theory', *International Organization* 41: 335–70.

Wight, M. and Porter, B. (eds) (1991) *International Theory: the Three Traditions*, Leicester: Leicester U.P.

World Resources Institute (1991) *World Resources 1990–91*, Washington, DC: World Resources Institute.

Young, O.R. (1989) *International Cooperation: Building Regimes for Natural Resources and the Environment*, Ithaca, NY: Cornell U.P.

# 5 International relations, social ecology and the globalisation of environmental change[1]

*Julian Saurin*

The conservative and conventional thinking of international relations (IR) has it that environmental problems are yet another set of pressing 'issues' to be addressed by students of international relations, whilst at the same time available for relegation to a tokenistic subset of concerns alongside questions of gender and racism (Smith 1993). The irreducible and timeless fundamentals of war, security and 'national' self-interest remain, in this portrayal, relatively undisturbed by the marginal, if endearing, frettings voiced by restless greenies around the world in general, and by some in the IR academic community in particular. Thus, the rejection of environmentalism arises from the conviction that environmental degradation does not undermine any of the foundations of the orthodox practice and theorisation of IR.

The prevailing approach of IR scholars to the environment remains state-centric. That is to say that the whole range of environmental concerns is theoretically and practically subordinated to, and dependent upon, the predetermined 'character' and 'interests' of the state. This predisposition is singularly pronounced in Brenton's *The Greening of Machiavelli* (1994), wherein the title alone makes it clear that the environment is contingent upon the Machiavellian turn, and not vice versa. However, it is also identifiable in the much more thoughtful work of Hurrell and Kingsbury (1992a, 1992b) and in the Chatham House-tempered volume by Thomas (1992), where it is made explicit in the former and implicit in the latter that the proper remit of an international relations of global environmental change is to be found in the manner in which *states*, through multilateral or other official arrangements – including the co-option of non-state actors – attempt to mediate and manage the global environment between states or through formally recognised international organisations.[2]

There remains a latent assumption that the rise of a worldwide environmental consciousness or the actuality of global environmental crises does not warrant a basic re-theorisation of international relations, but rather invites a modest means of accommodating such challenges within the existing preconceptions of orthodox IR. Contrary to this view, and the argument developed here is that the processes of global environmental change (GEC) are subversive of both the theory and the practice of orthodox international relations, if by 'international relations' is understood the conduct, regulation and management of relations between states across the world. The appearance of theoretical stability and security afforded to orthodox IR by the ascription of sovereignty to the political formation known as the modern state is radically undermined by the scale, spread, dynamics and complexity of global environmental degradation.[3] In this chapter, a case is made that is unequivocally against the arriviste theoretical complacency (Smith 1993) which suggests that GEC is yet another issue which, by design or default, may be added to the optional list of IR ephemera. For Smith, the evidence of the seriousness with which environmental 'issues' are taken is provided by the attention paid by political leaders or orthodox academia (Smith 1993: 44); from this line of reasoning, Smith derives an IR research agenda. However, this approach is far removed from the daily environmental concerns which inform the lives of the mass of humanity – from the radioactively poisoned residents (and their children, and their children's children, and their children's children's children) of Chernobyl and the Ukraine, to the tens of millions of children who die under the age of 5 from water-borne and preventable diseases, to the sufferings of malnutrition resulting from the normal operations of global food markets, to the racially biased daily deposition of toxic waste, to the forced marriages of male transmigrants to female tribals in Indonesia, or to the farmers whose sustainable agricultural practices have been subverted by the growing global intellectual-property-rights order. The analysis of these types of empirical and historical experiences, and the attempt to explain their global manufacture, distribution and remedy are, I argue below, where international theory should be developed and put into use.

Smith is entangled in a contradiction of his own making.[4] Whilst pretending to avoid a derailing of so-called 'low' politics by 'high' politics, he achieves this very derangement with great rhetoric effect. Thus, the concerns of many scholars of environmental change who wish to explain and account for the mundane and daily process of environmental degradation across the world, scholars who comprise the principal informants of the social, political and economic conditions of life across the world, are rendered as marginal and peripheral because they do not deal – allegedly – with the fundamental of the state system and its transcendence. Smith contends that 'the environment shares with gender and race the dubious privilege of being an issue in political and academic circles,' and that he 'wonder[s] whether that means anything more than that it is impossible not to pay lip-service to it'. That he can only pay lip service to it is a consequence of Smith's own problematisation of the environment, and of his own method of enquiry.

To avoid the theoretical and practical impasse which Smith establishes, an explicit attempt to problematise global environmental change in a global sociology is required. This means drawing up accounts of the global structures of power, articulations of capitalism and distribution of consumption, and not the a priori privileging of the 'high' politics of the state. Indeed, I share the point of departure which informs Redclift and Benton's *Social Theory and the Global Environment*, in which they argue that 'the social sciences are not equipped to play [an] enlarged imaginative and practical role without a radical rethink of their own inherited assumptions', and that this ill-preparedness continues to stand because 'serious attempts to come to terms with the issues posed by our environmental crisis expose to critical examination some very basic "settled" assumptions of the "mainstream" traditions of the social sciences' (Redclift and Benton 1994: 2). Thus, in part, what follows reflects the growing criticism of the fragmenting and reductionist traditions of social scientific enquiry in general, as well as the parochialism of IR in particular, which are so clearly revealed when global environmental change is analysed.

The root question which needs to be asked and responded to is: what is the principal object of enquiry in the IR of global environmental change? Is it the self-declared activities of states in the ambiguously, or at least contestedly, defined field of environmental affairs? Is it the inter-state management of issues which, by one history or another, have now been labelled environmental? Is it the examination of the practices of those organisations, be they state or non-state organisations, which declare themselves to be 'environmentalist' or environmentally concerned? Is it the analysis of environmental change in the light of a presupposed anarchical international society of states? Hurrell and Kingsbury pose the basic problem as follows:

> Underlying this analysis is a central question: Can a fragmented and often highly conflictual political system made up of over 170 sovereign states and numerous other actors achieve the high . . . levels of cooperation and policy coordination needed to *manage* environmental problems on a global scale? (emphasis added)
>
> (Hurrell and Kingsbury 1992b: 1)

Whilst these questions are of interest and may ultimately gain importance, managerialism can never be the purpose of critical academic enquiry. It is noticeable too that in Hurrell and Kingsbury's problematising of the environment, questions of causation and resolution are conspicuously absent from the remit of enquiry. The argument developed below is that an enquiry which seeks to establish whether any universal processes and practices have come about which obtain across the world (irrespective of the particularistic powers and characteristics of identifiable international actors) is indispensable. Whereas the greater part of the IR of global environmental change has focused upon the manner in which formal organisations, and notably states, have responded to the impact of environmental change – where the change is taken as given and relatively unproblematic – a thorough analysis of *causes* and of the *diffused* processes which engender environmental change should be regarded as the *sine qua non* of this field of enquiry.[5]

In the orthodoxy of IR, the primary object of enquiry is the manner in which states deal with and mediate amongst themselves the outcome of pre-given processes organised according to a distinction between internal and external, and between domestic and foreign, processes.[6] Thus, these processes, whatever they may be – trade, manufacturing, tourism, arms manufacturing, unemployment, migration, social upheaval, gender subordination – are typically brought into consideration if, and only if, they appear to disturb or impinge on the relations between states. One is left in no doubt that all is contingent upon the state. And one is reminded of Ralph Miliband's warning as to the distorting longevity of such essentialist views of politics when he wrote that

> The strength of this current orthodoxy has helped to turn these claims (for they are no more than claims) into solid articles of political wisdom; and the ideological and political climate engendered by the Cold War has tended to make subscription to that wisdom a test not only of political intelligence but of political morality as well.
>
> (Miliband 1973: 6)

Though the Cold War may be over, and though the Rio Conference was portrayed as the symbolic crowning of the new world order of cooperation and enlightenment, the empirical and intellectual legacy of statism remains well entrenched and resistant to any new wisdom and morality.

Atkinson similarly attributes the general inadequacy of our dominant intellectual tradition at accounting for social ecological change when he writes that

> Compartmentalised disciplining specialisms had grown out of the relatively stable set of post-war social and political arrangements and adopted a set of inter-related methodological approaches to knowledge – empiricism, behaviourism and pluralism – that could not easily come to terms with this new phenomenon [of global environmental crisis].
>
> (Atkinson 1991: 21)

The principal casualty, in IR, of an unreconstructed statism, empiricism, behaviourism and pluralism is the denial both of globalisation and of environmental crisis. Against this a priori privileging of the state, I want to argue for an empty slate which attempts not to prejudge an 'authentic' and 'proper' object of enquiry with its attendant reductionist and atomistic consequences, but rather to navigate through the social-economic-political-ecological web in which numerous and overlapping processes, communities and distributive criteria are embedded. In this, the terrain of enquiry is composed of the ideological representation and articulation of actual and historical material changes, and of the processes of material changes themselves. As Caroline Thomas unequivo- cally identifies, the environmental crisis is 'rooted in the process of globalisation under way' (Thomas 1994: 1), and she forcefully exhorts scholars in IR to focus on 'the underlying structure in which this process is played out' (ibid.: 2).

In responding to such a call, I will set out three interrelated areas of enquiry which seek both to identify those underlying structures and to suggest how the embedded process is played out. After first discussing (i) the processes by which the 'environment' is defined and come to be 'known', I will then focus attention on (ii) the relationship between the processes of global capitalist development and global environmental degradation, and (iii) on the processes by which environmental change (and degradation especially) has become global in character (where 'global' is not simply a trendy synonym for 'international').

## THE MEANING OF 'ENVIRONMENT'

Teasing out why and under what circumstances, and with what effect, contending conceptions of the environment are produced is of key importance for the IR of global environmental change. As Wolfgang Sachs aptly remarked

> After nearly everybody – heads of state and heads of corporations, believers in technology and believers in growth – has turned environmentalist, the conflicts in the future will not centre on who or who is not an environmentalist, but on who stands for what kind of environmentalism.
>
> (Sachs 1993: xvi)

Environmental degradation is not new, although the production and organisation of the global environmental crisis itself may be novel. What certainly is new is the rise of a particular form of ideological consciousness which carries the label 'environmental consciousness'. That this consciousness has arisen primarily in the West, in a particular set of forms and at a given historical moment, requires explanation. Environmental degradation is not, in this account, principally a consequence of accidents, errors or misunderstandings. Rather it is produced as a consequence of the structured and systematic usage of sources and sinks which is intimately bound up with the mode of production. In this sense, one can speak, without any hint of contradiction, of the *production* of environmental degradation. It is clearly not the case that degradation is new: it is the changed and changing production of that degradation – especially in its systematic and globalised character – and, crucially, the social responses to that degradation that must be central to any enquiry.

The debate over environmental change is in large part a battle in the social construction of knowledge and meaning which is fought out in a global arena. Whilst one can give immediate recognition to the 'environment' as an essentially contested concept, the question of which conceptions gain dominance in political and social discourse remains to be addressed. There is a large, fascinating and growing literature on environmentalism and political thought which need not be rehearsed here (see, for example, Pepper 1986; Dobson 1990; Atkinson 1991; Merchant 1992; Eckersley 1992; O'Neill 1993), but almost all of it is written as if there were no international world, nor even a globalised social world. Rather than reviewing these contributions, it is appropriate here to identify the more salient problems involved in establishing the meaning and significance of the environment. Establishing the meaning of 'environment' is necessary for two linked reasons: first, in order to move away from essentially quantitative assessments of environmental change – which deal with both the scale and rate of change – and towards qualitative assessments which address questions of value and valuation, identity, appropriation and distribution; and second, in order to distance oneself methodologically and politically from the crass neo-Malthusianism which constitutes the subtext of the prevailing IR of global environmental change. This neo-Malthusian hegemony manifests itself in the uncritical – and indeed profoundly anti-social and anti-historical – acceptance of the estimation of environmental impacts from the aggregation of individual impacts, quite regardless of the highly differentiated social origins of that change. In this second respect, we must avoid the seduction of the dangerous platitudes which grew out of the UNCED process and which abounded at Rio, such as appeals to 'our common future' or to 'save the planet', which imply an equality of responsibility both in causing environmental degradation and in facing the consequences of that global degradation. References to shared 'global' responsibility or to a common fate rely almost wholly on quasi-mystical appeals to some worldwide imagined community which does not and could not have any substantive historical presence. (As argued later, the very concept of 'global' removes in significant ways the possibility of shared agency and responsibility, but has therefore led to the increasing invocation of 'lifeboat ethics', authoritarianism, corporatism and centralisation.)

The meaning of the 'environment' in social sciences in general and IR in particular has been insufficiently theorised. Indeed, it is difficult to identify any IR scholars who have explicitly dealt with the theoretical implications of environmental change for the discipline of IR in the manner which is evident amongst other social scientists, including those in that equally conservative discipline, economics (see, for example, the journal *Ecological Economics* as well as the innovative work found in the interdisciplinary journal *Global Environmental Change*). Indeed, the prevailing linguistic practice of referring to 'environmental issues' performs the same function of subordination as that achieved by reference to gender as 'women's issues'. At one and the same time, the hoped-for recognition of its centrality in social analysis is casually dropped in favour of some unspecified yet assumed object of enquiry which lies deeper in the hierarchy of social determinisms. Implicit in this vernacular is the methodological premiss that one can take these issues or leave them depending on one's interests. Thus, a variety of apparently discrete environmental issues have been studied, for example, acid rain, climate change or environmental degradation in Eastern Europe or some other region. The origins of their separation invariably derive from their disparate physical, not social, characteristics. The categorisation of environmental issues seems to have occurred through an identification of final outcomes as the defining features. It has been built upon a scientific taxonomy which may defy critical analysis from social theory. Whilst this may make good research sense for natural scientists, it is erroneous and quite misleading for social scientists in general and IR students in particular to follow the research prescriptions implied by the transfer and inheritance of such a process of categorisation. In short, when it comes to the IR of global environmental change, one has to be suspicious of 'specialisation in an individual field where an account of [one's] position, [is] sustainable only by the very delimitation of its reference' (Young 1990: 156). What has occurred, in effect, is the nationalisation of inherited environmental issues so that they can be comfortably pressed into the service of statist interests and analysis.[7] Rather than accepting the science as 'given' – where science becomes the arbiter of social action over environmental concerns, and which, incidentally, is a licence for government inaction until 'scientific certainty' is confirmed – the scientific assessment of environmental change needs to be critically understood as part of a sociology of knowledge.

This questioning of the status of science reflects the need to overturn the working assumption that the environment amounts simply to a set of external data, a body of resources, or a range of sources or sinks. It is true to say that there are very few, if any, natural places left in the world, if, by this, is meant pristine habitats which have not been subject to some anthropogenic change. Our conception of nature and of what is natural is socially constructed, and is therefore socially, temporally and spatially contingent. Sayer reminds us that 'Non-social phenomena are impervious to the meanings we attach to them. Although one could say that such objects are "socially defined", they are not socially-produced' (Sayer 1992: 26). Nature in and of itself possesses no value or meaning; value and meaning are constituted through human interaction. Rather than counterpose nature against humanity, or dichotomise into the natural and the social, we should regard humanity as *constitutive* of nature. Cooper provides a useful distinction between two conceptions of the environment. The first is of the environment as simply the spatial surroundings of a being; the second is of the environment as the immediate milieu which a being inhabits and which is constituted through a field of significance comprising a 'referential totality' – i.e. all the objects and symbols which together constitute meaning for a person or social actor. It is this second, tighter social conception, wherein the environment, as a field of significance, is formed by 'the items within it [which] signify or point to one another, thereby forming a network of meanings' (Cooper 1992: 170), which needs to be explained. Therefore, when we analyse GEC, the environment should not be regarded as some objective external datum but as an ordered and manufactured set of meanings and values. The 'environment', then, is a complex of intersubjective, contingent but not arbitrary set of meanings. The crucial question is the manner in which we attribute value to the constituents and processes characteristic of the biosphere. As Benton and Redclift argue, 'Nature commands attention, and the "natural" has an ideological force, which takes us to the heart of the paradox of development itself' (Benton and Redclift 1994: xi). What needs explanation is how and with what consequence networks of meaning are produced; which meanings gain ascendancy and which are subjugated; what economic, cultural and social forms are constituted by contending networks of meanings; and how these material and ideological relations are articulated both globally and locally. (To pre-empt the discussion in the final section, in a globalised society, what comes to constitute the referential totality becomes extremely ill-defined and mercurial in character.) An international, actor-focused enquiry does not even begin to scratch the surface of these matters, because meaning is a question of social, and not individual, constitution.

A dispute over the range, content and significance of these networks of meanings lies at the heart of the environmental and developmental question. The task is to unearth the deeply embedded but differentiated understandings and practices about social development which are organised and articulated globally. A number of authors (Smil 1993; McCormick 1989; Pepper 1986; O'Riordan

1981) have traced the rise of 'environmentalism' over recent decades, and a dominant strand has been the neo-Malthusian conservationism whose principal ideological appeal is to a romantic signification of a fragile, innocent and vulnerable 'nature' (see Merchant 1980, and Jackson 1994, for feminist critiques of these portrayals) subject to the inexorable depredations of the human world. In this conception of the environment, humanity stands outside of nature with the resulting appeal to 'save', 'preserve', 'protect' or 'conserve' that which has been unsullied. This tradition, arising in the North, has been the principal ideological informant of the international environmental discourse, and may be characterised as one of enclosure and appropriation.

Against this tradition, and reflecting a much longer and heterogeneous, but subordinated, critique, have been the largely socialist, anarchist and anti-imperial strands which arose out of struggles for economic and political self-determination. This second critical tradition regarded 'environmental' concerns as part and parcel of the struggle for the control of resource use and resource distribution (see Redclift 1984, 1987; Pepper 1986; Merchant 1980, 1992; Bookchin 1990, 1991; Eckersley 1992; *Third World Resurgence*). In these views, environmental change was crucially determined by – in the currently unjustifiably unfashionable phrase – the ownership of the means of production and control over the criteria of exchange. By extension, what constituted the referential totality for this second tradition was not the rather arbitrary selection of environmental issues – involving say, the aesthetic and charismatic appeal of blue whales, the alarmism of population control or the chauvinist discourse concerning acid rain (all of which, ironically, are not immediately and directly experienced) – but the entirety of that which informed the systematically produced human condition – e.g. poverty, malnutrition, dispossession, proximity to toxic waste, a hazardous working environment, exposure to contaminated foods, etc. (all of which, by contrast, tended to be unavoidable and immediate). In short, the material transformation of the world necessarily entailed a corresponding social transformation of the world. The 'environment' in this second tradition was inseparable from the broader question of development. Thus, part of any rigorous social enquiry into environmentalism must include a deconstruction of how particular dominant conceptions of the environment arose and came to be naturalised, and why and in what ways such conceptions mask the socio-economic distribution of environmental benefits and degradations. Indeed, what is of interest are not the changed physical properties but the changed set of social relations – relations which carry with them new significations of environmental meaning and value.

What we consider to be 'environmental', as well as the very reference to 'environmental issues', are themselves social constructions. Lash and Urry rightly remind us that 'there are a variety of forms assumed by the nature/society relationship. This varies both historically and geographically' (Lash and Urry 1994: 294), and students of IR should resist the temptation of abstraction and of universalising what are actually historically contingent expressions. What students of IR consider worthy of enquiry, as well as the manner and the purpose to which this enquiry is put, are part of the material production of ideas, and not the neutral, value-free consequences of positivist scientific enquiry. The meaning of the environment is part and parcel of the production of degradation, and what counts as degradation needs to be clarified.

## GLOBAL ENVIRONMENTAL DEGRADATION AND THE GLOBAL CAPITALIST ECONOMY

The ideological meanings and significance given to the environment are embedded in the social expression of capitalism. The historical coincidence between the rise and spread of capitalism and industrialism and the generation of global environmental crises needs explanation. Whereas the IR of global environmental change has hitherto given primary causal explanation to actors and policy, I want to argue that environmental change – for which we can read 'the transformation and use of sources, sinks and resources' – on the scale which we have witnessed is not primarily the outcome of human agency (where agency means wilfulness, or purposive or intentional action), but is the cumulative or systemic consequence of a set of structured practices and processes. Attention paid to globalised reiterated practices reveals incomparably more about the organisation and administration of degradation than does a focus on the ad hoc and tangential responses witnessed in inter-state environmental negotiations. Bluntly stated, a focus on inter-state relations is largely irrelevant to the explanation of global environmental degradation, nor is an elaboration of inter-state relations likely to lead to any reversal of such degradation.

The approach and range of enquiry proposed here echo Bookchin's advocacy of social ecology (1990, 1991) which regards 'ecological degradation . . . in great part, [as] a product of the degradation of human beings by hunger, material insecurity, class rule, hierarchical domination, patriarchy, ethnic discrimination and competition' (Bookchin 1994: 17). There is, in Bookchin's view, an inseparability of social problems from ecological problems, and he thus proposes the term 'social ecology' as the remit of a proper environmental enquiry, or as the referential totality. Hitherto, accounts in the IR of global environmental change have privileged descriptions of what has happened in GEC in terms both of aggregated physical outcomes and of international institutional responses over *why* they happened – or even why they should be of any significance at all. Furthermore, the multitude of social relations associated with degradation have been lost to the singular concern of the state. A social-ecological account allows us to address the reasons for and the causes of change, along with the multiple manifestations and meanings of change, and in so doing broadens and enriches the account of what actually happened.

In this section I want to outline the socioeconomic principles which underlie environmental change in a capitalist world system, and from which we can thereby discern a social ecology. As Redclift neatly summarises, 'Capitalist development transforms nature and the environment within a logic which needs to be understood in global terms' (Redclift 1987: 46). Furthermore, he argues that the environment should be 'looked upon as process rather than form, as a result of a set of relationships between physical spaces, natural resources and a constantly changing pattern of economic forces' (ibid.: 79). Broadly speaking, capitalist ownership and capitalist allocative and distributive criteria have permeated the entire social world across the globe, although the extent to which these criteria are mediated, resisted and rearticulated remains highly differentiated. In other words, while capitalism is global in character, its character is not globally uniform (and there is, therefore, no substitute for detailed historical and empirical research). Nevertheless, a set of crucial constituents can be identified which illuminate that the key determinant of the dynamics of ecological degradation in a global capitalist economy is the relationship between capitalist expansion and the regulation of capitalism.

A central constituent of capitalism is the commodification of resources, be they material or ideational (including labour), and hence their privatisation. In broad terms, the process of capitalist expansion entails the displacing of myriad forms of use rights and property rights into *private* property rights (see Mandel 1990; *The Ecologist* 1992). The main ideal-typical characteristic of private property rights are exclusive rights to the use and alienation of the property in question, free from any other sociocultural constraints. For our purposes of environmental resource analysis, we can depict the twin pillars of capitalism as being generalised commodity production and commodity exchange, in which the constant accumulation of commodities is a necessary end in itself, one made possible through the social division of labour. The historical fact of multiple and competing capitals ensures the vitality and dynamism of this system of constant commodity expansion. Ecological tolerances are irrelevant to the capitalist logic of expansion.

Capital accumulation is a global structure, and not simply an aggregation of national capitals. Given this fact, it makes no sense to speak of the historical stage of national capitalism, nor to engage in a comparative analysis of the relative advancement or 'backwardness' of each unit (see Wallerstein 1991, and Saurin 1995). (It would, however, continue to make sense to analyse the mode of regulation by states of capitalist accumulation: this does not presuppose either the existence of national capitals or its organisation on national lines.) Similarly, it makes no sense to speak of national environmental conditions, since the specific form of degradation to which one is referring is a function on the one hand of the ecosystems or biophysical systems through which the physical transformation occurs (and which are not coincident with state jurisdictional boundaries), and on the other hand of the current expressions and articulations of global capitalism.

By way of example, the environmental, social and economic degradation consequent upon the introduction both of 'scientific forestry'[8] to Northern India in the first decades of the twentieth century under British imperial rule (Guha 1990) and of Green Revolution agriculture from the 1970s onwards (Shiva 1993) arose out of the commodification of production and labour and the modernisation of agriculture-based capital accumulation, as well as the wholesale privatisation of knowledge. The logic of accumulation was not national in character or manifestation, and nor were the principal beneficiaries of that modernisation. Instead, emergent global logics were evident, and are now much clearer. The development of the global agri-food complex, involving strong corporate vertical integration, grew in tandem with the commodification of agricultural labour and the privatisation of land and agricultural technologies, as well as with a process of incorporation into a parallel global chemical and biotechnology complex. The incorporation of people, local economies and environments into the global agri-food complex has much more to do with an unintentional process of incorporation into dominating logics of accumulation than with any wilful national policy.

The first point to make about the capitalist mode of production is that it is based upon the appropriation of profit (surplus value) from labour, wherein direct labour transforms the actual physical properties of the world whilst the economic value of that transformation is transferred or conveyed through the exchange process to other beneficiaries. This process of exchange results in the accumulation of capital which, by definition, is not under the control of direct labour. The strategic asset of accumulated and concentrated capital allows capitalists to determine the shape, content and direction of future investments irrespective of the needs or conditions of direct labour. Thus, whilst direct producers appear to be the immediate agents of environmental change (in which case, they generate a distinct and localised referential totality), as well as of a corresponding set of social relations of production, their autonomy is structured by principles of appropriation and exchange which they are not at liberty to overturn. At the same time, capitalists make investment decisions based on criteria generated through an entirely different referential totality. Thus, any capital investment, based on criteria which are of benefit to capitalists, involves the exploitation of sources, sinks and labour. The immediate and degrading consequences of that exploitation do not fall on the capitalist. They fall, instead, systematically and disproportionately heavily on direct producers, i.e. labour, and on 'displaced' labour or the reserve army of unemployed. In brief, the capitalist process of structured inequality in production produces continuous, but differentiated, social relations.

Second, the capitalist mode of production serves to commodify labour – into increasingly atomised and privatised forms – and therefore to permanently reconstitute labour into a structured and unequal market. The apparent disorganisation and fragmentation of labour (into 'free' labourers) mask the structured unity of the capitalist appropriation of wealth and the strategic concentration of decision-making powers amongst monopoly capitalists. This means that there is a global and social unequal distribution in the quality, composition and concentration of capital, from which particular degrading practices arise.

Capitalism is a global structure of material accumulation which simultaneously concentrates wealth and energy both in certain locales and at certain social levels by extracting and dispossessing from other locales and social levels. Eco- and biophysical systems act as material sources and sinks. As sources, these systems contain or provide raw materials as well as energy-synthesising services. As sinks, these systems absorb anthropogenically produced waste and re-assimilate materials and energy into these systems. To the extent that the rates of use of sources exceed the rates of assimilation of sinks, then environmental degradation is under way. Clearly, however, the location of sources, of transformative capacity (labour and technology) and of sinks need not coincide. The increasing lack of coincidence in this respect entails the redistribution of the externalised costs of production and consumption.

Furthermore, the historical separation of use value from exchange value, in large part through a monetised economy (see Sayer 1991; Lash and Urry 1994), has facilitated – indeed has been a precondition of – the rupturing of the material basis of economic growth away from local ecological and biophysical systems to global ecological and biophysical sources. The sphere of circulation increasingly integrates the world into a unitary capitalist market, whilst simultaneously alienating direct producers from control over production. Because commodity exchange and accumulation reflects exchange value and not use value, and because the process of capital accumulation entails the removal of investment and employment decisions away from direct producers, there is no imperative on capitalists to attend to either labour needs or local ecological propriety. For example, the destruction of Ogoni lands in Southern Nigeria by oil companies including, allegedly, Royal Dutch Shell satisfies the covetous and distanced shareholders and investors who derive huge financial benefit from the exploitation of these lands and people. At the same time, the Ogoni pay the permanent costs of ecological degradation and repression, whilst relinquishing control over what happens to their land, to the oil or to the product of their labour. Exchange value, as manifested increasingly in the world capitalist economy, is divorced from any capacity to reflect basic human needs and requirements. Instead, it compounds the possibility of market criteria, and of monopolies in particular, in such a way as to set the terms in which nature and labour are exploited. Such a process would involve the internalisation of otherwise socialised or externalised costs. In other words, with the expansion in the scale of capitalism, there has been an inexorable transferring of environmental control from the direct producer over to the monopoly capitalist.

The significance of this argument is that it cautions against identifying the direct agent of degradation – the *colono*, the woodfuel gatherer, the cattle herder, the fisherfolk, and so on – as the social cause of degradation. A given expression of degradation should not be mistaken for its cause. In the title words of a Friends of the Earth publication on deforestation, *Whose Hand on the Chainsaw?*, the global expressions of environmental degradation are the taken-for-granted conditions of conventional IR analysis. However, these socially generated and historically contingent conditions are precisely what need to be explained. As Marx, in his preface to *A Contribution to the Critique of Political Economy*, lucidly observed

> In studying such transformation it is always necessary to distinguish between the material transformation of the economic conditions of production . . . and . . . the ideological forms in which men become conscious of this conflict and fight it out. Just as one does not judge an individual by what he thinks about himself, so one cannot judge such a period of transformation by its consciousness.
>
> (Marx 1970: 20)

The distance between the site of degradation and the location of the benefit of that degradation leads to its own production of environmental understanding. As the net beneficiaries of distanciated environmental degradation, academic comment-ators on the international relations of GEC should not confuse our environmental understanding with the production of that understanding.

One is led, in the words of Sklair, to '[t]he hypothesis that there is a contradiction between capitalist development and global survival', and that this hypothesis has '. . . prima facie plausibility' (Sklair 1994: 220). Exploring this contradiction is a prequisite of the IR of global environmental change. But in what ways, if any, do explicitly environmental concerns shape the analysis of capitalism? In many ways, environmental concerns have simply drawn into the frame of analysis ecological and biophysical dynamics which were previously regarded as external to the explanation of material production and ideational production. However, one can now trace the lineage of capital accumulation – or global development – through shadow ecological costs. It is now evidently consistent to identify 'ecological debt' and 'ecological footprints' as necessary attributes of capitalist growth. The cumulative effect, and the growing structural consequence of capitalism, is the evolution of a globalised energy subsidy which relies on 'free' sources. And parallel to this energy subsidy is a global *material* subsidy, similarly relying on 'free' sources.

Whereas classical political economists recognised that such sources were 'free', there was no such recognition in respect of sinks. The belated recognition that *has* followed is, if anything, the novelty of environmental concern for economists and social theorists. In broad historical terms, the process of the extraction of energy for the transformation of materials has moved from local and relatively concentrated sources over to global and diffused sources. Evidently, these changes have been uneven and unequal, and necessarily so. All production therefore carries with it an ecological shadow – or, to repeat the above-mentioned metaphor, an ecological 'footprint'. This 'footprint' is social as well as physical in character, and must be understood as part of the analysis of the social relations of production.

The recent and important work of Richard Norgaard is clear on this matter. His development of the 'co-evolutionary paradigm' is one in which 'Nothing is exogenous' and 'everything is symmetrically related to everything else' (Norgaard 1994: 35), and in which 'Environmental subsystems are treated symmetrically with the subsystems of values, knowledge, social organisation, and technology in this co-evolutionary explanation of history' (ibid.: 36). The consequence of Norgaard's central thesis is that with the establishment of the hydrocarbon economy through the Industrial Revolution, there appeared to be an escape from the eco- and biophysical constraints of a primarily agricultural economy. Thus, the transformation of nature – previously achieved through low-energy technologies in which consumption rates roughly equalled regener-ation and assimilation rates – was accelerated by the use of hydrocarbon-based high-energy technologies. As a general rule, energy-intensive technologies act as substitutes for labour-intensive processes, but as high-energy sources are depleted in the locality, so sources must be sought further afield. Thus, the form of possession and the control of labour are intimately related to the choice of technologies used (Norgaard 1994), to the manner in which the natural world is transformed and to the distribution of environmental goods and bads. Benton rightly advises that '[w]hat *is* required is the recognition that each form of social/economic life has its own specific mode and dynamic of interrelation with its own specific contextual conditions, resource materials, energy sources and naturally mediated unintended consequences' (Benton 1989: 77).

This enquiry into global environmental change could equally lead to simply repeating again the incisive and inspired criticism contained in Marx's preface to *A Contribution to the Critique of Political Economy*, in which he was led to conclude 'that neither legal relations nor political forms could be comprehended whether by themselves or on the basis of so-called general development of the human mind, but that on the contrary they originate in the material conditions of life' (Marx 1970: 21). Thus, before we look at institutional responses, we must look at the global manufacture or production of degradation. Marx elaborates, furthermore, that

> in the social production of their existence men inevitably enter into definite relations, which are independent of their will, namely relations of production appropriate to a given stage in the development of their material forces of production. The totality of these relations of production constitutes the economic structure of society . . . and to which correspond definite forms of social consciousness.
>
> (Marx 1970: 21)

The systematic alienation entailed in capitalist accumulation involves the removal of the self-determination of the direct producers of material change. To the extent that production technologies and transformative practices are established by criteria determined by the effective demand on the part of global markets for the satisfaction of wants and desires (as against the provision for human need), so local practices which would otherwise ensure that the pace of development falls within eco- and biophysical tolerances are subverted.[9] Axiomatic to the argument made here is that people do not engage in environmentally degrading practices unless they are obliged to do so. (In contrast to the subtext evident in the nascent IR of global environmental change, I do not assume that the principal problematic factor for IR is that of the abuse of the so-called 'global commons' – which are, in fact, not commons at all but rather open-access regimes (this crucial difference is often ignored). Instead, I take the mundane and normal practices of degradation as being the object of critical enquiry.) If degrading practices occur as a matter of routine, how do we account for this?

## GLOBALISATION AND GLOBAL ENVIRONMENTAL DEGRADATION

Contrary to the assumption of anarchy which pervades orthodox IR, and from which the emergent sub-discipline of the IR of global environmental change inherits its principal intellectual baggage, I have argued that there are very powerful global ordering processes and sets of ordering principles which are intrinsic to the environmental debate. The use of the terms 'global' and 'globalisation' is problematic and needs explanation, as does their relationship to international relations. Having just argued that capitalism is a global historical process with peculiar environmental consequences, I want to turn briefly to the analysis of the significance of the globalisation of environmental degradation, and to a consideration of how orthodox IR fails to address these key problematics.

It is not self-evident what is meant in much of the literature when the terms 'global environmental change' or 'global environmental degradation' are used.[10] And an added confusion is to employ the term 'the international relations of global environmental change'. What we can, however, extract from these terms is that at least two logics and explanatory narratives are being invoked, but that these narratives are incommensurable. The first term – 'global environmental change' – most often refers to some rather vague or ill-defined but widespread change in environmental conditions, in its ambiguous characterisation of which it fails to draw upon any specific or explicit definition of a sociopolitical community. There is no self-evident sociopolitical identity carried in the term 'global environmental change', and thereby no such identity appears to be available for specification. Against this, on the other hand, the second term – 'the international relations of global environmental change' – invokes a readily identifiable set of political communities, namely sovereign states. However, the argument developed thus far is that the radical disjuncture between the dynamics and processes of environmental change and development and the territorially based authority of the state ensures the inappropriateness of looking at the state both as a basic causal unit of environmental change and as the most competent unit for the mediation of environmental change.

Globalisation should be understood as an analytical concept, and not as a descriptive term. It does not simply mean that behaviour is replicated around the world. It refers, instead, to the form in terms of which the world is ordered (see Robertson 1992). It suggests a causal relationship between distanciated social agents, that is, between agents who not only may never come into physical contact with each other but are unlikely even to *know* of each other, and who are furthermore not subject to the same jurisdictional powers. Nevertheless, in an important sense, the life of a distanciated social agent may be intimately entangled in the lives of all other social agents. Globalisation entails the restructuring of the locality through globalised relations of power over which no central, let alone jurisdictional, authority has control.

Globalisation means that social ordering is under way, not as a consequence of the presence of either a singular global authority or an inter-state authority, but as a consequence of the 'fostering [of] relations between "absent" others' (Giddens 1990: 18) and of the growing reliance upon the coordination of time and space. This capacity for global coordination is predicated upon a capitalist world economy in which the principles of commodification and exchange are firmly embedded across the world. Thus, capitalists are able to exploit the abstract labour and abstract economic relations quite regardless of local social, cultural, economic or environmental conditions. The relative security of capitalist economic relations globally may be contrasted with the growing insecurity of localised customs and practices – which would otherwise value more highly ecological or environmental integrity. As Giddens reminds us, upon this bedrock of globalised capitalist relations, ' . . . coordination serves to open up manifold possibilities of change by breaking free from the restraints of local habits and practices' (ibid.: 20). 'Breaking free' also means breaking free of local source, transformation and sink capacities, through the utilisation of globally spread source, transformation and sink capacities instead. Thus, the abuse or collapse of local ecosystems poses little threat to production since globalised sources and sinks can be used in their place.

When Raymond Williams observed that contemporary states are too large to deal with the local problems of modern life and too small to deal with the global problems of modernity (Williams 1983), he was primarily referring to the non-correspondence between the causes of socioeconomic change and the regulatory mechanisms that are meant to be applied to those changes. The process of globalisation, more than any other factor, has ensured the non-correspondence between state and inter-state regulation and global environmental integrity. It is as meaningless to speak of national economies as it is to speak of national environmental problems. Just as 'it was a characteristic of organised capitalism that a whole range of economic and social problems was thought to be soluble at the level of the nation-state', so, in an increasingly globalised socioeconomic order, '[d]isorganised capitalism disorganizes such national strategies' (Lash and Urry 1994: 293). The social and spatial distribution of benefits differs consider-ably from the social and spatial distribution of costs. What is clear is that the distributive principles or allocative criteria of a globalised capitalist system cut across state boundaries and are, in many respects, only marginally affected by state regulatory authority. For example, it is the scale, quality and dynamics of beef production and consumption on a global market that determine the patterns of environmental and socioeconomic degradation, and not the particular admini-strative authority or jurisdiction (though the administrative authority *will* give a particular set of incentives to that market). Two issues are at stake here. The first is the extent or spread of jurisdictional powers – that is, over what territorial space do administrative authorities have competence? The second is: what is the actual effectiveness of the administrative authority in question? I would contend not only that jurisdictional authority is subverted by globalisation but also that, in any case, the capacity and effectiveness of jursidictional authorities are typically weak or severely compromised (see Gill and Law 1988; O'Brien 1992; Dunning 1993; Sklair 1991).

Still, the portrayal of problems as being global, and of their putative solutions, also, as being global, is of key ideological significance. It is worth noting Buttel and Taylor's argument that the appeal to the 'global' has two principal facets: first, that 'in so far as environmental goods tend to be public goods, "saving" the environment is in everyone's interest, and hence no-one's in particular, leading to a very difficult collective mobilisation problem'; and second, that 'Global formulations permit "packaging" of multiple environmental problems and concerns within a common overarching rubric, at the same time they convey the legitimacy and persuasiveness afforded by their being rooted in science' (Buttel and Taylor 1994: 242). The history of international relations encourages the belief that so-called 'public goods' are essentially problems of a political nature, i.e. of state concern, and therefore incorporated into the debate about state regulation. The aggregate effect of all states attempting to regulate such public goods is to transfer the worldwide management of environmental public goods into a problem of inter-state environmental regulation (q.v. Hurrell and Kingsbury 1992a; Young 1989, 1994). Thus, for example, when Bush made his boastful assertion at Rio that the strictest environmental laws in the world applied in the USA, he could only do so by entirely ignoring the globalised nature of the world economy. Reference to the United Nations Environment Programme Register of International Treaties confirms that of the 152 multilateral environmental agreements, 102 were concluded between 1970 and 1990. However, it is much more difficult to confirm the effectiveness of these agreements, and considerable scepticism remains as to their substantive contribution to reducing environmental damage. Thus, in brief, despite the rapid increase in formal state involvement in environmental questions, the formal and discrete contribution of the state to controlling global environmental damage remains at best marginal and at worst irrelevant (Chatterjee and Finger 1994). Strict territorially based environmental laws usually have the effect of simply shifting the production or disposal of the offending product or process into another jurisdictional area. This calls into question what constitutes effective environmental laws or regulation: effective for what, or for whom? And at what price to what, or to whom? An analysis of inter-state environmental relations tells us virtually nothing about the mechanisms and processes by which environmental use and environmental risks are routinely distributed.

## CONCLUDING REMARKS

Any examination of social change must involve at least two fundamental enquiries: first, an identification of the causes of social change, and second, an analysis of the understanding of and the response to that change. The broad claim of the argument developed above can be sketched out as follows: the scale, spread and dynamics of contemporary environmental degradation are historically unique and global in nature. The characteristics of global environmental degradation are such that their attempted incorporation into unreconstructed theories of social change, including those implied in IR, reflects a grave misunderstanding both of environmental change and, more especially, of the environment–society nexus. Once again, rather than start the analysis with a study of how states respond to environmental change, we need to start our examination with a study of how social, economic, cultural and political practices across the world generate environmental change through the transformation and disposal of matter and energy.

The foregoing argument has not been one of ignoring actors in general and states in particular. It has been argued that a global sociology can remove the false promises of an analysis of 'high' politics, in which the IR of global environmental change is narrowly interpreted as a concern with the ad hoc responses of officialdom to environmental change. Rather, a global sociology must be able to explain how mundane and structured practices create environmental change, and how such changes are understood and reflected upon. Hence, it is with a determination of the principles and criteria by which social life is organised, and nature transformed and redistributed, that the enquiry must commence.

All actors are agents of environmental change, whether or not they declare this to be their intention. To accept the self-description of actors as 'environmentalist' and to disregard, on the other hand, all so-called 'non-environmental' actors is to misidentify the sources and consequences of environmental change. Marx's proposed method of enquiry is worth further consideration. To repeat:

> Just as one does not judge an individual by what he thinks about himself, so one cannot judge such a period of transformation by its consciousness, but, on the contrary, this consciousness must be explained from the contradictions of material life, from the conflict existing between the social forces of production and the relations of production.
>
> (Marx 1970: 20)

However, the focus on actors arises, in large part, due to the inheritance of the realist predisposition of making 'actor' equivalent to 'agent', and 'policy' equivalent to 'agency'. Rosenberg correctly observes that 'Historical *agency* is almost always reducible in Realist writings to *policy*' (Rosenberg 1990: 286; italics in the original). In this way, the transformation of the social world is predominantly interpreted as a matter of intent, and not as a consequence of unintentional action or behaviour. The current rejection of the traditional focus on actors results, however, from the contention that unless one understands the mundane and routine processes of global economic and social change which make up environmental degradation, then the milieu out of which actors arise, upon which they act, and by which they are transformed, will be discounted.

The approach advocated here is one which pays attention to the actual historical material change and the socioeconomic process which together allow the accumulation and concentration of transformative power. It is difficult to see an analytical case for paying greater attention to those already-constituted actors in IR who shout the loudest about environmental change. Unlike Molière's bourgeois *gentilhomme* who was shocked to find that he had indeed been speaking prose throughout his life, students of IR should not be surprised to find that all social life constitutes environmental change, and that all social agents are environmental agents.

To adopt a method of analysis which presupposes that a particular set of administrative, bureaucratic and expert scientific organisations lies at the centre of environmental regulation, and will be manifested predominantly through the state system, is to ignore the realities of diverse and complex social, economic and cultural processes across the world. A latent assumption behind these top-down approaches is that, in the end, the 'environment' is an external problem which simply has to be investigated technically, and appropriated and managed by a standard set of bureaucratic and legal resolutions. The history of both developmental change and environmentalism has been one where, in the words of Norgaard, 'Agencies . . . were established under the pretence that they merely had to uncover the facts, rationally determine solutions, and efficiently implement projects and programmes (Norgaard 1994: 4). The fact that it is in the underlying processes of production and accumulation that the roots of degradation are to be found has been ignored in favour of ephemeral and reactive attempts at the regulation of that degradation.

The central problem with traditional IR approaches to environmental change is that they elevate an ignorance of the vast range of social, cultural and economic processes at work into an essential methodological precondition. The latent universalist claims which have come to characterise IR seem to run contrary to the complexity, diversity and particularism which mark out environmental conditions. Complexity and diversity are marginalised in order to press standard generalised procedures into the service of official state regulation. As Panario and Prieto insist, 'We . . . have to resist the attempt to reduce the environmental problem to a new package of techno-bureaucratic rules and strategies, in the hands of the same structures of power' (Panario and Prieto 1992: 175). The critique of traditional IR in this chapter stems from two concerns: first, that traditional IR fails fundamentally to deal with environmental change because, by persisting with its traditional focus on the state and on related organisations, it ignores the socioeconomic processes involved in that change; and second, that in searching for solutions to that environmental crisis by continuing to focus on those institutional practices of modernity which have caused the environmental crisis in the first place, prevailing scholarship misses the opportunity to step outside the premises of its own entrapment. Despite his protestations to the contrary (Smith 1993: 29), Smith invokes the usual realist techniques of marginalisation by suggesting that the environmentalists and gender analysts can maintain their critique because they do not 'pay sufficient attention . . . to the "realities" of political and economic power' (Smith 1994: 29). To paraphrase Rosenberg's (1990: 291) compelling critique of Realism, whilst Smith is busy watching these 'realities' being played out, the global struggles over the environment, patriarchy, accumulation and distribution are mediating wholesale transformations of the form and conditions of social power in the world.

## NOTES

1 In addition to thanking participants of the British International Studies Association Global Environmental Change seminars, I would particularly like to acknowledge the useful discussions with Dr Marc Williams. This chapter was completed whilst the author was an ESRC GEC Programme Research Fellow, and this support is gratefully acknowledged.

2  It is worth reminding ourselves that whilst Non-Governmental Organisations (NGOs) have had a growing input into the process of advising on and formulating international environmental policy – especially through contributions to 'technical' or 'scientific' issues – it remains the case that only *states* formally deal with each other as sovereign and equal parties to international agreements.

3  I would also argue that orthodox IR has been extremely reluctant to address international, or rather 'global', political economic processes, despite facing criticism, on this point, that ranges from the modest objections of, for example, Susan Strange to the stronger objections raised by Stephen Gill and David Law or Robert Cox.

4  Unfortunately, a close critique cannot be entered into here of the contradictions, the misinformation and the cursory and mistaken analysis which characterise the ten factors which Smith claims consign 'environmental politics' to the periphery. This must be the subject of another work.

5  The atomistic, methodological individualism of orthodox social science and traditional IR needs to be contrasted with the concern with structures, systems and processes which informs much of environmental and ecological studies.

6  See Justin Rosenberg's (1990) sharp and neat rejection of Realism in 'What's the matter with Realism?' (*Review of International Studies*). A number of the methodological and historical objections he raises are pertinent to the current criticism. They are more fully developed in his (1994) *The Empire of Civil Society*.

7  By 'the nationalisation of environmental issues' I mean problematising environmental issues as if they could be articulated as national interests and subjected to nationalist interpretation. For a critique of intellectual nationalism in international theory, see Saurin 1995. I am not arguing here that the scientific debate is settled and given, but that science itself is pressed into national service, and that a nationalist scientific agenda can still be pursued pending the 'definitive' conclusions of scientific enquiry.

8  'Scientific forestry' involved the application of standardised models of forestry management that were based on North European – especially German – forestry practice. This method derived from ecological conditions characterised by relatively low biodiversity and limited tree species, and from economic relations characterised by private property, commodification and the specialisation of labour, but it was subsequently transferred to ecological conditions marked by relatively high biodiversity and by complex and non-standardised economic arrangements. See Shiva (1993) for related commentaries on biodiversity and biotechnology.

9  This is a major claim which cannot be properly addressed in the space available. Central issues of economic democracy and self-determination are at stake here.

10  See Turner *et al.* 1990 for useful definitional distinctions for the term 'environmental change'.

## BIBLIOGRAPHY

Atkinson, A. (1991) *Principles of Political Ecology*, London: Belhaven.
Benton, T. and Redclift, R. (1994) 'Introduction', in Redclift, R. and Benton, T. (eds) *Social Theory and Global Environmental Change*, London: Routledge.
Bookchin, M. (1990) *The Philosophy of Social Ecology*, Montreal: Black Rose.
—— (1991) *The Ecology of Freedom*, revised edn, Montreal: Black Rose.
—— (1994) *Which Way for the Ecology Movement? Essays by Murray Bookchin*, Edinburgh: AK Press.
Brenton, T. (1994) *The Greening of Machiavelli: the Evolution of International Environmental Politics*, London: Earthscan Royal Institute of International Affairs.
Buttel, F. and Taylor, P. (1994) 'Environmental sociology and global environmental change: a critical assessment', in Redclift, M. and Benton, T. (eds) *Social Theory and the Global Environment*, London: Routledge.

Chatterjee, P. and Finger, M. (1994) *The Earth Brokers: Power, Politics and World Development*, London: Routledge.

Cooper, D. (1992) 'The idea of the environment', in Cooper, D. and Palmer, J. (eds) *The Environment in Question: Ethics and Global Issues*, London: Routledge.

Cox, R. (1987) *Production, Power and World Order*, New York: Columbia U.P.

Daly, H. (1992) *Steady-State Economics*, 2nd edn, London: Earthscan.

—— and Cobb, J. (1990) *For the Common Good: Redirecting the Economy Towards Community, the Environment and a Sustainable Future*, London: Green Print.

Dobson, A. (1990) *Green Political Thought*, London: HarperCollins.

Dunning, J. (1993) *The Globalisation of Business*, London: Routledge.

Eckersley, R. (1992) *Environmentalism and Political Theory: Towards an Ecocentric Approach*, London: UCL Press.

*The Ecologist* (1992) 'Whose common future?', special issue, 22: 4.

Engel, J.R. and Engel, J.G. (eds) (1990) *Ethics of Environment and Development: Global Challenge and International Response*, London: Belhaven.

Giddens, A. (1990) *The Consequences of Modernity*, Cambridge: Polity.

Gill, S. and Law, D. (1988) *The Global Political Economy: Perspectives, Problems and Policies*, Hemel Hempstead: Harvester Wheatsheaf.

Guha, R. (1990) *The Unquiet Woods*, New Delhi: O.U.P.

Hurrell, A. and Kingsbury, B. (eds) (1992a) *The International Politics of the Environment*, Oxford: O.U.P.

—— (1992b) 'The international politics of the environment: an introduction', in Hurrell, A. and Kingsbury, B. (1992) (eds) *The International Politics of the Environment*, Oxford: O.U.P.

Jackson, C. (1994) 'Gender analysis and environmentalism', in Redclift, M. and Benton, T. (eds) *Social Theory and the Global Environment*, London: Routledge.

Lash, S. and Urry, J. (1994) *Economies of Signs and Space*, London: Sage.

McCormick, J. (1989) *The Global Environmental Movement*, London: Belhaven.

Mandel, E. (1990) 'Introduction' to Marx, K. *Capital: Volume 1*, Harmondsworth: Penguin.

Marx, K. (1970) *A Contribution to the Critique of Political Economy*, London: Lawrence & Wishart.

Merchant, C. (1980) *The Death of Nature: Women, Ecology and the Scientific Revolution*, San Francisco, Cal.: Harper & Row.

—— (1992) *Radical Ecology: the Search for a Liveable World*, London: Routledge.

Miliband, R. (1973) *The State in Capitalist Society: an Analysis of the Western System of Power*, London: Quartet.

Norgaard, R. (1994) *Development Betrayed: the End of Progress and a Coevolutionary Revisioning of the Future*, London: Routledge.

O'Brien, R. (1992) *Global Financial Integration: the End of Geography?*, London: RIIA/Pinter.

O'Neill, J. (1993) *Ecology, Policy and Politics: Human Well-Being and the Natural World*, London: Routledge.

O'Riordan, T. (1981) *Environmentalism*, 2nd edn, London: Pion.

Panario, D. and Prieto, R. (1992) 'Autonomy, ecology and development', in Norberg-Hodge, H. and Goering, P. (eds) *The Future of Progress: Reflections on Environment and Development*, Bristol: International Society for Ecology and Culture.

Pepper, D. (1986) *The Roots of Modern Environmentalism*, London: Routledge.

Redclift, M. (1984) *Development and the Environmental Crisis: Red or Green?*, London: Methuen.

—— (1987) *Sustainable Development: Exploring the Contradictions*, London: Methuen.

—— and Benton, T. (eds) (1994) *Social Theory and the Global Environment*, London: Routledge.

Robertson, R. (1992) *Globalisation: Social Theory and Global Culture*, London: Sage.

Rosenberg, J. (1990) 'What's the matter with Realism?', *Review of International Studies* 16(4): 285–303.

—— (1994) *The Empire of Civil society: a Critique of the Realist Theory of International Relations*, London: Verso.

Sachs, W. (ed.) (1993) *Global Ecology: a New Arena of Political Conflict*, London and Nova Scotia: Zed Books/Fernwood.

Saurin, J. (1993) 'Global environmental degradation, modernity and environmental knowledge', *Environmental Politics* 2(4): 46–64; also in Thomas, C. (ed.) (1994) *Rio: Unravelling the Consequences*, London: Frank Cass.

—— (1995) 'The end of international relations? The state and international theory in the age of globalisation', in Linklater, A. and Macmillan, J. (eds) *Shifting Boundaries: New Directions in International Relations*, London: Pinter.

Sayer, A. (1992) *Method in Social Science: a Realist Approach*, 2nd edn, London: Routledge.

Sayer, D. (1991) *Capitalism and Modernity: an Excursus on Marx and Weber*, London: Routledge.

Seager, J. (1993) *Earth Follies: Feminism, Politics and the Environment*, London: Earthscan.

Shiva, V. (1993) *Monocultures of the Mind: Perspectives on Biodiversity and Biotechnology*, London and Penang: Zed Books/Third World Network.

Sklair, L. (1991) *Sociology of the Global System*, Hemel Hempstead: Harvester Wheatsheaf.

—— (1994) 'Global sociology and global environmental change', in Redclift, M. and Benton, T. (eds) *Social Theory and the Global Environment*, London: Routledge.

Smil, V. (1993) *Global Ecology: Environmental Change and Social Flexibility*, London: Routledge.

Smith, S. (1993) 'The environment on the periphery of international relations: an explanation', *Environmental Politics* 2(4): 28–45; also in Thomas, C. (ed.) (1994) *Rio: Unravelling the Consequences*, London: Frank Cass.

Strange, S. (1988) *States and Markets: an Introduction to International Political Economy*, London: Pinter.

Thomas, C. (1992) *The Environment in International Relations*, London: Royal Institute of International Affairs.

—— (1993) 'Beyond UNCED: an introduction', *Environmental Politics* 2(4): 1–27; also in Thomas, C. (ed.) (1994) *Rio: Unravelling the Consequences*, London: Frank Cass.

—— (ed.) (1994) *Rio: Unravelling the Consequences*, London: Frank Cass.

Turner, B., Kasperson, R., Meyer, W. *et al.* (1990) 'Two types of global environmental change: definitional and spatial-scale issues in their human dimensions', *Global Environmental Change*, December: 14–22.

Wallerstein, I. (1991) *Unthinking Social Science: the Limits of Nineteenth Century Paradigms*, Cambridge: Polity.

Weizsacker, E.U. von, (1994) *Earth Politics*, London: Zed Books.

Williams, R. (1983) *Towards 2000*, London: Chatto & Windus.

Young, O. (1989) *International Cooperation: Building Regimes for Natural Resources and the Environment*, Ithaca, NY: Cornell U.P.

—— (1994) *International Governance: Protecting the Environment in a Stateless Society*, Ithaca, NY: Cornell U.P.

Young, R. (1990) *White Mythologies: Writing History and the West*, London: Routledge.

# 6 Gender and environmental change

## Are women the key to safeguarding the planet?

*Charlotte Bretherton*

> If there must be a war, let the weapons be your healing hands, the hands of the world's women in defence of the environment. Let your call to battle be a song for the earth.
>
> (Mostafa Tolba, Director, United Nations Environment Programme (UNEP), addressing the 'Women Nurture the World' workshop, Nairobi, 1985)

Mostafa Tolba's words are amongst many thousands which claim some particular relationship between women and the environment. Frequently, such words evoke an image of women which accords with traditional gender stereotypes; hence implying specific roles, responsibilities and expectations. In consequence, the imputation of links between women and the environment, and the conceptualisation of women as playing a central environmental role, raise fundamental gender issues which have implications for theory, policy and action – in relation both to women and to the environment.

Gender analysis provides fruitful insights into the causes of environmental change and degradation. By re-examining the evolution of Western cultural values, it exposes the essentially masculine bias of our thinking about the natural world, and about the exploitation of its resources, which underlies contemporary, dominant models of economic development. Similarly, gender analysis highlights the gendered nature of the assumptions which have underlain the development of social and political institutions and which inform the policy-making of organisations at all levels, from the local community to the United Nations. In consequence, it is argued, successful implementation of environmental policy will depend upon the extent to which its formulation reflects an analysis both of the social construction of gender and of the ascription of gender roles; and attempts not only to redress the gender imbalance of decision-making fora but also to challenge the gendered assumptions which underlie the policy-making process.

This chapter, before addressing these issues, charts briefly the emergence of women–environment links as an aspect of the global political agenda, and outlines three distinct approaches which attach particular significance to such links.

## EVOLUTION OF WOMEN–ENVIRONMENT LINKS

During the 1970s, feminists, primarily from the West, began to theorise about gender–environment relationships. A variety of ecofeminist approaches developed which posited a special affinity between women and the natural world. Meanwhile, the United Nations Decade for Women (1975–85), in stimulating contact between Western and Third World women, widened this debate to include the special concerns and the activism of Third World women. Of particular significance was the negative impact of environmental degradation and pollution upon large numbers of Third World women. Consequently, the closing conference of the Decade placed particular emphasis upon the significance, globally, of links between women and the environment.

The impact of feminist perspectives articulated during the Decade for Women is evident from the sharp contrast between the respective treatments of gender issues in the proceedings and Declarations of the two United Nations Conferences on the Environment in 1972 and 1992. The final Declaration of the 1972 Conference on the Human Environment referred only to men, the first of its twenty-six Principles asserting:

> Man had the fundamental right to freedom, equality and adequate conditions of life, in an environment of a quality that permitted a life of dignity and well-being, and he bore a solemn responsibility to protect and improve the environment for present and future generations.

By the time of the 1992 Conference on the Environment and Development (UNCED), women had been acknowledged as part of the human race. Indeed Principle 20 of the Rio Declaration maintained that

> Women have a vital role in environmental management and development. Their full participation is therefore essential to achieve sustainable development.

In addition to this statement of principle, Agenda 21 (the Conference's broad statement of policy) included a chapter on 'Global action for women towards sustainable and equitable development' (Chapter 24) which demands that UN agencies involved in implementing Agenda 21 'ensure that gender considerations are fully integrated into all policies, programmes and activities'. Furthermore, specific reference is made to the special position of women in no less than 147 other clauses of the Agenda.

This comprehensive incorporation of women and environment links into Agenda 21 attests to the success of women's activism since the end of the UN Decade in 1985, which culminated in a period of intense activity in preparation for and during the Rio Earth Summit.[1] Perhaps it demonstrates, also, a recognition of the relevance of gender issues to global environmental politics.

## THE NATURE OF WOMEN–ENVIRONMENT LINKS

An emphasis on the significance of women's environmental role is shared by feminists and environmentalists alike. Nevertheless, assessments of the nature and value of women–environment links vary. Feminist activists and theorists tend to place positive emphasis upon women's links with the natural world, and upon their practical contribution to environmental management and protection. Other commentators, however, have tended to emphasise women's role as consumers, or, more particularly, to problematise women's reproductive role.

Clearly, these divergent approaches to women and the environment derive from different approaches to social analysis. They involve, also, rather different policy implications. In order to assess these implications, both for women and for the environment, the assumptions underlying the interconnection of women and the environment require examination. These fall broadly into three categories: women as the problem; women as victims; and women as saviours.

## Women as the problem

Discussion of the potential for a global environmental crisis associated with increasing pollution and resource depletion identifies two broad causal problems: excessive consumption in the developed world and population increase in the South. In both these 'problem' areas, women may be identified as bearing particular responsibility.

Attempts to address the problem of consumption in the developed world have focused around the notion of green consumerism, which has both attracted the support of and targeted women. This approach, with the apparent aim of environmental protection, has the effect of reducing women to the role of consumers, objects of influence whose genuine concerns about environmental issues are manipulated in order to change their purchasing habits. Recommendations in green consumer guides for environmentally friendly products promoted elsewhere by explicitly sexist advertising are cited as evidence of this manipulation (Hynes 1991: 475–8).

Green consumerism has been successful in that the demand for environmentally friendly products has increased considerably. In supplying this demand, however, changes in marketing, involving much 'green' labelling and packaging of products, have tended to substitute for changes in production. Thus, for a variety of reasons, green consumerism seems unlikely to succeed in reversing or even reducing the rate of environmental decline. It is a reductionist, market-oriented approach which seeks to change consumer preferences rather than reduce levels of consumption.

Despite the evidence that overconsumption in the developed world is currently the principal factor contributing to environmental change, this factor has not been the principal concern of researchers or environmentalists. Attention has focused, rather, upon the issue of population growth, in particular estimates of potential growth in the developing world. The work of biologists Ann and Paul Ehrlich exemplifies an approach which identifies population growth as the source of all environmental ills:

Global warming, acid rain, depletion of the ozone layer, vulnerability to epidemics and exhaustion of soils and groundwater are all related to population size . . . . We shouldn't delude ourselves: the population explosion will come to an end before very long. The only remaining question is whether it will be halted by the humane method of birth control or by nature wiping out the surplus.

(Ehrlich and Ehrlich 1990: 17)

The Ehrlichs' preferred solution to the population problem involves targeting Third World women through literacy programmes. The principal aim of this policy is to promote the acceptance and use (by women) of artificial birth-control methods. This approach is also favoured by the World Bank, whose 1992 *World Development Report* advocated 'Expanding educational programs for girls to promote demand for smaller families'. Apparently, 'Investments in female education have some of the highest returns for development and the environment' (International Bank for Reconstruction and Development 1992: 25–7).

In this approach, women are again objectified. As the least developed members of less developed societies, they are now to be 'developed' – to facilitate manipulation of their reproductive choices in the interests of the environment. Their designation in Non-Governmental Organisation (NGO) reports as 'acceptors' or 'rejectors' of family planning demonstrates this. Moreover, Third World women continue to be subjected to contraceptives, such as Depoprovera, which have been banned in the USA for their carcinogenic qualities. Severinghaus, in his study of Nepal (1990), found Depoprovera to be the most used non-permanent birth-control method. Permanent population control in the form of sterilisation similarly involves women to a disproportionate extent. Thus, despite the relative safety and low cost of vasectomies, International Planned Parenthood Federation (IPPF) reports indicate that tubectomies remain ten times more common. Traditional rewards (coconuts and steel utensils) are apparently available to women who undergo sterilisation (Rao 1991: 7–8). In these circumstances it is unsurprising that, in India, poor women are reluctant to approach official health providers, believing that 'all health care messages are family planning messages in disguise, and that family planning only means sterilization'(Sharma 1994: 23).

The emphasis on population control has further negative implications for women. Cultural norms and socioeconomic factors, particularly in traditional, rural societies, have generated a preference for male children. In such circumstances women may be obliged to continue child-bearing until at least two male infants seem assured of survival. In circumstances where this pressure conflicts with strong external pressure to reduce family size, as in China and India, the result has been widespread female infanticide or, more recently, foeticide.[2] Meanwhile new 'advances' in reproductive technology have made possible the option of sex preselection or 'breeding male', a solution to the population problem originally advocated by biologists some twenty years ago, when it was argued that 'Countless millions of people would leap at the opportunity to breed male (particularly in the third world) and no compulsion or even propaganda would be needed to encourage its use, only evidence of success by example' (Mies 1986: 124). This scenario both underlines the centrality of women to the environmental debate and demonstrates the urgent need for a comprehensive, women-centred approach to the issue of population growth. Such an approach was strongly urged at the September 1994 United Nations International Conference on Population and Development in Cairo. Sadly, however, women's voices were eclipsed by the publicity afforded an unprecedented alliance between the Roman Catholic Church and militant Islamists. Indeed, seven of the Conference's nine days were dominated by the efforts of these organisations to reverse or dilute the proposals contained in the draft Programme painstakingly formulated during the pre-conference process.[3]

The developments at the Cairo Conference demonstrate, once again, the manner in which women, whether in their reproductive or their consumption roles, or both, continue to be treated as objects of policy, and as a problem to be addressed.

## Women as victims

The relationship between poverty on the one hand and exposure to environmental pollution or degradation (or both) on the other has been well documented, both for developed and for less developed countries. According to statistics produced by USAID, the majority of the world's poor are women, and female-headed households constitute the poorest group in every country (Dankelman and Davison 1991: 18).

Residents of the inner cities of the developed world are subjected to various forms of environmental hazard. In the USA, for example, the urban poor are substantially more likely to live near a toxic waste dump than their more affluent, suburban neighbours (Hynes 1989: 73). The majority of the adult urban poor are women who, in addition to suffering increased exposure to hazards, are responsible for caring for other victims of pollution, particularly children. This combination of poverty and domestic responsibilities considerably reduces physical mobility, thus denying access to more healthy environments. In addition, women are victimised in their reproductive role through their being identified as the principal cause of foetal contamination. The risk that pregnant women may be exposed in the workplace to ionising radiation and a range of chemical substances is already resulting in job discrimination against those of child-bearing age. Evidence that foetuses are particularly vulnerable in the early stage of pregnancy, when awareness of the pregnancy is likely to be low, has resulted in attempts by large chemical producers in the USA to exclude women of child-bearing age from the workplace, or to require their prior sterilisation. In the European Union, also, this issue has been the subject of debate during the formulation of health and safety policy. At present, the indications are that foetal protection rather than equality of opportunity will be the major emphasis of any EU directive on this issue (Conroy Jackson 1990: 63).

It is in the context of the Third World, however, that the relationship between women, poverty and environmental degradation has been most fully documented. Much of the research in this area is associated with the Women in Development movement, and concentrates largely, but not exclusively, on women in rural areas. Here, despite the considerable diversity of women's experience both across and within the various Third World countries, women's domestic/reproductive roles are somewhat broadly conceived. Thus, in addition to family health care, women typically bear responsibility for the collection of fuel and water (and for attendant water-purification and water-sanitation measures) and the production as well as the preparation of food. Indeed, it is estimated that women produce more than 80 per cent of food for sub-Saharan Africa and between 50 and 60 per cent of Asia's food, forming the majority of the world's subsistence farmers, but owning only 1 per cent of the world's land. Moreover, this contribution to food production is believed to be systematically underestimated, both because it is unpaid work deemed to constitute part of women's reproductive role and because the survey evidence is gathered from male heads of households or village elders, who fail to recognise or choose to obscure the contribution made by women (Charlton 1984: 38–43).

Women's overwhelming responsibility for the provision of fuel, water and food indicates a close relationship with, and dependence upon, the local environment – and hence a particular vulnerability to environmental change. This has proved to be the case. Deforestation, desertification and the diminution/pollution of water supplies have had devastating effects. Forests, in addition to fuel, have traditionally provided women with food, medicinal plants and materials for shelter, and their loss has greatly affected women's subsistence needs. Moreover, as forests diminish and water supplies dry up, women are obliged to make increasingly longer journeys to fetch water and fuel, and this renders their already heavy work burden intolerable. Desertification, in reducing the quality and availability of cultivable land, has also affected women disproportionately; their exclusion from land ownership has ensured that they are increasingly relegated to marginal plots, or denied access to land altogether.

Land and water shortages are also associated with increased male migration from the countryside (sometimes referred to as drought migration), which leaves women with the sole responsibility for providing for their children. Indeed, there has been a dramatic rise in female-headed households throughout the Third World (as high as 50 per cent in Kenya, Ghana, Sierra Leone and Botswana), whilst in some regions the extent of the male exodus has produced serious social-destabilisation effects (Monimart 1991).

In the Third World, women's suffering as victims of environmental degradation has been experienced not only in terms of increased hardship but also in terms of diminished social status, as women's expertise in land, water and forest conservation has been marginalised and devalued. In the context of India, Vandana Shiva maintains that environmental degradation and the associated diminution in the status of women are closely linked to the increasing violence and deprivation suffered by women and girls. Additional work burdens and lowered food entitlement damage women's health and reduce life expectancy, while forms of direct violence against women include dowry murders, the selective abortion of female foetuses and female infanticide. Indeed, it has been estimated that, in the absence of the systematic decline in the sex ratio resulting from the murder or neglect of female infants and the ill treatment of women, there would have been almost 30 million more women alive in India than actually live today (Shiva 1988: 118–20). Further evidence that women suffer disproportionately as victims of environmental degradation would be gratuitous.

Feminist explanations (whilst varying considerably in emphasis) have explicitly identified both women and the environment as victims, focusing upon the interconnection between economic exploitation and political oppression that is inherent in the concept of patriarchy. Thus, it is argued, contemporary models of economic growth and development are founded upon the domination and exploitation both of the natural world and of women, whilst the contribution of each to human well-being has been undervalued precisely because it is without a price (recent efforts by economists to 'price' them both notwithstanding).

In the context of the developed world, Patricia Hynes, a former official of the US Environmental Protection Agency, has stated simply, but vividly, her views concerning the cause of environmental pollution:

> Almost exclusively, all polluters and environmental criminals are men; women don't hold positions of power to make and carry out those decisions . . . hazardous waste exists because men never learned to clean up after themselves.
>
> (Hynes 1989: 73)

Writing in the context of the Third World, Vandana Shiva has emphasised the impact, on women and on the environment, of externally generated development policies, in particular the increase of intensive, commercial agriculture and the so-called Green Revolution. For Shiva, such policies constitute a model of 'maldevelopment' based on Western, patriarchal thought which emphasises the virtue of technological and scientific intervention and assesses traditional agriculture as 'unproductive'(Shiva 1988: 73). In consequence, traditional, sustainable agriculture is being supplanted by resource-depleting, market-oriented production which has marginalised the small producer in general and women in particular.

The identification of women (and children) as the principal victims of environmental degradation has clear policy implications. Attention tends to focus upon the plight of the women rather than upon the causes of that plight, so that the problems emanating from the disruption of women's traditional relationship with the natural world are neither identified nor addressed. Rather, women are objectified as passive recipients of welfare, and provided with alternative means of subsistence for themselves and their families. This 'welfare' approach, in consequence, reinforces the imposition of a narrow, Western interpretation of women's reproductive role. Additionally, the targeting of women for support has tended to encourage male migration, since the responsibility for families' survival is seen to rest with women and aid agencies.

Clearly, the 'women as victims' approach fails to generate any kind of policy which recognises and enhances women's role in environmental conservation. Nevertheless, despite the persistence of a welfare orientation in many aid programmes, considerable attention has focused upon women's practical, day-to-day contribution to environmental management. Attempts have been made to involve women in schemes aiming to protect or repair the environment, and to the extent that such schemes stress a utilisation of the special knowledge and skills possessed by women, this approach accords with the notion of women as saviours of the environment.

## Women as saviours

Feminists' concern for environmental issues is frequently expressed through a 'women as saviours' approach. This shares certain assumptions with, but develops upon, the 'women as victims' approach. Thus, it is argued that there exist fundamental links, indeed a certain equivalence, between women and the natural world; and that this equivalence represents a primary source of the domination and exploitation of both. Marilyn French's assertion exemplifies this view:

> The primary manifestation of the relationship between humans and nature is the way a society sees men and women. Most cultures associate women with nature . . . and men with humanness, which is seen as a condition permitting transcendence – superiority over, freedom from, control of nature.
>
> (French 1985: xvi)

Moreover, it is argued that the status differentiation between women and men, seen as the source of all other forms of social stratification, was considerably reinforced as a consequence of the development of Western industrial civilisation. This analysis forms part of the broader critique of those ideas and modes of thought associated with the Enlightenment and with the scientific revolution.

Men's enhanced ability to control and exploit the earth's natural resources was contemporaneous with women's subordination and domestication as the social (and sexual) division of labour became entrenched. The mythology of the separate spheres, and associated stereotypical representations of femininity and masculinity, served to legitimise this process of division, and became both deeply embedded in social institutions and formalised within the legal and political systems.

While much contemporary feminist analysis identifies gender as the fundamental social division, there is considerable divergence between feminists in their treatment of gender difference. Thus, feminist approaches range from those which seek to minimise or transcend gender differences to those which emphasise such differences but seek to revalorise feminine and masculine characteristics. In relation to the environmental debate, ecofeminism tends to exemplify this latter approach. Women's identification with the natural world arises, it is argued, from shared experience of exploitation, exploitation which will end only when social esteem is attributed to the feminine values of cooperation and nurturance rather than to the masculine values of competition and dominance.

The work of the historian of science Carolyn Merchant exemplifies ecofeminist approaches. Merchant has carefully documented changing attitudes towards the natural world and towards women from the sixteenthth century onwards, illustrating the gradual rejection of a holistic world-view in favour of a dualistic separation of nature and culture. In this evolving system of thought, women were identified with nature, with wilfulness, passion and traditional knowledge ('witchcraft'); whilst culture – involving rationality, science and progress – was the domain of men. Merchant's work abounds with evidence that this separation of nature and culture involved the systematic domination and exploitation of women and nature. An early example, from Francis Bacon's 'The masculine birth of time', is colourful but by no means untypical: 'I am come in very truth leading to you nature with all her children to bind her to your service and make her your slave' (Merchant 1982: 170). Merchant's work examines the development and application of science, the industrialisation process and the rise of capitalism, tracing their impacts upon women and upon the natural world. These include the expropriation by men of the qualities of creativity and productivity – which had formerly been associated with women and nature, and the assignment to both women and nature of a passive role as objects of exploitation. The result has been a suppression of the talents of half the world's population and environmental crisis. She concludes: 'Perhaps the ultimate irony in these transformations was the new name given them: rationality' (Merchant 1992: 170).

Ecofeminism, then, shares with other contemporary radical perspectives a fundamental critique of traditions of thought and notions of progress deriving from the Enlightenment. Two aspects of this critique – feminist approaches to the concept of rationality and the feminist rejection of dualistic modes of thought – will be examined further, and their implications for women's action as 'saviours' explored.

## COMMUNAL RATIONALITY

Many feminists reject the liberal view of individual, instrumental rationality on the grounds that it is a gendered conceptualisation which universalises essentially male, market-oriented behaviour. Women's unpaid work in the provision of basic needs, in households and in the subsistence sector of the Third World does not conform to this model; nor can the concentration of women in low-paid, caring professions be explained by reference to profit maximisation. A feminist reconceptualisation of rationality in order to embrace women's lived experience, would emphasise interdependence and the need for mutually supportive, cooperative behaviour – that is, communal rationality.

This interpretation, in relation to global environmental issues, has considerable implications for the much-rehearsed debate concerning the 'tragedy of the commons'. Hardin's (1968) apocalyptic metaphor of the profit-maximising herdsmen overgrazing and inevitably destroying the medieval commons has been criticised for both its historical inaccuracy and its lack of contemporary relevance (Cox 1985; Reader 1988). Additionally, feminists would point out that Hardin's interpretation of his herdsmen's conduct is based upon a gendered and highly tendentious approach to rationality. Had the communal values of herdswomen prevailed, the global commons would not now be so imperilled.

Vandana Shiva has explored the issue of the commons in the context of India, tracing the process of appropriation and privatisation back to the colonial period. The classification of uncultivated common land as unproductive 'wasteland', irrespective of its value to and use by local communities (and particularly women), ensured its availability land grants to colonists. Subsequently, the 'wasteland' designation facilitated the development of the forest commons for private commercial forestry, a process culminating in the activities of the World Bank-funded Wasteland Development Board, established in 1985. The Board's projects involve the extensive (5,000,000 hectares) privatisation of village commons for commercial development – particularly the cultivation of eucalyptus for the wood and fibre industries. This replaces, in many cases, indigenous, mixed forested or semi-forested areas which have for centuries provided women with sources of food, medicine, fuel and shelter and grazing land (Shiva 1988: 86–9). Shiva maintains that the designation of the commons as wasteland has been, and remains, associated with a failure to recognise its contribution both to ecological balance and to the needs of village communities. Far from women's activities having depleted the commons, their close relationship with and understanding of the natural world ensured both the successful management of the village commons and the maintenance of local ecosystems. In contrast, 'wastelands development' through eucalyptus cultivation has been ecologically disastrous, resulting in soil exhaustion and the depletion of water resources; indeed, it is better named a programme of 'wasteland *creation*', one which has reflected masculine values and individual instrumental rationality rather than feminine values and communal rationality.

## HOLISTIC VS DUALISTIC MODES OF THOUGHT

Equally central to feminist critiques of dominant modes of thought is the rejection, particularly emphasised by ecofeminists, of philosophical dualism. Ecofeminists reject as essentially masculine the dualistic and hierarchical assumptions inherent both in the separation of nature and culture, of human and non-human species, and in the construction of gender stereotypes. Such separation makes possible the creation and objectification of the 'other' which becomes, according to the tenets of patriarchal rationality, worthy of consider- ation only in so far as it can benefit the subject.

Ecofeminists adopt a holistic approach emphasising the essential inter- connection, and equal value, of all life forms. Such an approach, which was exemplified by the work (see Carson 1963) of Rachel Carson (who was not writing from an explicitly feminist perspective) typifies much subsequent ecological thought. Nevertheless, ecofeminists also stress the particular insights that derive from women's experience – shared by the natural world – of exploitation and oppression. This common suffering, deriving from a common source, places upon women a special responsibility to oppose and undermine dualism in all its forms, and to promote in its stead the feminine principle of ecological holism – in the interests both of the natural world and of women. Typical of this approach is Judith Plant's assertion:

> We know that when we resist the rape of the earth, we are fighting the same mentality that allows the rape of women.
>
> (Plant 1989: 49)

Ecofeminists, then, in linking feminist and ecological thought, explicitly place upon women the role of saviour and the burden of safeguarding the planet. Examples abound of women, from many parts of the world, who have appeared willing to shoulder this burden.

## WOMEN'S ACTION IN DEFENCE OF THE ENVIRONMENT

There is no doubt that women have contributed significantly to environmental activism. In addition, women's environmental movements can be shown to have reflected the principles of communal rationality and ecological holism; and to have clearly embraced the notion of women's particular responsibility in relation to the environment.

In the developed world, women have been prominent in instigating campaigns on a wide range of issues, including the dumping of hazardous wastes and the use both of toxic chemicals in agriculture and of chlorine in sanitary products and nappies. All of these issues directly link the health of the environment with human health, drawing particular attention to contradictions between production and reproduction. As the Director of the Medical Research Council Reproductive Biology Unit reminds us, somewhat laconically, these contradictions may be fundamental:

> Much interest centres on the 50 per cent fall in the human sperm count in the developed world. This has little consequence as yet for fertility, but it does focus our attention on the vulnerability of the human foetus to environmental toxicants . . . some of which are found in the modern kitchen.
>
> (Lincoln 1993: 2)

Whether or not such arguments will be used to deny women access to the kitchen (as they have been in relation to the workplace) remains a matter for conjecture. While Professor Lincoln's research may demonstrate that ecofeminist calls for action to sustain life on earth are not untimely, it is in the less developed world that links between environmental and human health are most immediately evident and, as has been demonstrated, impinge most specifically upon the lives of women. It is in the less developed world, also, that some of the most effective women's environmental movements have emerged.

In India, women's activism has been particularly apparent, and is specifically linked to a non-Western, holistic world-view 'in which nature is Prakriti, a living and creative process, the feminine principle from which all life arises' (Shiva 1989: xviii). The best-known example of Indian women's activism is undoubtedly the Chipko Andolan (the hug-the-trees movement) involving the revival, in contemporary form, of an ancient link between women and their sacred trees. Thus, in Uttar Pradesh (UP) in 1973 a group of women physically prevented the felling of three hundred ash trees, a protest mirrored throughout the UP state during the next two years, sometimes in direct opposition to the preferences of male members of the community. Following an official enquiry, the UP government banned tree-felling in the Reni forest area for ten years. The Chipko movement has survived as a grass-roots women's movement, repeating its modest successes and spreading to several other parts of India (Philipose 1989: 67–75).

Indian women are also active in the Manna Rakshana Koota (the movement for saving the soil), a popular resistance movement dedicated to the protection of the village commons from the wasteland development programme. Action here has involved the uprooting of newly planted eucalyptus seedlings and successful demands for their replacement with more appropriate varieties. The regenerated commons in these cases have been managed exclusively by women (Shiva 1989: 94).

A further example of non-violent direct action led by Indian women is the Narmada Bachao Andalan (the save-Narmada movement) which is protesting against the construction of a series of dams on the Narmada River. In addition to wide-scale disruption of sensitive ecosystems, this would cause an inundation of farmland in three states. In August 1993, four hundred activists were arrested to prevent them carrying out a threatened mass drowning in the Narmada River, and the leaders of the movement were driven underground (*The Guardian*, 6 August 1993).

The Green Belt Movement of Kenya provides an example from a different context of successful action by women on behalf of women and the environment. Developed under the auspices of the National Council of Women of Kenya, the movement espouses a self-consciously holistic philosophy which aims to reunite individuals with their cultural roots and with nature, whilst encouraging the movement's own spread beyond Kenya and linking Kenyan experience with wider issues, including the prospect of global environmental change. Based on tree-planting as a focus for active popular participation, with the aim of stimulating broadly based environmental consciousness, the movement has established more than a thousand tree nurseries, tended by approximately 50,000 women, and has issued millions of tree seedlings for planting by small-scale farmers and voluntary organisations (National Council of Women of Kenya, undated).

Relatively large-scale movements in India and Kenya provide important examples of women's role in environmental issues. However, there are, in addition, numerous examples of community groups and indigenous NGOs which work at the local level, both in the developed and developing worlds. Many of these women's environmental groups can claim successes; indeed, UNEP has published a compendium of some 200 success stories (UNEP 1991). Nevertheless, the record is mixed – in Malaysia, for example, women's protests at continuing deforestation have been met with repression – whilst any assessment of the achievements of women activists must acknowledge a failure to reverse the overall trends concerning the non-sustainable exploitation of natural resources in the interest of export-led economic growth.

These broad issues of women/environment/development have been addressed by women's NGOs over the past several years, and analysis has increasingly focused upon the manner in which they are linked. This was reflected in the women's agenda at the 1992 Earth Summit, which included panels on debt and trade, and on militarisation. Indeed, the final Declaration (of 10 June 1992) on behalf of Planeta Femea demonstrated the inclusive nature of the women's analysis through its explicit reference to the environmental implications of the GATT Uruguay Round, and to the problems of militarism and nuclear testing, all of which were excluded from the Earth Summit's official agenda. The Declaration emphasised, also, the necessity of recognising 'the centrality of women's roles, needs, values and wisdom to decision-making on the fate of the Earth and the urgent need to involve women at all levels of policy-making, planning and implementation on an equal basis with men' (Planeta Femea: Declaration, Article 1).

At all levels, then, from local grass-roots action to policy formulation at the global level, women are demonstrating their concern over environmental issues, and are adopting a position which emphasises the centrality of gender analysis to our understanding of these issues. In relation to policy and action, this position consistently reflects the values of communal rationality and a holistic approach, whilst assigning to women a key role as saviours of the environment.

## THE IMPLICATIONS OF STRESSING WOMEN–ENVIRONMENT LINKS

The implications of stressing women–environment links will tend to be reflected in the interests and policy agendas associated with the three broad approaches outlined above.

The 'women as the problem' approach emphasises the significance both of women as consumers and of women in their reproductive roles. Women are specifically targeted as the objects of policy, formulated in the interests of the environment rather than of women. The principal emphasis is upon changing women's behaviour rather than actively involving women in policy-making and policy implementation. This approach is not based upon gender analysis, and in consequence it isolates women from their social context. There is no appreciation of the complexity and variety of factors determining the different roles, responsibilities and activities of women and men in any given society. Without such an appreciation, attempts to influence attitudes and behaviour cannot succeed, particularly in sensitive areas such as reproductive behaviour. As the Third World women's network Development Alternatives with Women for a New Era (DAWN) has stated:

Women know that childbearing is a social not purely personal phenomenon: nor do we deny that world population trends are likely to exert considerable pressure on resources and institutions by the end of the century. But our bodies have become a pawn in the struggles among states, religions, male heads of households, and private corporations. Programs that do not take the interests of women into account are unlikely to succeed.

(DAWN 1985)

In contrast with the 'women as the problem' approach, the 'women as victims' approach focuses upon the needs and interests of women, particularly in the Third World. Emphasising women's disproportionate suffering as victims of environmental change, this approach is associated with policies aiming to provide assistance and support for women. Such policies have typified the responses of NGOs and United Nations agencies. They can be divided into two broad categories: welfare provision and Women in Development (WID).

A welfare orientation, involving a prioritisation of the immediate practical needs of women and their families, has been the traditional approach, and remains a common feature of agency programmes. This approach is associated with a narrow conception of women's reproductive and domestic responsibilities which again reflects an inadequate gender analysis. Hence, there has been a failure to recognise the extensive agricultural and commercial roles fulfilled by women in many societies, or to examine the structures of political and economic power which determine land-ownership patterns. In consequence, the negative effects of environmental degradation upon women's social status and economic independence have been overlooked; indeed the situation has been exacerbated by the creation of welfare dependence. Women have, once again, been marginalised; identified as objects of policy rather than agents of change.

The deficiencies of the welfare approach were highlighted during the UN Decade for Women, when the WID approach became widely accepted in principle and, to a somewhat more limited extent, applied in practice. This approach has extended to environmental policy, and involves a conscious effort to include women in environmental programmes, with varying results.

Patricia Thomas, in her consultancy report on the IUCN's (International Union for the Conservation of Nature and Natural Resources) Women and Natural Resources Management Programme, provided a broad assessment of the WID approach. She found that, whilst women had become more visible in programme planning, they were rarely targeted for mainstream activities with large budgets. Typically, 'women's components' were peripheral to the major projects, which allocated subordinate (and frequently unpaid) roles to women. As a consequence, women's already substantial workloads were further increased, with a concomitant reduction in their ability to participate in income-generating activities. In addition, there was a failure to recognise women's important traditional role as environmental managers in the subsistence sector, which again indicates the inadequacy of the gender analysis involved in the project designs. Thus, whilst women were included in environmental programmes, the opportunity was lost to utilise their special knowledge and expertise and, as a result, to begin to address their status and independence needs (Thomas, September 1991–June 1992).

Once again, despite the explicit aim of the WID approach, women have largely remained objects rather than initiators of policy, an outcome likely to prove disadvantageous both to women and to the environment. A response from Third World women has, again, been articulated by the DAWN network:

> Our capacity to sustain our livelihoods and care for our families, our link with our communities and the earth is being destroyed. Our knowledge of the earth and its care is being undermined and we are now told that we have to be taught about the environment.

(Wiltshire 1992: 4)

The gender blindness of these approaches is not shared by perspectives which emphasise women's potential as saviours of the environment. Here, in contrast, analysis of gender provides the basis both of theorisation and of action. Far from marginalising women as passive objects of environmental policy, ecofeminist approaches accord to women and to feminine principles a central role in safe-guarding the environment. Essentially, this involves action to promote funda-mental changes in the way stereotypical gender characteristics are perceived and evaluated; with the aim of promoting life-enhancing, feminine values of nurtur-ance and community, and a feminine, holistic world-view. Ecofeminism, in linking feminist and ecological thought, identifies women as agents of change but prioritises the natural world in terms of policy and action. Thus, whilst the interests of women and of the environment are regarded as complementary, ecological concerns may vie for attention with, and indeed take precedence over, the interests of women. In consequence, despite its apparently positive ecological implications, this approach has provoked rather unhelpful divisions between ecofeminists, on the one hand, and on the other, feminists, whose concern for the environment comes secondary to their commitment to furthering the interests of women. These divisions focus around two broad areas: eco- feminists' alleged failure adequately to prioritise the interests of women, and the potential conse-quences for women of assuming a central role as saviours of the environment.

The first division between feminists, then, arises as a consequence of equating women and the natural world. Thus, for example, ecofeminists apply to dis-cussion of environmental pollution/degradation the language and imagery of male violence against women. The frequent references to the 'rape' of nature are, however, seen by many feminists as deeply insulting to women victims of male sexual violence. As Patricia Hynes has argued, 'ecofeminism is braver, more explicit, angrier, and more effective about the threat of nuclear winter than the fact of an epidemic in male violence against women' (Hynes 1990: 170).

The rejection of 'speciesism' by ecofeminists has also angered Third World women, who have seen their children's hunger less highly prioritised than the needs of unnamed endangered species (Wiltshire 1992). A particularly divisive issue has been the relationship between population and the environment, which was the subject of controversy at Planeta Femea during the 1992 Earth Summit. Here, ecofeminists' concern for the survival of non-human species has led them to be identified with the population lobby, and hence distanced from feminists who support the principle of women's right to reproductive self-determination.

The second broad issue dividing feminists again concerns the implications for women of ecofeminist perspectives. Whilst stressing the need to reassert and revalorise feminine principles, ecofeminists tend to emphasise the differences between female and male gender characteristics and roles. The consequences of this are twofold, and are epitomised by the slogan 'Women Nurture the World': traditional gender stereotypes are reinforced, whilst women appear to stand alone in the fight to save the planet. Having suffered jointly with the natural world at the hands of men, women are deemed to have privileged insights into ecological imperatives, and are accorded a special, potentially onerous, responsibility for pursuing them.

This interpretation of women's environmental role appears to have much support – for example, in the words of Mostafa Tolba at the start of this discussion. Women, too, have accepted with apparent enthusiasm the responsibility for saving the planet:

> We have the capacity to give life and light. We can take our brooms and sweep the earth . . . . We can seal up the hole in the ozone layer. The environment is life and women must struggle for life with our feet on the ground and our eyes toward the heavens. We must do the impossible.
>
> (Merchant 1992: 205)

This statement by Chilean activist Isabelle Letelier reflects the ecofeminist view of women as life force. It does not address the problem of how women, who are everywhere amongst the poorest and least powerful members of society, are to combat the structures of political and economic power and the associated ideologies which continue to legitimise their oppression and exploitation – as well as the degradation and pollution of the environment. In the absence of a solution to this problem, women's struggles to safeguard the planet will remain confined to clearing up men's messes.

## CONCLUSION

That there are significant links between women and the environment is evident from all three approaches discussed above. Women's traditional domestic roles encompass both consumption and reproduction, behaviours which can be shown to have negative environmental impacts. At the same time, women in all parts of the world suffer disproportionately from environmental degradation. Finally, women and the natural world do suffer under a common mode of domination and exploitation developed from and legitimated by masculine systems of thought.

The *implications* of these links are also significant, both for women and for environmental policy. Women will be considerably disadvantaged if they assume environmental responsibilities in circumstances of disempowerment. At the same time, environmental policy cannot succeed unless the interconnections between women and the environment are understood and acknowledged, and the active support of women secured. Attempts to change women's consumption habits, to alter their reproductive behaviour or to preserve and utilise their traditional knowledge and skills in environmental management will fail if these behaviours are addressed in isolation from the social context in which they occur.

It is evident, then, that social gender analysis must precede the formulation of environmental policy. This would involve a consideration of the different but interdependent and overlapping roles and responsibilities of women and men; of their different life experiences, knowledge and skills; and of the power and status differences which separate them. An understanding of these factors facilitates the identification of supports for, and impediments to, policy implementation – in particular the processes by which women's contributions and expertise have been marginalised or obscured. These processes operate at all levels and are not confined to state or corporate decision-making. Indeed they have been encountered by women with a WID brief working with development NGOs (Ashworth 1988), and amongst the larger, well-funded environment groups, or 'eco-establishment', which increasingly set the environmental agenda (Seager 1993).

Women's NGOs and women activists within international agencies have recognised both the need for gender analysis in environmental policy formulation and the links between gender and the political marginalisation of women. Indeed, the inclusion of these issues in Agenda 21 of the Rio Earth Summit is the outcome of extensive and sustained networking and lobbying by women. The women's NGO networks now face the major challenge of monitoring compliance by UN agencies with the provisions of Agenda 21, in an attempt to ensure that the rhetorical statements of Chapter 24 are translated into policy. Similarly, the plan of action emanating from the 1994 Conference on Population and Development provides only the starting point of a broadly based strategy for the inclusion and empowerment of women, in the interests of women and the environment (see Note 3).

At the UN level, the appointment in 1992 of Elizabeth Dowdeswell to succeed Mostafa Tolba as Executive Director of UNEP represents a welcome departure from the male domination of senior UN positions, but it is unlikely to present a major challenge to the patriarchal culture of the organisation. Meanwhile, UNEP and Unifem are jointly convening an 'International Consultation to Promote Cooperation, Coordination and Strategic Planning' to support the implementation of Chapter 24, and, together with the NGOs, are utilising the preparatory stages of the 1995 Fourth World Conference on Women to maintain the impetus of activism on gender–environment links (Martin-Brown, undated).

Clearly, then, women's activism on environmental issues will continue, as will women's disproportionate suffering as victims of environmental change. Because of their distinct life experiences, women do bring a different perspective to the environmental debate, and the interests of the environment and of women will be served if their voices are heard. A stress upon women's special insights into environmental problems should not, however, lead to any assumption of a particular responsibility for addressing them. This is both unfair and unrealistic in a situation where women are everywhere underrepresented in decision-making processes. Ecofeminists are not alone in rejecting the instrumental rationality of 'economic man', nor in embracing a holistic world-view; it is not in the interest of women to assume singular or disproportionate responsibility for safeguarding the planet. But it is in the interest of us all to challenge those gendered assumptions which underlie social attitudes and behaviour, which legitimise structures of economic and political power, and which persuade us that the natural world is a resource to be exploited rather than a living system of which we are a part.

## NOTES

1 Since 1985, gender issues have received at least formal recognition on the agenda of global environmental politics, and have been widely reflected in international fora. Examples include:

- The appointment by the United Nations Environment Programme (UNEP) of a Senior Women's Advisory Group on Sustainable Development in 1985.
- The promotion by Unifem (United Nations Development Fund for Women) of the Women, Environment and Development Programme, which includes a series of women's 'Summits'.
- An emphasis on women–environment links by a wide range of Non-Governmental Organisations (NGOs); for example: the International Planned Parenthood Federation (IPPF); the International Union for the Conservation of Nature and Natural Resources (IUCN); the Asian and Pacific Development Centre.
- The establishment of a range of 'dedicated' NGOs – for example, the Women and Environment Education and Development (WEED) Foundation and the Women's Environmental Network (WEN)). Also, the Organisation for Economic Cooperation and Development (OECD) Conference on Women and the Environment, Paris, 1989.
- The Global Assembly of Women and the Environment, held in November 1991 and coordinated by UNEP's Senior Women's Advisory Committee. The shared information concerning women's roles in environmental management and sustainable development formed part of women's input to the 1992 Earth Summit.
- The formation of the Women's International Policy Action Committee (IPAC) to coordinate women's participation both in the UNCED preparatory process and at the Earth Summit itself, and whose actions included the organisation of Planeta Femea, the women's forum attended daily by more than 1,200 women throughout the period of the Summit.
- The comprehensive inclusion of women/environment/sustainable-development links on the agenda of the UN International Conference on Population and Development in September 1994. See also Note 3 below.

2 The development of amniocentesis, a procedure intended to assist in the early detection of certain foetal abnormalities, has also provided the ability to ascertain the sex of the foetus. In countries where male children are particularly highly valued, such as India and China, the availability of amniocentesis has led to the large-scale abortions of female foetuses solely on the grounds of their sex. This *foeticide*, in consequence, might also be referred to as *femicide*.

3 This determined 'religious filibuster' succeeded in removing a number of important provisions from the Programme, including those on 'sexual rights', on an 'alternative to early marriage' and on equal inheritance rights for women. Nevertheless, the

replacement of 'family planning' by the concept of 'reproductive health' (defined as 'complete physical, mental and social well-being . . . in all matters relating to the reproductive system and to its functions and processes') was maintained. Included, also, were a number of general statements linking improvements in women's political, social and economic status with strategies for sustainable development (Hooper 1994). For a discussion of the issues raised during the pre-conference process, see UNEP's (1994) *Our Planet*: passim.

## BIBLIOGRAPHY

Ashworth, G. (1988) 'An elf among the gnomes: a feminist in North–South relations', *Millennium: Journal of International Studies* 17(3): 497–505.

Asian and Pacific Development Centre (1992) 'Women, environment, development', *Issues in Gender and Development* 4 (September) .

Berry, R.J. (ed.) (1993) *Environmental Dilemmas, Ethics and Decisions*, London: Chapman & Hall.

Biehl, J. (1988) 'Ecofeminism and deep ecology: unresolvable conflict?', *Our Generation* 19(2): 19–32.

Caldecott, L. and Leland, S. (eds) (1983) *Reclaim the Earth: Women Speak out for Life on Earth*, London: The Women's Press.

Carson, R. (1963) *Silent Spring*, London: Hamish Hamilton.

Charlton, S.E. (1984) *Women in Third World Development*, Boulder, Col.: Westview.

Collard, A. with Contrucci, J. (1988) *Rape of the Wild*, London: The Women's Press.

Conroy Jackson, P. (1990) *The Impact of the Completion of the Internal Market on Women in the European Community*, Brussels: Commission of the European Communities.

Cox, S.J.B. (1985) 'No tragedy on the commons', *Environmental Ethics* 7: 49–61.

Dankelman, I. and Davison, J. (1988) *Women and Environment in the Third World*, London: Earthscan.

—— (1991) 'Land: women at the centre of the food crisis', in Sontheimer, S. (ed.) *Women and the Environment: Crisis and Development in the Third World*, London: Earthscan, pp. 3–31.

Davison, J. (1989) 'Restoring women's link with nature', *Earthwatch* 37: 2–4.

Development Alternatives with Women for a New Era (DAWN) (1985) *Development, Crisis and Alternative Visions: Third World Women's Perspectives*, Delhi: DAWN.

Eckersley, R. (1992) *Environmentalism and Political Theory: Toward an Ecocentric Approach*, London: UCL Press.

Ehrlich, P. and Ehrlich, A. (1990) *The Population Explosion*, New York: Simon & Schuster.

French, M. (1985) *Beyond Power: on Women, Men and Morals*, London: Sphere Books.

Grant, R. and Newland, K. (eds) (1991) *Gender and International Relations*, Buckingham: Open University Press.

*The Guardian* '400 Indian dam protesters held', 6 August 1993.

Hardin, G. (1968) 'The tragedy of the commons', *Science* 162: 1243–8.

Hooper, J. (1994) 'Big issues slip past religious filibusters', *The Guardian*, 14 September.

Hynes, P.H. (1989) *The Recurring Silent Spring*, New York: Pergamon.

—— (1990) 'Pornography and pollution', *Women's Studies International Forum* 13(3): 169–76.

—— (1991) 'The race to save the planet: will women lose?', *Women's Studies International Forum* 14(5): 473–8.

International Bank for Reconstruction and Development (1992) *World Development Report 1992: Development and the Environment*, New York: O.U.P.

IPPF, UNFPA, IUCN 'Special report: educating girls', *People and Planet* 2(1).

International Union for the Conservation of Nature and Natural Resources (1991) *Workshop Report: Population and Resources*, 18th Session of the General Assembly, Social Sciences Division, Gland: IUCN.

International Women's Tribune Centre (1993) 'Women, environment and development part II', *The Tribune* (Newsletter) 49 (February): IWTC.

Lincoln, D. (1993) 'Reproductive health: a key to sustainable development', *The Globe* (15) (October): 2–4.

McFadden, M. (1984) 'Anatomy of difference: towards a classification of feminist theory', *Women's Studies International Forum* 7(6): 495–504.

Martin-Brown, J. (undated) *UNEP and the Role of Women: the Way Ahead*, Washington, DC: UNEP.

Merchant, C. (1982) *The Death of Nature: Women, Ecology and the Scientific Revolution*, London: Wildwood House.

—— (1992) *Radical Ecology: the Search for a Liveable World*, London: Routledge.

Mies, M. (1986) *Patriarchy and Accumulation on a Global Scale*, London: Zed Books.

—— and Shiva, V. (1993) *Ecofeminism*, London: Zed Books.

Monimart, M. (1991) 'Women in the fight against desertification', in Sontheimer, S. (ed.) *Women in Third World Development*, Boulder, Col.: Westview, pp. 32–64.

Moser, C.O.N. (1991) 'Gender planning in the Third World: meeting practical and strategic needs', in Grant, R. and Newland, K. (eds) (1991) *Gender and International Relations*, Buckingham: Open University Press, pp. 83–121.

National Council of Women of Kenya (undated) *The Green Belt Movement*, Nairobi: NCWK.

Philipose, P. (1989) 'Women act: women and environmental protection in India', in Plant, J. (ed.) *Healing the Wounds*, Philadelphia: New Society, pp. 67–75.

Plant, J. (ed.) (1989) *Healing the Wounds*, Philadelphia: New Society.

Rao, S. (1991) 'Focusing on women', *People* 18(2): 7–8.

Reader, J. (1988) 'Human ecology: how land shapes society', *New Scientist*, 8 September: 51–6.

Seager, J. (1993) *Earth Follies: Feminism, Politics and the Environment*, London: Earthscan.

Severinghaus, J. (1990) *Is Reproductive Health a Sustainable Rural Development Strategy?*, Oklahoma City: World Neighbours.

Sharma, K. (1994) 'Population panic damages women', *Our Planet* 6(3): 22–3.

Shiva, V. (1988) *Staying Alive: Women, Ecology and Development*, London: World Books.

Sidel, R. (1987) *Women and Children Last*, Middlesex: Harmondsworth.

Sontheimer, S. (ed.) (1991) *Women and the Environment: Crisis and Development in the Third World*, London: Earthscan.

Steady, F.C. (undated) 'Agenda 21: an easy reference to the specific recommendations on women', in *Women, Environment, Development*, New York: Unifem, pp. 4–5.

Thomas, P.F. (September 1991–June 1992) *Consultancy on the Reorientation of IUCN Women and Natural Resources Management Programme: Compilation of Major Reports*, Gland: Social Sciences Division, IUCN.

Tickner, J.A. (1991) 'On the fringes of the world economy: a feminist perspective', in Murphy, C.N. and Tooze, R. (eds) *The New International Political Economy*, Boulder, Col.: Lynne Reiner, pp. 191–206.

Turner, R.K. and Powell, J.C. (1993) 'Economics – the challenge of integrated pollution control', in Berry, R.J. (ed.) *Environmental Dilemmas, Ethics and Decisions*, London: Chapman and Hall: 172–203.

United Nations Development Fund for Women (Unifem) (undated) *Agenda 21: An Easy Reference to the Specific Recommendations on Women*, New York: Unifem.

—— (undated) *Strengthening Partnerships: Action for Agenda 21*, New York: Unifem.

United Nations Environment Programme (UNEP) (1991) *Success Stories of Women and the Environment*, Washington, DC: UNEP.

—— (1994) 'Population and environment', *Our Planet* 6(3).

Wiltshire, R. (1992) *Environment and Development: Grass Roots Women's Perspectives*, Kingston: DAWN.

Womankind Worldwide 'We and the land are one: women and the environment', *Women's Lives* 6.

Women and Environments Education and Development (WEED) Foundation (1993) *Building Women's Networks for Sustainability*, July, Toronto: WEED Foundation.

World Neighbours (1993) 'Women's literacy: freeing voices', *Neighbours*, Spring.

—— (1993) 'Making motherhood safe', *Neighbours*, Winter.

# 7 Who cares about the environment?

*Peter Willetts*

A study of the politics of global environmental change invites us to revisit and rethink the three 'Great Debates' of international relations. In the 1940s, the debate between Idealism and Realism forced us to ask whether we should plan for a better world of international peace and cooperation or reluctantly accept that conflict was inevitable. In the 1960s the choice was between attempting to study the social sciences by using the epistemology and methodology of the natural sciences or remaining rooted in the disciplines of history, law and philosophy. In the 1970s and 1980s we faced a wide-ranging debate between Realism and globalism (or pluralism) about the nature of the international system. In global environmental politics, we immediately confront the following questions that comprise the three main debates: what is our idea of a better world, and can we hope to achieve progress through international cooperation? What is the politics of science, and what is the science of politics? And do states and inter-state relations determine outcomes, or do companies and pressure groups have an independent influence? In each of these debates, the current concern for distinct environmental values contributes to the argument that the analysis of differing contentions over values should be central to our study of global politics.

## IDEALISM, INTERESTS AND VALUES

Many people care passionately about the environment, and few people would deny that they have some concern. A multitude of pressure groups, or Non-Governmental Organisations (NGOs) as they are referred to in UN diplomacy, have sprouted throughout the world both to articulate ordinary people's desires and to challenge current policies and practices. The failures of the natural scientists, the technologists and the economists have to be overcome by a new discourse that gives priority to environmental values. Surely it is self-evident that a new spirit of idealism is putting values on the agenda again? This argument is false. Values have never been absent from politics; indeed, the most useful and all-encompassing approach is to define politics, as Easton does, in terms of the authoritative allocation of values (Easton 1965: 50).

For the classic realist, Morgenthau, value questions were superficial in relation to the analysis of politics. States pursue their interests, and these are defined in terms of power (Morgenthau 1960: especially 4–11 and 233–71). A few academic writers continued during the Cold War to maintain the idealist position of earlier years (Clark and Sohn 1966; Falk 1971). Their approach is now being echoed in the current calls to democratise the United Nations, by forming a directly elected assembly, to make the UN more responsive to ordinary people's environmental concerns (Falk, Kim and Mendlovitz 1991; Heinrich 1992; Childers 1994). In a less radical form, the environmental idealists want UN diplomacy to be more open to NGO participation (UN, Agenda 21, paras 23.1, 23.2 and 38.43).

A recent textbook on environmental politics could almost be quoting Morgenthau in saying that one of its themes was 'the nature and significance for international environmental protection of the conflicts between states over power, over the distribution of the costs of environmental management, and over questions bearing upon state sovereignty and freedom of action' (Hurrell and Kingsbury 1992: 11). The main change that contemporary state-centric power theorists have made to traditional realism is to broaden the concept of 'national interest', from a central focus on military security, to cover economic interests as well. However, the same assumptions are made that rational state actors are pursuing objective interests, and the same problem of promoting inter-state cooperation in an anarchic world is addressed (ibid.: 5).

Both sides to this debate misunderstand the nature of their own arguments: there is no dichotomy between 'interests' and 'values'. Although there is no well-developed theory of values, 'some of those which have been identified and sought through time and across space are wealth, physical security, order, freedom/ autonomy, peace, status, health, equality, justice, knowledge, beauty, honesty and love' (Mansbach and Vasquez 1981: 58). Assertions that an objective 'national interest' in the pursuit of power cannot be affected by subjective values are in reality assertions that the value of security should be given higher priority than other values such as equality and beauty. If interests are defined in economic terms, then the pursuit of these interests is the result of deciding to give priority to the material value of wealth. Alternatively, the defence of sovereignty involves making autonomy and status the highest values. Interests are not objective. They are simply a particular subset of values that are often maximised by the control of concrete stakes such as territory and physical resources.

It is true that the pursuit of security and wealth regularly conflicts with the realisation of environmental values. (The discussion of what is meant by 'environmental values' is left until the next section.) It would be naive idealism to say that environmental values should always override interests, because that would imply that security, wealth, autonomy and status should never have any consideration. Equally, most political actors would say that it is only in the most severe life-threatening situations, such as war or famine, that environmental values can be ignored. Given the complexity of human nature and of human value systems, the pursuit of interests has to be analysed in the context of other values that are relevant to the political actors in a particular situation. There can be no rational pursuit of an objective national interest. The selection of what values are to be pursued is a matter of subjective choice, not of rational choice, and different sectors of society usually differ on which values should be given priority. It would be possible to define the 'national interest' as covering all values that a government endorses, including environmental values. However, the statement that governments pursue the national interest would then become a tautology.

It is clear that many environmental questions, such as those about the ozone layer, climate change, resource depletion, marine pollution and species conservation, are seen as global questions. In as much as common interests are asserted, it is not 'the national interest' but the importance of the 'global commons', or 'the common heritage of mankind', that is invoked. Such a value then generates the presumption that the proper locus of authority lies at the global level and not the country level. There is such a range of international regimes covering global environmental questions that it would be nonsense to start research with an unchallengeable axiom that all authority lies with governments pursuing security and wealth. Such an assumption would prevent an investigation of the nature of these regimes. It would rule out the possibility that new phenomena are arising in global politics. Two of the most important questions raised by environmental politics are: when do environmental values assume higher priority than security or wealth? And under what conditions is authority transferred to the global level?

## VALUES, SCIENCE AND POLITICS

The behavioural revolution encompassed several distinct challenges to traditional epistemology. The most important was a move away from detailed, supposedly atheoretical, historical studies. Instead, there was an explicit attempt to formulate general theory. Overall, this goal is not controversial in the discipline. Authors as diverse as Hedley Bull and John Burton have been identified as being highly hostile to behaviouralism (Bull 1966; Burton *et al.* 1974), but nevertheless they themselves have produced general theory (Bull 1977; Burton 1965, etc.). The second challenge offered by behaviouralism was for theory to become more formal, with concepts being defined precisely and the relationships between them being specified in a manner that could be subject to verification or falsification. On the model of the natural sciences, this was seen as requiring sophisticated quantitative measures and complex statistical techniques, though in fact neither is essential for hypothesis-testing.

The strongest reaction against behaviouralism was, and still is, against its positivist epistemology. If we can only study objective reality, how can we study political processes that are perceived in a subjective manner by different people who make different evaluations of these processes? If the core of politics is contention over values, how can we be objective about the study of them? Those who ask such questions tend to conclude that there can be no value-free study of politics in the same way as there is a value-free study of physics. As Humphreys has pointed out in this volume, the anti-positivist position takes an even more radical form in contemporary ecologism. It is argued that environmental values cannot be measured and cannot be compared with economic values. Scientific claims to universal knowledge are a form of ideological imperialism, while knowledge and understanding are only derived from the local community's experience of its own environment. This epistemology seems to base knowledge on a mystical communion with nature. (For the broader debate about ecology and epistemology, see both Atkinson 1991 and Sachs 1992.)

In the chapter on climate change in this volume, Paterson follows Cox and engages in a rather different attack. He argues that positivism is associated with the analysis of stability and hence privileges the values that uphold the status quo. Both links in this argument are merely asserted by Paterson, but neither point is self-evident. There is no reason to deny the possibility of a positivist analysis of dynamic change, nor does the attempt to understand stability preclude the desire to promote destabilising political change.

The various anti-positivist positions are based on a misinterpretation of the fact–value distinction. Clearly it is correct that political scientists must study values. However, the empirical data on the values of political actors is not subjective: it is part of the objective reality of politics. (This is adopting the ontological realist position, but this phrase will not be used, to avoid confusion with analytical realism in the study of international relations.) The values of the analyst and the values of those who sustain the analyst will enter our study of environmental politics, as with any study of politics, when the decision is made to allocate time, money and effort to that study. The values of the analyst and of other political actors will also determine the use of the results. Research that concludes with a challenge to the conventional wisdom on how we perceive the world can have a significant political impact. How large are the reserves of a non-renewable resource? Is a renewable alternative available? Is a species endangered? Does the electorate endorse an environmental policy? Do the tax-payers accept the costs of a policy? These questions *in principle* have objective answers, but the answers can have consequences that lead to a re-evaluation of social and political relationships.

The arguments are easy to appreciate in the natural sciences. The nuclear physicists who developed the first atomic bomb were part of a massive political enterprise: the defeat of German and Japanese fascism. The political consequences were profound, and the existence of nuclear weapons was one of the defining features of the Cold War. Many people have taken the position that the design, the production and the maintenance of such horrific weapons were totally unjustifiable. Einstein himself regretted that his pioneering work had made the existence of these weapons possible. Nevertheless, whatever position one takes on the politics, and the morality, of the origins and consequences of these weapons, it is sensible to take it as an unquestionable objective reality that the weapons do cause a massive explosion.

Neither the motives for undertaking research on global environmental politics nor the consequences of that research can be separated from the political process itself. Nevertheless, the identification both of what values people use to take positions on environmental questions and of how they mobilise support for those values can be studied by a value-free methodology. The resulting knowledge can be expressed in a manner that has the same meaning for anybody who reads it, whatever their own values. The question is not whether scientists can avoid the study of values, nor whether they can become value-free individuals, nor whether the research has a political impact. Instead, we must ask whether it is a feasible goal for a social science to achieve a value-free study of values, as a collective enterprise. The positivist claim is solely that the validity of knowledge is assessed in terms of the researcher's methods, not the researcher's values.

By the mid-1970s the debate on behaviouralism had come to an end in a stalemate, with only a minority maintaining the positivist position (see particularly Nicholson 1983 and 1989). The publication of the second edition of Kuhn's *The Structure of Scientific Revolutions* was taken as a refutation of Popper's *The Logic of Scientific Discovery*. In fact, the two approaches were not contradictory, and were reconciled by Lakatos. He argued that theories can accommodate a limited range of empirical anomalies. The choice of which of two or more competing research programmes survives is determined by 'sophisticated methodological falsification'. The crucial question is whether the accommodation of anomalies expands the explanatory power of the theory or causes it to degenerate to a lower level of utility (Lakatos 1970).

A decade later, the debate resumed under different labels: postmodernism and critical theory. (For a discussion of the literature, see Brown 1994, and for a selection of readings, see Hoffman and Rengger 1995.) Brown distinguishes the two approaches by arguing that postmodernists have abandoned the 'Enlightenment Project' with its search for explanation and theory through rationality and science, while critical theorists only wish to integrate normative and explanatory theory. Hoffman and Rengger make the same distinction, but as two approaches within critical theory. Their wording will be used below. Unlike the debate in the 1960s, little attention is given to quantification and methodology. However, positivism is again an explicit target, but with more emphasis now on denying its ontology than on denying its epistemology.

The major insight of all critical theorists is that we cannot be assured of any direct knowledge of empirical reality. Such theorists restate the philosophers' old 'argument from illusion': all we can perceive is the information from our senses. In its most radical form, this argument becomes a denial of any reality outside the observer: therefore all knowledge is subjective (Flood 1990). The statement that we only have sensory perceptions is an obvious truism. The deduction that we cannot know that there is any reality might be logically valid, but it is pushing logic to the point of absurdity.

In the less radical versions of critical theory, the communication of knowledge from one observer to another is seen as being problematic, because this is done via language and language is socially constructed. This too is an obvious truism, but one of profound importance that an empiricist should never forget. For this reason, scientific theorists, aspiring to achieve intersubjective communicability, must be formal in their approach, with a rigid adherence to verbal and operational definitions of concepts. The social sciences have difficulty in separating their statements from many of the subjective cultural assumptions contained in the language in which social science is expressed. Nevertheless, the difficulties involved in using language should not lead to the conclusion that value-free theory cannot be attempted. A deconstruction of orthodox theory by critical theorists can help us to expose an inadequate social science, but it does not substantiate their axiom that positivism is impossible.

Indeed, the challenge posed by critical theorists gives us an empirical basis for recognising fundamental political change. Something significant is happening in a political system when the language of political debate changes. This can be seen in global environmental politics. The United Nations Charter was written in 1945, and it contains no mention of the environment nor any form of words covering the subject. When the first consideration of environmental issues arose in the postwar years, it was done as 'conservation of nature' under the heading of 'science' in either the UN or UNESCO. In December 1972 the UN established the United Nations Environment Programme (UNEP), and in February 1993 it established the Commission on Sustainable Development. No doubt, the vocabulary of the news media and of academic journals would also show the same change from non-consideration to conservation, to environment, to sustainable development. These shifts in the language of environmental politics do embody a widespread cultural shift in the perception of the problems faced by humankind. Both the physical conditions that we perceive and the changing perceptions have been an empirical reality.

## REALISM, GLOBALISM AND VALUES

The argument so far leads to the conclusion that we need an empirical theory of values. From that simple conclusion many difficult questions follow. What are the major values that humans pursue? How may they be classified? How do values become salient to different types of actors? How do value-preference schedules become or established? And what are the dynamics of changes in the values of individuals and groups? These questions cannot be answered within the confines of this short essay, but it is clear that we will not understand environmental politics until we do address such questions. To do this effectively, it becomes necessary to take a position in the third 'Great Debate' in favour of a pluralist global political approach and against a realist approach (Willetts 1990).

As a starting point, we can assume that concerns for beauty, human health, the conservation of biodiversity and the avoidance of suffering among animals are basic, abstract values that are frequently invoked and contested in environmental politics. They are not the only values in environmental politics, however, as the pursuit of wealth is also often involved. Nonetheless, there *are* several important features to these first four values. First, with the exception of health, they are relatively new to politics at the global (as opposed to the country) level. Second, they are particularly central to environmental issues: it is difficult to imagine any issue being considered environmental without one or more of these values being invoked; and those who give high priority to one of these values will tend to give high priority to the others, and also to be opposed to those political actors who give the highest priority to materialism. And third, realists do not address the politics of these values. For them, the 'high politics' of security and diplomacy is assumed to dominate the 'low politics' of environmental issues.

A deconstruction of realism shows that it is based on a view of human nature that takes aggression, conflict and 'masculine' values for granted (Elshtain 1985). It takes as axiomatic that 'states' are coherent actors, but that world politics is incoherent. Both these axioms help to maintain the status quo by maintaining the authority of governments. By the distinction between high politics and low politics, the concerns of governmental actors are given priority over the concerns of non-governmental actors. Clearly, a range of conservative values is embedded in realism. Rather than jumping to the conclusion that the only alternative is to adopt a theory that sustains liberal or socialist values, it is possible to reject realism on empirical grounds and to construct a better representation of reality.

The concept of 'states' is useful for the purposes of international law, but political science cannot progress by a reification of this abstract concept. Two different meanings are given to 'the state' – namely, the country as a supposedly unified 'nation state', and the government in its broadest sense as a holistic entity – but neither concept is useful. The idea that political systems of individual countries are sufficiently coherent to be considered as unitary actors is empirically false in anything but the most extreme circumstances. Countries must be disaggregated into governments and civil societies. The concrete empirical referents for the world of diplomacy are governments and not states. This shift in terminology provides for open systems rather than closed systems, and helps to analyse change rather than emphasising continuity. On the other hand, international organisations are empirical realities that act as a focus for decision-making and do give some coherence to global systems. There is an ontological inconsistency, therefore, in taking it as axiomatic that states are holistic entities while inter-state relations are anarchic. There is ontological *consistency*, on the other hand, in regarding governments, companies, NGOs, countries, international organisations and global politics as all being constituted as open systems that are interconnected and analysable at different levels of resolution.

Instead of simplifying human nature, one can draw on the disciplines of psychology and sociology to demonstrate that human nature is complex. As has already been argued, humans seek much more than just security and wealth. The various arguments about values are so central to politics that the alternative paradigm that is now offered in certain areas of contemporary literature could reasonably be called a values paradigm. The realist paradigm is of states pursuing security and economic interests, and the heirs of Marxism entertain a structuralist paradigm of capitalist interests being pursued within a global system. Both of these can be subsumed and refined within a paradigm of diverse political actors pursuing any value that is salient to them. Other writers have focused on the different elements of such an approach under a variety of headings: a world politics paradigm (Keohane and Nye 1972), a pluralist perspective (Smith, Little and Shackleton 1981), an issue paradigm (Mansbach and Vasquez 1981), a global politics paradigm (Willetts 1982, 1990) and an interdependence and transnationalism perspective (Little and Smith 1991). The Eastonian definition of politics, as the authoritative allocation of values, was only intended to cover politics within countries. To adopt a value-based paradigm for international relations is thus to automatically deny the axiom that domestic politics and international relations are fundamentally different. Using the label Global Politics (in capitals as the proper name of what Lakatos would call a research programme) helps to remind us that this analytical barrier is being broken down. It also seems appropriate for analysing what is commonly called global environmental politics.

As with so many aspects of the Global Politics paradigm, Rosenau was the pioneer, years ahead of other academics, in considering values and issues. He suggested that political behaviour would vary from one 'issue area' to another. This term was purely an abstract, analytical concept used to divide issues into four categories, according to whether the actors used tangible or intangible means to mobilise support, and according to whether they sought to allocate tangible or intangible values (Rosenau 1966). Unfortunately, Rosenau's scheme does not work because actors do not restrict themselves to one or another method of mobilising support, nor do they concentrate their behaviour on a single type of value.

Mansbach and Vasquez were the first authors to make the pursuit of values the basis of a Global Politics 'issue paradigm'. Actors were seen as trying to gain control over stakes in order to realise their values. Stakes may be concrete, as with territory or economic resources, or they may be abstract, as with diplomatic recognition or support for political statements. Day-to-day politics is concerned with the multitude of decisions taken on the allocation of specific stakes. In this paradigm, an 'issue' is a central simplifying concept: 'an issue consists of contention among actors over proposals for the disposition of stakes among them' (Mansbach and Vasquez 1981: 59). Other authors before and since, including Rosenau, have tended to take the concept of an issue for granted, but generally one may assume that they would accept the definition offered by Mansbach and Vasquez. It is now commonplace to use the term 'issue area' to cover a cluster of related issues. It should be emphasised that this is totally different from Rosenau's categorisation of issues. The current usage is firmly rooted in political behaviour: 'When the governments active on a set of issues see them as closely interdependent and deal with them collectively, we call that set of issues an issue area' (Keohane and Nye 1977: 65).

All these authors have made major contributions to an issue-based paradigm. It should be noted that they have in common the idea of aggregating the details of day-to-day politics. Stakes aggregate into issues, and issues aggregate into issue areas. And one might add that issue areas aggregate into the totality of global politics. However, the various authors have caused confusion by failing to analyse actors' perceptions of issues separately from the analysis of actors' *interactions* on issues. This distinction is recognised by Rosenau in his use of types of values and types of actions as the basis of his four categories. It is also recognised by Mansbach and Vasquez (1981: 60) when they argue that perceptions of stakes and competition between actors provide alternative bases for constituting an issue. In the case of Keohane and Nye, they have simply interpreted different actors' perceptions of issues as being interdependent, such actors dealing with issues collectively. It is necessary to follow Rosenau in recognising perceptions and behaviour as two different dimensions that apply simultaneously, but independently, to issues. This distinction is so important that it would be useful to abandon the concept of an issue area in favour of two separate concepts, issue systems and policy systems.

A pattern of contention over the degree of support that should be given to a particular value determines the existence of an issue system. Anything to do with the conservation of African elephants, whenever and wherever it occurs, constitutes part of a single-issue system. Similarly, there is an Amazonian-parrots issue system and a polar-bears issue system. The habitat, the food and the wildlife, provide the concrete stakes for these conservation issue systems. The ability to conrol these stakes reflects one underlying abstract environmental value, the conservation of biodiversity. Through this value, the various more specific issues can be perceived as being linked together in a wider issue system, a biodiversity issue system. At this higher level of aggregation, the stakes may become more abstract – examples may include the endorsement of biodiversity or the ratification of CITES (the Convention on International Trade in Endangered Species of Wild Fauna and Flora). At each level, however, there is coherence in two ways: both the political actors and the outside analyst perceive that a common value is invoked. At the lower level, however, there is not necessarily any behavioural connection. In principle, one could imagine that none of the participants in the politics of African elephants, Amazonian parrots or polar bears are active in more than one of those issue systems. In practice, however, the World Wide Fund for Nature (WWF), for example, *has* worked on all these issues. Not all actors in these specific issue systems will regard biodiversity as important. Traders in ivory or in tropical birds are giving priority to wealth creation for themselves, but even they can be presumed to recognise that biodiversity is at issue.

In saying this, one must not allow the analysis to become subjective. The analyst's presumptions about what values are invoked by a set of political choices must not create any *ex cathedra* analytical system. It might be logical to assert that the elimination of the smallpox virus and the elimination of anopheles mosquitoes are biodiversity issues. In practice, however, they have to be classified instead as health issues. Indeed, they cannot be classified by a positivist as biodiversity issues unless political actors are observed to be invoking the value of biodiversity. Even if some 'deep Greens' do wish to conserve the smallpox virus in the name of maintaining biodiversity, their argument has not been taken up sufficiently for the World Health Organisation to feel the need to address it. An issue system based on contention over a value has to be grounded in empirical reality.

In behavioural terms, an issue system is an analytical abstraction that does not encompass all the complexities of real world events. The aggregation of behaviour on the basis of the perceptions that a common value is invoked yields an issue system. In a particular time and place, politics is often about 'What is to be done?', i.e. the formulation of policy. The definition by Mansbach and Vasquez of an issue, quoted above, is best seen as the definition of a policy system rather than that of an issue system. The disposition of stakes constitutes policy-making. The aggregation of interactions designed to determine decision-making and the actual decision-making process itself constitute a policy system. It will be argued below that four different processes can link different issues and affect how decisions are taken. As a result, policy systems normally lie at the intersection of several issue systems.

The crucial interactions may often be specified as taking place in the meetings of an organisation on a certain day in a certain room. In a domestic system, this may be, for example, a bureaucratic committee, a political party, the cabinet or the legislature. In a global system, it may involve a meeting of international civil servants, diplomatic working groups, caucuses, UN meetings or specialised international regimes. However, we ought here to follow the literature on domestic politics in particular, with its concept of 'policy networks' (Marsh and Rhodes 1992). It would be too narrow to restrict our definition of a policy system to that of a system in which the final decisions are taken. A policy system consists of all those actors' interactions, occurring in a formal or an informal manner, that are designed to affect the final policy.

The complexity of politics is due to the fact that different actors support different values and give them different priorities. When policy is to be made, these differences will become evident. The possibility exists that a particular policy will only invoke one value, but this is unlikely to occur. Issue systems and policy systems are not necessarily co-terminal. At the extreme, a single simple yes-or-no policy decision may invoke a large number of values. Whether or not to build the Channel Tunnel between Britain and France was an environmental issue, concerning how to dispose of the spoilage from digging the tunnel and where to route the rail-link; it was a health issue, with respect to the fear of wildlife spreading rabies; it was an identity issue, in providing a symbolic link between Britain and Europe; and it was an economic issue for both the construction industry and traders. Thus, the one policy involved at least four different issues.

Having separated perceptions from behaviour, we must now ask what links together the millions of discrete events each year around the globe, and what links perceptions to behaviour. There are four different linkage processes.

1  *Value linkages* have already been mentioned. These occur when we perceive different events to be part of the same issue, because the same value is invoked.
2  *Functional linkages* arise when one action inevitably has a variety of consequences that cannot be separated. In some cases the link may even be a physical one, totally devoid of any political cause; the example has been given of the Channel Tunnel: the act of digging a large hole linked environmental, health and economic issues.

3  *Actor linkages* will occur when one and the same set of actors is involved in different issues and positions are taken in response to the status of the actors. We might expect virtually all policy in the Antarctic Treaty system to concern environmental and economic values. However, the participation of the South African government as a consultative party ineluctably placed the issues invoked by apartheid within the Antarctic policy system.

4  Finally, the process of political interaction will lead to *bargaining linkages* by which various actors agree to form coalitions to support each other's goals. One major example, in which environmental issues have been linked to other very diverse issues, is the UN Convention on the Law of the Sea. None of the gains negotiated can be realised unless the whole package is implemented, so none of the linkages can be broken by individual actors. (For a more detailed discussion of issue linkages, see Willetts 1994.)

All four types of linkage may serve to create a policy system. Value linkages, by definition, only operate within a single-issue system, whereas the other three processes are more likely to create linkages between a number of different issues. These three latter processes are still, nonetheless, subjective. Responses to other actors and to bargaining processes are obviously themselves determined on the basis of value preferences, though the different participants in a policy system are probably not all responding to the same values. Both by definition and in terms of the actual effects of a policy, functional linkages are clearly objective in nature. However, these kinds of linkage will not affect politics, nor will they link different issues together in a policy system, until their objective features are *subjectively* perceived. For example, nobody in the 1960s was linking the health issue of skin cancer to the economic issue of producing refrigerants. Until the objective process of the erosion of the ozone layer was perceived to exist and the subjective evaluation was made that action should be taken to reduce CFCs in order to reduce deaths, there could be no political linkage.

The traditional Realist approach can easily accommodate the idea that politics consists of various issues that are related to each other through actor linkages and bargaining linkages. This appears to be a restatement of their concern with military and economic power. Functional linkages would here just be seen as physical constraints on the exercise of power. The major departure from Realism made by a value-based paradigm is the idea that an independent subjective process exists in which actors choose values to support, pursue stakes to realise those values and mobilise other actors to support those values. The Global Politics approach is to assume that the pursuit of values is the reason for attaining power, rather than that the pursuit of power is the reason for adopting value positions. The idea that value preferences determine action is not compatible with the idea of politics being reducible to no more than the pursuit of power. To separate value linkages from actor linkages and bargaining linkages is to claim that one central process, the process of perceiving the world, is not determined by power. A Realist cannot accept 'the power of ideas', nor can he or she accept that an actor without military or economic capabilities can have communication resources and communication skills and hence can influence outcomes.

Through asking what values create issues and what issues are salient in policy systems, we can approach a general theory of global politics that can easily handle environmental values and conform to the positions taken above in the three 'Great Debates'. Policy systems can be seen as the focus for resolving conflicts between environmental values and security or economic values. Neither the Idealist presumption that international cooperation can and should occur nor the Realist presumption that security and economic conflicts will limit such cooperation has to be adopted. The outcome will depend on the priority accorded by political actors to the values that can best be maximised through cooperation. It is not necessary to reject a positivist approach to the study of actors mobilising support for their values. It is possible to assert that the processes by which we perceive reality are central to the way in which policy problems are socially constructed, and to the way in which these problems embody different issues, but this does not require an acceptance of the ontology of critical theorists. Finally, by putting both values themselves and our changing perceptions of the linkages between those values at the centre of politics, we are denying the realist's static approach. The rise of environmental politics was possible because there is no static objective national interest, and because there is no constant ranking of values into issues that involve either 'high politics' or 'low politics'.

## ENVIRONMENTAL VALUES AND ENVIRONMENTAL NGOs

At the country level of analysis, governments are of great importance because they are the focus for nearly all collective decision-making. Environmental outcomes may be significantly determined by market processes, involving the aggregation of many separate decisions, but governments are expected to set the framework within which these markets themselves operate. Most values are salient to governmental actors, in one way or another. Furthermore, other political actors may demand that governments take a firm position on a certain issue. It is only when an issue is of low salience to most members of society, or at least of low salience to the constituencies on which the government relies for support, that that government can avoid adopting a position in relation to the values invoked by an issue. Conventional political science tends to emphasise that governments have legislative authority and can exercise coercion, and tends to forget that both authority and coercion have first to be legitimised, at least within the government itself. An alternative emphasis is on governments as the institutions created for the purpose of the collective allocation of values. It is this feature of governments, that they may be involved in all issues, rather than just that of 'power', which distinguishes them from other actors.

At the other extreme, specialist non-governmental organisations (NGOs) may be devoted primarily to the pursuit of a single value. The WWF promotes the conservation of biodiversity; Amnesty International promotes freedom of expression;

companies strive to promote wealth creation; the International Federation for Animal Welfare seeks to alleviate animal suffering; and Health Action International promotes human health. It is not, however, a defining feature of NGOs that they promote a single value. The Red Cross, motivated by the desire to minimise the human suffering caused by war, has the two values of health and peace central to all its work; and when the health of refugees is threatened by famine, this organisation then has to make a major effort to pursue a *third* value, wealth, to mobilise economic resources in order to provide food and medicines. (This is a functional linkage.) As NGOs gain experience, various linkages become more apparent to them and they then expand their values or activities, or both, accordingly. With its campaigns against torture and the death penalty, Amnesty moved to include freedom from suffering, alongside freedom of expression, as a value to pursue. And the Red Cross similarly moved from a concern for the health of the victims of war to include support for the victims of natural disasters.

Some NGOs are engaged in tasks which have such complex ramifications that a wide range of values are promoted as a result. The International Planned Parenthood Federation (IPPF), in promoting family planning, is also promoting the health of women, the health of children, equality for women, wealth accumulation for the Federation's own activities, wealth accumulation to improve general living standards, knowledge to improve standards of education, freedom of expression, knowledge of sexuality and freedom of choice with respect to child-bearing. Not only are these values diverse, but most of them generate issues in more than one policy system. Through multiple linkages, the IPPF is effectively concerned with women's rights, development and many environ- mental issues, and it collaborates on a regular basis with the World Conservation Union and the WWF. Its concerns are not much less extensive than those of developing-country governments.

Despite the range of issues involved, an NGO such as the IPPF remains different from a government because it can choose how wide or narrow the range of its activities should be. It does not have to make an authoritative allocation of resources or non-material values within the wider political system, and it does not have to make any of its opponents implement its decisions. An NGO, as a body with voluntary membership, remains highly cohesive, compared to society as a whole. Its main asset is the commitment of its members to its values. When members do dispute the NGO's values, they may seek to change the NGO or they may cease to be members, but even a severe crisis may be resolved by the NGO splitting into factions that form new NGOs, a process that is not uncommon.

The normal response to a situation where governments act as the focus for decision-making is to concentrate on governmental behaviour as the core of international politics. Most studies of environmental politics that are empirically based have to acknowledge the growth in the numbers of NGOs, the strong popular base of the largest ones and the range of their different types of inter-actions with governments. However, as a recent book has pointed out, 'there has been little conceptualisation of the NGO phenomenon as a political development in its own right' (Princen and Finger 1994: x). Generally, the implicit response has been that NGOs are only important in as much as they influence governments. One could respond that governments are only important in as much as they influence NGOs. (Effective governance must mean having an impact on society and hence an impact upon NGOs.) The Global Politics paradigm, with its emphasis on values and issues, gives a sound theoretical basis for the instinctive feeling, on the part of environmental researchers, that NGOs really are important in a more fundamental way.

When NGOs select the values they will advocate, they are doing something that governments cannot do. They are setting a clear schedule of value preferences, so that, in principle, they always know what are their priorities. (This is an analytical description. Some NGOs do not explicitly agonise over their values, and are 'action' orientated. Nevertheless, the choice of what activities to undertake is, indirectly, determined by the set of values chosen.) As a direct consequence, NGOs commit themselves generally and on a long-term basis to those particular issue systems in which they will be active. At the same time, however, they remain free to decide, as a matter of short-term tactics, what policy systems they will target. NGOs can select the ground on which their opponents are weakest and seek to achieve change there. Governments do not have this freedom. Most governments, most of the time, have to respond to the full range of issues and policy problems on the global agenda.

The effects of these differences are self-reinforcing. NGOs have clear priorities, can limit their activities and therefore can set their own agendas and continually keep their priorities in focus. Governments may have clear priorities when they assume office, but usually they have to respond to a domestic and global agenda over which they have little control. They thus suffer from agenda overload and lose direction, unless they have a remarkably clear ideology and strong leadership. (For a while, in the late 1980s, Mrs Thatcher had the ability to set her own agenda, but that was exceptional.) In particular, NGOs are free to consider new problems, develop new perspectives and promote new policies to attain their values. On the other hand, governments have to focus on current problems, work within current perspectives to maintain the support of their constituencies and work within current bureaucratic structures that are generally only modifying the status quo (Rose 1994).

As a result, NGOs are more likely to be the source of new ideas, and where they have their own operational programmes, they can be the test-bed for new policies. At a more fundamental level, if values start to change in society, it will be NGOs that have the greatest freedom to adopt the new value-preference schedules. If existing NGOs do not change, then new ones can form to articulate the new priorities. A value-based theory gives a basis for asserting that NGOs are important, and are not just an interesting quirk of some case studies in environmental politics. NGOs are important because they set the agenda for change: they provide the dynamics of global politics.

From this Global Politics paradigm one can re-evaluate the major changes of recent decades. The process of decolonisation, the increased attention given to human rights, the changing status of women, the redefinition of development –

from GNP growth to human development – and the collapse of apartheid are all policy processes that, like the rise in environmental concerns, have made the contemporary world unrecognisable from the world of 1945. (Two of these processes, the rise of human rights and the rise of environmental concerns, were central to the delegitimisation of communism and the end of the Cold War.) In each of these policy systems, governments have taken part in a diplomatic debate and produced decisions at the United Nations reflecting a massive shift in generally endorsed values. But, prior to the diplomatic debate, the shift in values was in each case initiated by NGOs. Because value changes are so slow, the world may seem relatively static on a month-by-month basis. When we consider change over the decades, however, it is clear that global politics has been highly dynamic, and that NGOs have been at the centre of this dynamic process.

Thus, the traditional emphasis on an 'inter-state system' in which sovereignty has not given way to supranational authority is misplaced. Governments are still the focus of policy-making, but the systems of interaction have fundamentally changed, not only in terms of the values that are dominant but also structurally. Governments have new bureaucracies and new responsibilities; they interact in a more dense system of communications; and they are members of new global organisations, some of which act as regimes. The empirical content of the concept of a 'state' in the mid-1990s has little similarity to a 'state' of fifty years ago. Structural changes and the ability of NGOs to change governmental agendas mean that the concept of sovereignty is a distortion of the current empirical content of statehood. We are not living in coherent, relatively autonomous, hierarchical systems. Governments are nodes of communication and decision-making, interacting with domestic NGOs, international NGOs, local and transnational companies, other governments and intergovernmental organisations.

It is important that global communications are not only dense but also very cheap. This factor gives any two people who have some minimum resources, wherever they may be on the globe, the ability to speak to each other, to exchange documents and funds rapidly, to travel to meet face to face and, hence, to work together in transnational structures. Environmental NGOs have been at the forefront of the communications revolution, networking both through simple organisations, producing newsletters, and through the use of the Internet. Overall, the number of NGOs has expanded rapidly (Willetts 1993, 1995; Princen and Finger 1994).

State-centric researchers are able to recognise that 'The activities of environmental NGOs have assumed an important place in issue identification, agenda-setting, policy formation, normative development, institution building, monitoring and implementation' (Hurrell and Kingsbury 1992: 10). What they do not seem to recognise is that such processes are not meaningful either within the realist paradigm or within any modifications of realism. The acceptance of the global nature of environmental problems in a 'seamless web of ecological interdependence' (ibid.: 4); the addition of NGOs as significant actors; the focus on decision-making in regimes; and the consideration of the interplay between economic, security and status values on the one hand and environmental values on the other hand – these analytical shifts together constitute a paradigm shift.

Global environmental politics, in relation to any specific problem, is readily described and understood in terms of a variety of governmental actors, companies, non-governmental actors and international organisations, all interacting to mobilise support for a diverse range of values. The international policy systems are complex because they have to handle a variety of issues. Descriptions of the politics of ozone depletion, tropical-forest utilisation, atmospheric pollution and various threats to biodiversity can be generalised into a common theoretical paradigm. Global policy-making in the fields of human rights or development politics would demonstrate the same empirical patterns. Many problems such as East–West disarmament negotiations or Palestinian–Israeli relations are not normally described in these terms, but a generalisation from global environmental politics would also suggest a very different research programme for the investigation of these policy systems.

## CONCLUSION

From revisiting the idealist–realist debate, we can conclude that politics involves both the pursuit of economic, security and status values (not objective interests) and the pursuit of other values, including internationalism and environmental concerns. Revisiting behaviouralism, in the light of the study on the part of natural scientists and social scientists of different aspects of humankind's interaction with the environment, leads to the conclusion that both the data on ecosystems and the data on environmental values can be studied in a value-free manner. And a consideration of critical theory makes us aware that some theory may privilege the values of those who do not care about the environment. Theory, and the language by which it is expressed, is a distortion of reality rather than a representation of reality if it does not allow us to study the actions of those who wish to promote change.

We can start from the presumption that political actors do seek both concrete material values and more abstract values. Some values are maximised by engaging in conflict, but other values are realised through cooperation. Value preferences are not identifiable, through rationality, as an objective feature of an actor's situation. They are the subjective choice of that actor. Values are socially constructed: as society changes, so values change. Nevertheless, they are also an empirical reality. A focus on the resolution of issues in policy systems offers a positivist approach for an alternative Global Politics paradigm.

## BIBLIOGRAPHY

Atkinson, A. (1991) *Principles of Political Ecology*, London: Belhaven.
Brown, C. (1994) 'Critical theory and postmodernism in international relations', in Groom, A.J.R. and Light, M. (eds) *Contemporary International Relations: a Guide to Theory*, London: Pinter.
Bull, H. (1966) 'International theory: the case for a classical approach', reprinted in Knorr, K. and Rosenau, J.N. (eds) (1969) *Contending Approaches to International Politics*, Princeton, NJ: Princeton U.P., pp. 20–38.

—— (1977) *The Anarchical Society: a Study of Order in World Politics*, London: Macmillan.

Burton, J.W. (1965) *International Relations: a General Theory*, Cambridge: C.U.P.

—— (1968) *Systems, States, Diplomacy and Rules*, Cambridge: C.U.P.

—— (1972) *World Society*, Cambridge: C.U.P.

—— *et al.* (1974) 'The study of world society: a London perspective', Occasional Paper No. 1, Pittsburgh, Penn.: International Studies Association.

Childers, E. with Urquhart, B. (1994) 'Renewing the United Nations system', *Development Dialogue*, 1994: Issue 1.

Clark, G. and Sohn, L.B. (1966) *World Peace Through World Law*, Cambridge, Mass.: Harvard U.P.

Cox, R. (1981) 'Social forces, states and world order', *Millenium: Journal of International Studies* 10: 126–55.

Easton, D. (1965) *A Framework for Political Analysis*, Englewood Cliffs, NJ: Prentice Hall.

Elshtain, E.J. (1985) 'Reflections on war and political discourse: realism, just war and feminism in a nuclear age', in Little, R. and Smith, M. (eds) (1991) *Perspectives on World Politics*, 2nd edn, London: Routledge.

Falk, R.A. (1971) *This Endangered Planet: Prospects and Proposals for Human Survival*, New York: Random House.

——, Kim, S.S. and Mendlovitz, S.H. (1991) *The United Nations and a Just World Order*, Boulder, Col.: Westview.

Flood, R.L (1990) *Liberating Systems Theory*, New York: Plenum.

Heinrich, D. (1992) *The Case for a United Nations Parliamentary Assembly*, New York and Amsterdam: World Federalist Movement.

Hoffman, M. and Rengger, N. (eds) (1995) *Critical Theory and International Relations: a Reader*, Hemel Hempstead: Harvester Wheatsheaf.

Hurrell, A. and Kingsbury, B. (eds) (1992) *The International Politics of the Environment*, Oxford: Clarendon.

Keohane, R.O. and Nye, J.S. (eds) (1972) *Transnational Relations and World Politics*, Cambridge, Mass.: Harvard U.P.

—— (1977) *Power and Interdependence*, Boston, Mass.: Little, Brown.

Knorr, K. and Rosenau, J.N. (eds) (1969) *Contending Approaches to International Politics*, Princeton, NJ: Princeton U.P.

Kuhn, T.S. (1970) *The Structure of Scientific Revolutions*, 2nd enlarged edn, Chicago: University of Chicago Press.

Lakatos, I. (1970) 'Falsification and the methodology of scientific research programmes', in Lakatos, I. and Musgrave, A. (eds) *Criticism and the Growth of Knowledge*, Cambridge: C.U.P.

Little, R. and Smith, M. (eds) (1991) *Perspectives on World Politics*, 2nd edn, London: Routledge.

Mansbach, R.W. and Vasquez, J.A. (1981) *In Search of Theory: a New Paradigm for Global Politics*, New York: Columbia U.P.

Marsh, D. and Rhodes, R.A.W. (1992) *Policy Networks in British Government*, Oxford: Clarendon.

Morgenthau, H.J. (1948) *Politics Among Nations: the Struggle for Power and Peace*, 3rd edn (1960), New York: Alfred A. Knopf.

Nicholson, M. (1983) *The Scientific Analysis of Social Behaviour: a Defence of Empiricism in Social Science*, London: Pinter.

—— (1989) *Formal Theories in International Relations*, Cambridge: C.U.P.

Popper, K.A. (1959) *The Logic of Scientific Discovery*, London: Hutchinson.

Princen, T. and Finger, M. (1994) *Environmental NGOs in World Politics*, London and New York: Routledge.

Rose, R. (1994) *Inheritance and Public Policy: Change Without Choice in Britain*, New Haven, Conn.: Yale U.P.

Rosenau, J.N. (1966) 'Pre-theories and theories of foreign policy', reprinted in (1971) *The Scientific Study of Foreign Policy*, New York: Free Press.

Sachs, W. (ed.) (1992) *The Development Dictionary: a Guide to Knowledge as Power*, London: Zed Books.

Smith, M., Little, R. and Shackleton, M. (eds) (1981) *Perspectives on World Politics*, 1st edn, London: Croom Helm.

United Nations (1992) 'Report of the United Nations Conference on Environment and Development, 3–14 June 1992', UN document A/CONF.151/26.

Vasquez, J.A. (1979) 'Colouring it Morgenthau: new evidence for an old thesis on quantitative international politics', *British Journal of International Studies* 5(3): 210–28.

Willetts, P. (1982) *Pressure Groups in the Global System*, London: Pinter.

—— (1989) 'Interdependence: new wine in old bottles', in Rosenau, J.N. and Trope, H. (eds) *Interdependence and Conflict in World Politics*, Aldershot: Gower.

—— (1990) 'Transactions, networks and systems', in Groom, A.J.R. and Taylor, P. (eds) *Frameworks for International Co-operation*, London: Pinter.

—— (1993) 'Transnational actors and changing world order', Occasional Paper Number 17, Yokohama: International Peace Research Institute Meigaku.

——, with Bentham, M., Hough, P. and Humphreys, D. (1994) 'The issue of issues in regime theory', mimeo paper, London: City University Transgovernmental Relations Research Group.

—— (ed.) (1995) *We the Peoples: the Influence of Non-Governmental Organisations at the United Nations*, London: C. Hurst & Co.

# 8 The environment and the United Nations

*Mark F. Imber*

This chapter does not offer a complete institutional review of the UN's activities in the field of environmental protection. Such works exist elsewhere, and the issue deserves fuller treatment than can be afforded in one chapter.[1] The purpose of this chapter is to explore the conceptual and institutional limitations of global, intergovernmental cooperation on environmental questions. Thereafter, its purpose is to identify the larger picture of continuing negotiations and institutional reforms which have followed from the 1992 United Nations Conference on Environment and Development (UNCED) – the so-called 'Earth Summit'. These conceptual and institutional issues will be combined in a discussion of the attempt to develop both definitions and measures of sustainable development.

UNCED, and more particularly the follow-up process, represented an attempt to invest the United Nations with major responsibilities in the promotion of sustainable development. First, the post-Cold War UN is able to address the environmental agenda more thoroughly than at any time since the Stockholm Conference of 1972. Second, both Third World political pressure groups and the scientific community now acknowledge the explicit connections between environmental degradation and patterns of economic development (between mass poverty in the South and unsustainable patterns of consumption in the North). Third, and most ambitiously, sustainable development may come to acquire the status of a new normative campaign within the UN (one comparable to decolonisation in the 1960s and anti-apartheid in the 1980s), and this will create a definitive post-Cold War purpose for the organisation. This may also be a typically liberal-institutional objective. Elsewhere in this volume, Humphreys refers to sustainable development as a 'rescue hypothesis'. Others are still more dismissive of the inattention both to the structural dimension (Smith 1993) and to the co-option of private-sector interests which sustainability implies (Doran 1993). There is indeed something both millenarian and functionalist about the recasting of the organs of global governance around a new organising principle. There is also something deeply nostalgic and reminiscent of Bretton Woods 1944 about such proposals, except that the process of *reforming*, as opposed to inventing, the machinery of the United Nations has to overcome a half-century of barnacle-encrusted practice and precedent. Precedent is not always encouraging. Despite the apparent novelty of UNCED, and the unreal level of expectations which surrounded it, two important precedents do exist for this attempt to shift the normative basis of the UN towards a more environmental, if not ecologist, perspective. These precedents show the need to think in terms of decades as regards the evolution of a normative consensus into legal standards. Rio 1992 was the second such global conference on environmental issues to be convened by the UN. Stockholm 1972 had focused on a narrower agenda, but even then the immutable connections to Third World development were apparent, especially in the explicit connections that were made in Principles 8-11 of the Stockholm Declaration (UN 1972). The second precedent is the common-heritage-of-mankind principle, now widely recognised as an appropriate regulatory mechanism for the protection of global 'life-support systems' such as the ozone layer and the climate system. It is over twenty-five years since the common-heritage idea was *first* mooted in the United Nations, although it was then applied to a different context, namely the exploitation of the deep-sea bed (Imber 1994: 48–54; Sanger 1986: 70–89). Arvid Pardo's 1967 General Assembly speech set in motion twelve years of negotiation, which was concluded by the adoption of the United Nation's Convention on the Law of the Sea in 1982. A further twelve years were to elapse before the Convention secured the sixty acts of ratification necessary for it to enter into force in November 1994. During the time that common-heritage ideas in relation to the Law of the Sea remained in abeyance (with consequent harm to high seas, straddling and pelagic fish stocks), an elaborate regime for the protection of the ozone layer and the first Framework Convention on Climate Change were successfully implemented under UN auspices. (See chapters in this volume by Ogley, Paterson and Owen.) Both rested upon the common-heritage proposition that global environmental systems cannot either be annexed by states or be left *res nullius* (without the law), for they would then be liable to destruction by unregulated overexploitation – the so-called 'tragedy of the commons' (Hardin 1968: 1243–8).

Sustainable development, derived from the 1987 Brundtland Report of the World Commission on Environment and Development (Brundtland 1987: 8), was the central ideology of UNCED. The Rio Declaration, adopted at the close of the Conference, confirmed this commitment. The two-part definition maintained that:

- The right to development must be fulfilled so as to equitably meet develop-mental and environmental needs of present and future generations (UN 1993: Principle 2).
- In order to achieve sustainable development, environmental protection shall constitute an integral part of the developmental process and cannot be con-sidered in isolation from it (UN 1993: Principle 3).

Twenty years after the Stockholm Conference had addressed the *human* environment, UNCED attempted to deploy a grand linkage strategy combining environmental protection and economic development, two factors thought by some from the 1970s limits-to-growth school to be irreconcilable (Meadows *et al.* 1983; Martell 1994: 24–40). The Northern interest in a number of global environ-mental issues *was* unavoidably linked to the Third World's determination to resurrect the agenda of development after the frustrations of the 1980s. Not only was the imperative political, in that the consensus procedures of the UN system would not allow the two issues to be debated separately, it also reflected *scientific* evidence that a number of so-called environmental issues such as climate change, ozone-layer depletion, deforestation and toxic-waste pollution were intimately associated with *unsustainable* patterns of development; namely fossil-fuel and CFC use, land tenure, indebtedness and the relocation of polluting industrial processes in Third World countries. The last (the Bhopal Syndrome) reflected the risk inherent in the globalisation of the world economy.

Two perspectives are dominant in assessing the role of the UN in any multilateral venture: the forum/actor perspective and the instrument/executor perspective (Archer 1983: 130–41). First, the UN may be perceived as an *arena* or *forum* for global bargaining between governments. It is only in a public and universal forum of this kind that sovereign actors may be persuaded to endorse cooperative ventures, and so relinquish the temptations to play the 'free-rider', to pass on 'external costs' and to play the persistently uncooperative role in the many 'prisoner's dilemma' scenarios that characterise global environmental change.[2] Second, the UN may be characterised as an *instrument* for implementing or executing the policies of its members. These two limited schemes deliberately sidestep the cosmopolitan aspiration that the UN can somehow operate as an autonomous *actor* beyond the ken of its creators. When operational autonomy does arise, such as in the immediate response of a peace-keeping force under fire, or with the decisions inevitably devolved upon aid and refugee workers delivering humanitarian relief, it occurs in strictly limited circumstances. The UN does not have its own tax base to finance peace-keeping and humanitarian programmes. The organisation is international, not supranational, and as such the UN depends upon the policy decisions and funding of its members. As will be shown, particular difficulties arise when those members decline to finance what in previous resolutions they have committed themselves to support. The UN is not a leviathan. Its separate legal corporate existence is a deceptive piece of flattery. It does not *make* policy, nor does it *enforce* the agreements made by its members and adopted in its name. This fact applies to sustainable development as much as it applies to other pretended competencies such as collective security. Central to an understanding of the limited UN role in global environmental management are two propositions so basic as to be clichés. However, clichés derive their influence from their tested status. The first, concerning the arena perspective, is that the United Nations is literally the *only* place where global negotiations on environmental protection can be conducted. The second cliché concerns the UN's status as an instrument. The UN machinery, its funding and its organisational culture are, as currently constituted, inadequate to undertake the tasks it has been assigned by the outcome of the 1992 UNCED. The UN, in other words, has been set up to fail. These assertions will be substantiated by detailed reference to the UNCED mandate later on. It is first necessary, however, to establish the conceptual framework in which the UN exists and operates, as an arena and as an instrument of its member's creation.

## THE CONCEPTUAL RATIONALE

The UN's role in the environmental field derives from the clearly transboundary and sometimes global nature of many threats to the environmental security of the state. The boundaries of sovereign states do not coincide with the boundaries of the ecological systems which sustain them. Therefore, any attempt by a sovereign state to regulate ecological systems is bound to have only limited success. This creates a crisis of legitimacy for the state, because it cannot deliver complete security. One solution to this dilemma has been the functional approach to international organisations, an approach latterly restyled by some as 'liberal institutionalist'.[3] Even the most apparently isolated island republic, such as the Maldives or Tuvalu, depends upon external climate systems and oceanic currents to create and sustain its variety of fauna and flora, and indeed its pattern of human migration and settlement. Furthermore, these small island states are, more than any other countries, threatened by the global environmental change caused by processes and events that occur literally half a world away, such as North American, Japanese and European fossil-fuel use. Some environmental threats to the security of the state are completely beyond the capacity of any one state to resist or to alter. No one country can legislate for the protection of the ozone layer above it, or command the obedience of the level of the sea lapping at its shores. Countries that do legislate for sustainable-development policies will be subject to pressures caused by transboundary flows originating abroad. Some countries are likely to be more sinned against than sinning in this particular balance of trans-boundary pollution (Saetevik 1988). Air quality in the Netherlands is clearly affected by discharges from the German Ruhr basin. Similarly, water quality in the Rhine–Maas river system is determined, for downstream riparians, by the behaviour of upstream riparians, namely Germany, Belgium, France and Switzerland.

Functional organisations have, since the creation of the Rhine Commission in 1815, attempted to reconcile the imperfect fit between jurisdictional boundaries and so-called natural or functional boundaries. Some of the earliest examples of functional cooperation were associated with the international river commissions for the Rhine, Scheldt and Danube. These *can* be described as 'natural', in the sense of being hydrological systems defined by geographical rather than political boundaries. These nineteenth-century projects were a successful precedent for the global application of the functional approach to fields of human cooperation such as the Universal Postal Union, the Food and Agricultural Organisation and the International Civil Aviation Organisation, in which standard-setting and economies of scale suggested a rational basis for intergovernmental cooperation. Attempts to apply the vocabulary of 'natural functions' or 'technical self-determination' to other social and economic aspects of international cooperation – for example, the World Bank – have invited criticism that functionalism is either teleological (Haas 1964) or hegemonic (Keohane 1984). However, some dimensions of contemporary global environmental change, such as climate change, ozone-layer depletion and the control of oceanic pollution, fit well with the functionalist logic, invoking the case for global regulation by organisations of global reach.

Functional cooperation can only operate under the conditions of complex interdependence identified by Keohane and Nye (1977). UNCED addressed a complex agenda: Agenda 21 itself extended over forty substantive chapters. Pre-conference positions were well established. The North promoted climate change, forestry conservation and the preservation of biological diversity as its priorities. The South approached Rio keener to promote pledges on concessionary finance and technology transfer, trade reform, action on desertification and protection from waste-dumping, and sought to avoid stigmatisation on forestry and demographic questions. The UNCED process recognised the crucial role of numerous stakeholders and parties in the implementation of, and the follow-up to, the agreements which were made. Agenda 21 also recognised the role of numerous so-called 'major groups', mostly obviously local authorities, women, indigenous peoples, youth, the corporate sector, trade unions and the scientific community (though despite this, these groups were poorly represented in the state-centric *decision-making* structures of the Conference). UNCED was (like all similar global conferences) predicated on the parties' recognising the near irrelevance of military power in resolving the disputes that arose in addressing the agenda.

Although typically associated with relations of mutual dependence, the above conditions need not imply *symmetrical* relations. On the contrary, in UNCED, as in many North–South arenas, the parties were configured in a profoundly *asymmetrical* relationship of power. Despite a substantial rhetorical investment in both environmentalism and globalism, the Northern countries maintained their control of global financial resources. The South's need for concessionary finance, debt relief, trade liberalisation and technology transfers was considerably more pressing than the North's need for Southern signatures on measures to limit those global environmental changes which were, anyway, overwhelmingly Northern in their industrial causation (changes such as ozone-layer damage and climate change). In this situation, the South was compelled to recognise not only that half a loaf was better than none but also that *crumbs* (like the Global Environmental Facility – GEF) were better than none. The South maintained its dignity, nonetheless: it left some crumbs on the table when threatened with scapegoating on the issues of forestry and population.

It is possible to make three broad predictions concerning the conduct of multilateral diplomacy under such conditions as the above.

- *Package deals*. The complexity of the agenda will lead the parties to strike compromises based upon complex 'package deals'. Interests and priorities will be traded off against each other. No party will take the risk of making concessions on one item of the agenda without making gains elsewhere.
- *Consensus*. Package deals in turn create the need to proceed by consensus rather than by votes. Voting creates winners and losers, issue by issue. A climate-change treaty without US, Russian, Chinese and Indian consent and

support would omit those countries responsible for nearly 50 per cent of carbon dioxide ($CO_2$) emissions. Their absence, furthermore, would undermine the incentive for other responsible parties to join. The complete breakdown of negotiations for a forestry convention at Rio illustrates this thesis. The nature of a global conference is such that nothing is agreed until everything is agreed, because every individual agenda item remains a potential bargaining chip until the whole deal is agreed.

- *Intransigence.* Proceeding by consensus to an overall package deal creates the third characteristic of the UN conference method. Both preceding characteristics tend to reward intransigence in negotiation. In a vote, the minority of one is an exposed loser. When assembling a package by consensus, however, the minority of one can attract disproportionate concessions from the other parties to achieve a final deal. Since all can behave likewise, this tends to reward the dogmatist, the insomniac and the plain bloody-minded. It is a characteristic of UN life which punishes the pragmatist, the tired and the gullible.

These aspects of conduct are not peculiar to the UN system. Something very similar characterises bargaining within the EU Council. The scale is, however, proportionately larger when encompassing over 190 governments within a consensus framework on an agenda which is divisive. When the rapidity of international agreement on the Montreal Protocol is contrasted with the more contentious climate-change issue (or with the even more contentious forestry or demographic issues), the characteristics which encourage or discourage agreement become relatively predictable (see Figure 8.1).

In addition to the well-established impulse to cheat in the matters of free-riding and external costs, more complex compulsions to cause environmental damage also exist. Deudney (1990) has shown the difficulty of confronting environmental damage when to a greater or lesser extent 'we are the enemy', in other words when our actions harm ourselves as well as others. This is recognised in the game-theory construct of the prisoner's dilemma. Individual acts of self-interest, such as commuting by car and watering the lawn in a drought, do not

| *Factors encouraging multilateralism* | *Factors discouraging multilateralism* |
| --- | --- |
| Urgent issues | Non-urgent issues |
| Scientific consensus | Scientific doubt/dispute |
| Win–win outcomes | Win–lose outcomes |
| Progressive distribution effects | Regressive distribution effects |
| Verification credible | Verification weak/uncertain |

*Figure 8.1* The incentives to negotiate multilateral agreements

work to the individual's advantage because every other member of society makes the same individually rational (i.e. selfish) decision. As a result, we get stuck in traffic jams and reservoirs run dry, because the 'hidden hand' of the market does *not* always yield optimal results. List and Rittberger have pointed out other categories which mix self-harm and social harm. 'Victims' are damaged by others but do not inflict harm on others. The case of receiving transboundary pollution flows, such as with acid rain or downstream river pollution, illustrates this category. 'Hara-kiri' is self-harming behaviour, as in the case of a local land-fill of toxic wastes involving no leakage into the water table of other jurisdictions but creating a fearsome middle-range problem for the sustainable re-use of that particular land. This could be said to be primarily harming other generations, but it is also *self*-harm in the sense that the political community affected is that of the perpetrator. 'Kamikaze' behaviour consists of that which harms others *and* destroys the perpetrator. An example would be a spectacular nuclear accident (Hurrell and Kingsbury 1992: 101).

Although, as mentioned, the UN is not a leviathan, it could be said to be an imperfect analogue of a civil society in which the member states consent to be bound by rules which they have freely negotiated between themselves. In the UN, as a global forum, each state is confronted with the costs of failing to agree to collective solutions to shared problems. Each is also provided with a glimpse of the freely negotiated alternative, namely treaties, binding on each party, that create mutual obligations. Like a military alliance or a mutual insurance fund, such treaties spread the risks and costs of environmental protection among a larger number of subscribers.

The language of globalism can sometimes be revealed as rhetoric rather than analysis. In one sense, the environmental factors which cause the death of over 12 million Third World children every year are parochial (Imber 1994: 1–2). Water-borne diseases, open sewers and inadequate access to paediatric medicine and family planning do to an extent constitute self-contained disasters. However, a structuralist analysis of international relations would locate the responsibility for this new holocaust (32,000 preventable child deaths per day) within the world-system of neocolonialism. In the structuralist view, the plight of these countries has been created by a 400-year process of Western capital accumulation, the expropriation of raw materials, the distortion of primary product markets and, now, by 'reverse aid' in which Third World debt servicing massively outstrips Overseas Development Aid (ODA) (Vallely 1990; Miller 1991; George 1992). However, so far as the political mainstream is concerned (including the liberal roots of functionalism and institutionalism), errors of omission such as the shortfall in promised ODA are always regarded as less culpable than acts of commission. Furthermore, the causal links between, say, protectionism and infant mortality are indirect and tenuous when set beside the more direct health impacts of ozone depletion, climate change and tropical deforestation. Despite the South's participation in UNCED, and its implied recognition of the agenda of interdependence, UNCED could be represented as a *confrontation* between the structuralist and the pluralist paradigms of international relations.

The poorest of Third World delegations presented the environmental crisis in terms of massive and contemporary human disadvantage. The South's priorities were in the fields of health, life expectancy and poverty, with the appropriate policy emphases on concessionary finance, debt relief and technology transfers, using a vocabulary of rights and equity. In contrast, the Northern governments, and the Northern-dominated media, were inclined to promote an agenda which emphasised climate change, biological diversity and forestry primarily as a crisis for the 'environment', as if somehow disconnected from *human* tragedy. Media interest appeared to be more concerned with the fate of telegenic (i.e. cute) animals than with the fate of children. When the Northern countries admitted the connection between the environment and development, the mechanisms which they favoured to reconcile the two were pluralist – that is, market-led – and consistent both with the emerging consensus of the Uruguay round of trade negotiations and with the promotion of private capital flows to augment the OECD's clearly indifferent performance in ODA finance over the past decade (Middleton, O'Keefe and Moyo 1994; see also Saurin in this volume).

The conceptual approaches to explaining the UN's role are therefore contested. Something of this is shown in the follow-up to UNCED, and in subsequent attempts to define and implement the concept of sustainable development.

## UN TASKS 1: DEFINING SUSTAINABILITY

The work of the whole UN system must, logically, rest upon implementing an agreed definition of sustainable development. This is not so straightforward as it might appear. The parallel to the UN's collective-security mandate of 1945 is instructive. Despite the explicit textual definition contained in the Charter, the implementation of collective security was rendered unworkable by the tensions of the Cold War and by the procedural wrangles that accompanied the Korean decisions in 1950. These served to emasculate collective security, from which there emerged the valid but altogether more limited genre of peace-keeping. Without consistent political and intellectual attention to the meaning of sustainable development, a similar fate will overtake this new post-Cold War imperative.

The debate over 'sustainable development indicators' (SDIs) is one such attempt to define sustainable development in a consensual way that will allow meaningful international comparisons. It combines conceptual and empirical elements in providing national governments, the EC and the UN with the means to *measure* sustainability. And it seeks to identify in a rigorous and systematic way which indicators of economic and social activity could be used to measure progress towards sustainability and (the corollary) which present indicators (such as GDP) are poor or misleading indicators of sustainability.

Certain economic activities, counted as growth, are destructive of environmental quality (for example, increased expenditure on commuter-mileage petrol). Other activities, regarded as a cost to the public purse, may nonetheless support sustainable development, such as subsidies to more fuel-efficient mass-transit systems. Furthermore, certain consumer decisions may be recorded as involving a reduction in economic activity (such as walking to work rather than driving), and these are desirable contributions to sustainability. Sustainability indicators seek to record activities, inputs or outcomes that more reliably indicate those changes in development which affect environmental quality, both adversely and favourably.

The UN first addressed these issues in the preparatory committee (or 'Prepcom') of the Rio Conference, and they may be traced to a UN General Assembly resolution of 1989 (UNGA 44/228: para. 15). This exercise sought to combine economic and environmental-quality indicators into the concept of integrated economic-environmental accounting (IEEA). Two particular concerns were to establish numerical and financial values for the role of the environment both as a source of natural capital and as a sink for by-products. In particular, the UN efforts confronted the dilemma that

> traditional systems of national accounts, focussing on market transactions do not record changes in the quality of the natural environment and the depletion of natural resources. These effects are particularly relevant for the measurement of an adjusted concept of value added in production, which is compatible with long term environmentally sound and sustained economic growth, and of an adjusted concept of net income, which takes into account the welfare aspects of environmental depletion and degradation.
>
> (UN A. CONF. 151: para. 7)

Agenda 21 mandated both the UN Statistical Office (UNSTAT) to pursue this question (Agenda 21: 40, 6) and the relevant organs to thereafter use SDIs (Agenda 21: 40, 7). The task has in fact been tackled, more or less simultaneously, not only by UNSTAT but also by the OECD, the Economic Commission for Africa (UNECA), leading NGOs such as the New Economics Foundation (NEF) and a small number of concerned national governments (NEF 1994).

UNSTAT and the UN Environment Programme (UNEP) collaborated in a consultative process initiated in December 1993. Bedrich Moldan, the Vice-Chairman of the Commission on Sustainable Development (CSD), promoted a paper which sought agreement around a number of indicators measuring both environmental quality and changes in the following clusters: the atmosphere, fresh water, marine water, sanitation, land/soil use, biological resources, mineral resources, human settlements, population and health care, natural disasters, economic policy, education and international cooperation. The great majority of measures proposed comprised hard statistics potentially embarrassing but not arguable, e.g. green-house gas emissions in tonnes per year, industrial waste discharge to coastal waters (tonnes per $m^3$), fertiliser use (tonnes per $km^2$), etc. Other proposals were more controversial and involved qualitative judgements, e.g. the projected lifetime of non-renewable energy resources at given rates of exploitation, flows of environmental refugees and the percentage of the population living in absolute poverty.

A related aspect of the indicators debate which is central to international relations concerns imported sustainability or the 'international footprint' of a particular society or sovereignty. Some societies might achieve a commendable performance under a system of 'sustainability indicators' by first importing energy-intensive or pollution-intensive goods and then performing higher-value-added stages of production which are *less* energy- and pollution-intensive. Assembling automobiles using steel components manufactured elsewhere would be an example. The energy-use, ore-extraction and air-pollution aspects of the steel industry are recorded as having occurred in the original steel-milling country. Only the 'clean' stages of final assembly are recorded in the country of nominal manufacture. Imported sustainability has radical implications. Sustainable development is unavoidably predicated upon the redistribution of income. The current gulf in living standards between rich and poor is an acute reflection of profound inequalities in environmental quality. Variations between North and South – such as the per capita consumption of fossil fuels, twenty-four times higher in the USA compared to India (Paterson and Grubb 1992: 298), and the net transfer of wealth created by a debt-servicing flow that exceeds ODA – are both aspects of imported sustainability in the North. This issue also forces advocates of sustainability to consider the regressive implications of carbon taxes such as VAT on fuel. Policies to encourage sustainability *can* be distributionally neutral or even progressive; take, for example, the transfer of resources from road construction over to public transport, which better assists the mobility of the car-less poor (von Weizsacker 1994: 129–40). In these ways, the significance of Agenda 21 can be appreciated. It requires the holistic treatment of sustainable development at all levels of the policy process – local, national and international.

## UN TASKS 2: ORGANISING SUSTAINABILITY

The institutional reforms of the UN machinery set in motion by the 1992 UNCED were contained in the recommendations of Chapter 38 of Agenda 21. In brief, the governments participating in UNCED reaffirmed a hierarchy of political accountability, with the UN Environment Programme (UNEP) and the UN Development Programme (UNDP) obliged to cooperate with each other (Agenda 21: 38, 32). Both are explicitly accountable to the newly created Commission on Sustainable Development (CSD), itself a subcommission of the well-established Economic and Social Council (ECOSOC), which is in turn an organ of the General Assembly. Within this hierarchy, Agenda 21 enlarged the competence of UNEP, whilst assigning a particular leadership role to the UNDP in capacity-building and finance, and also agreed to continue funding the newly created tri-agency, Global Environmental Facility (GEF).

The mandate granted to UNEP was not surprising. By 1992 the programme had established a reputation for conducting its small programmes in an efficient manner. Donor confidence was high, especially amongst the more sceptical American and British governments which regarded UNEP (by UN standards at least) as a paragon of focused activities and tight budgetary restraint (USGAO 1989). The dilemma facing advocates of an expanded role for UNEP was how to encourage the so-called 'catalytic' role pioneered by the programme whilst releasing UNEP from the Sisyphean task of 'coordinating' UN environmental activities on a system-wide basis (Imber 1994: 82–3). The original 1972 Resolution of the General Assembly which created UNEP also burdened it with a dual mandate. The Governing Council was directed to 'promote international cooperation in the field of the environment and to recommend, as appropriate, policies to this end; to provide general policy guidance for the direction and coordination of environmental programmes within the UN system' (UNGA Res. 2997 (XXVII)). The constraints upon a small secretariat based in Nairobi with only 250 professional staff and a budget of approximately $60 million per annum are obvious. With its scientific staff matching that of a middle-sized British university, it would have been quite unreasonable to expect UNEP to operate at the cutting edge of basic science as ranked by global criteria of excellence. Hence the development of Mostapha Tolba's incumbency of the niche role in unique functions such as Global Earth Monitoring (GEMS), INFOTERRA and the management of the secretariats of the Convention on International Trade in Endangered Species (CITES) and the International Register of Potentially Toxic Chemicals (IRPTC). These represented genuinely global functions appropriate to the Programme and mindful of its limitations. Equally clearly, UNEP could not be expected to coordinate a variety of autonomous UN programmes. UNEP, as noted, is formally subordinate to ECOSOC and the General Assembly. Meanwhile, the UNDP operates a budget approximately thirty times larger than UNEP (over $900 million), and the World Bank disperses funds measured annually at over $10 billion. The degree of 'greenness', or otherwise, of these two autonomous organisations therefore largely determines the environmental impact of the UN's system-wide efforts. Encouraging the UNDP and the World Bank towards sustainable-development policies is therefore a more important task than tinkering with the pretence of UNEP 'coordination'. Agenda 21 promotes UNEP's role as 'strengthening its catalytic role in stimulating and promoting environmental activities and considerations throughout the United Nations system' (Agenda 21: 38, 22 (a)). This 'think tank' role is compatible both with the modesty of UNEP's place in the organisational structure of the UN and with its level of funding. UNEP is also assigned other responsibilities: the development of natural-resource accounting systems, the dissemination of global data and 'the coordination and promotion of relevant scientific research' (Agenda 21: 38, 22(e)).

In a wide-ranging reform of the UN headquarters' secretariat initiated in 1992, staff numbers were actually reduced and reorganised into a smaller number of departments. The Department for Policy Coordination and Sustainable Development was created under the direction of Under-Secretary General Desai. This department provides the full-time staff which services the CSD. The UN General Assembly has also asserted its pre-eminence in this field, a move it is entitled to make since all structures not accountable to the Security Council are ultimately accountable to UNGA. Agenda 21 specifically cites the Assembly as 'the highest level intergovernmental mechanism . . . the principal policy-making and appraisal organ on matters relating to the follow-up to the conference' (Agenda 21: 38, 9).

A recognition of the need to impose system-wide coordination in the pursuit of sustainable development persuaded the otherwise reluctant Anglo-Saxon delegations to endorse the creation of the aforementioned Commission on Sustainable Development (CSD). Charged with the role of following up the Rio Conference, both in the general sense of coordinating the UN's own organs and agencies' programmes for sustainable development and in a more formal, institutional sense, the CSD is thus responsible for organising the 1997 Review Conference for UNCED (Roddick and Dodds 1993).

The system-wide coordination of UN activities is both a long-standing and a frequently cited problem. It is in part a consequence of the illusion that the UN is an *actor*. In truth, only the *members* can coordinate their own activities – within organs which *they* have created. And the UN is, in fact, quite crowded with organs created for this purpose. The Administrative Committee on Coordination (ACC), the Committee of International Development Institutions on the Environment (CIDIE), the Designated Officers on Environmental Matters (DOEM) and (as already seen) both ECOSOC and UNEP were all originally mandated to undertake greater or lesser burdens of coordination (Bertrand 1988: 193–219; Taylor 1988: 220–36; Imber 1994: 107–8). Now these mechanisms have been joined by the CSD.

The fifty-three-member CSD was brought into being during 1993, and holds annual sessions each Spring. These sessions extend over two weeks, concluding with the so-called High Level Segment, conducted at a ministerial level prior to ECOSOC sessions. The CSD has adopted a programme of work which, over the five years remaining until the 1997 Review Conference, will review the member states' progress in the implementation of Agenda 21 (Imber 1994: 104–9). The CSD's programme has, like that of the UN Commission on Human Rights, adopted the practice of receiving national reports from the members as well as instigating cross-sectoral reviews of the Agenda 21 chapters.

Roddick has demonstrated that the CSD's prospects have been blunted by the indifference of two major constituencies. The large Southern states, such as China, Brazil and India, remain suspicious of the implications of national reporting, and generally fearful of 'anti-growth' environmentalism. Among the developed countries, the 'dirty old men', viz the USA, Russia and, some might add, France and the UK with their rhetorically supportive but practically hypocritical positions, have combined to deprive the CSD debates of major sponsors. The CSD's proponents, on the other hand, are the middle-sized and small Third World countries, and the committed 'green' developed countries such as Canada, the Netherlands, Germany and the Nordic countries – all aided by NGOs and the academic community (Roddick 1993: 13–14).

## THE LIMITATIONS OF THE UNITED NATIONS

The UN is both the best and the worst place in which to conduct environmental diplomacy. It is the best place because, it is the *only* global forum or arena in which norms and laws for the management of global environmental change can be negotiated. The UN is constituted as a global forum, it expressly recognises the legitimacy of the smallest and most vulnerable states and it has, over a half century of piecemeal reform, created machinery, such as ECOSOC, the CSD, UNEP and the UNDP, explicitly structured to promote and monitor the implementation of 'development' – redefined since 1992 in the language of 'sustainable development'. It is at the same time, however, the worst place in which to advance this essential project. Precisely because it is an organisation of member *states*, it does not include all of the stakeholders in the process of sustainable development. Despite elaborate provision for consultation and observer rights, the NGOs are not party to binding international conventions. Meanwhile, the fact that indigenous peoples, national minorities, women and youth are cited in Agenda 21 is a backhanded compliment only, one which recognises and institutionalises their marginalisation.

The UN's structure, comprising over thirty organs and sixteen autonomous specialised agencies, each responsible for programmes in fields as diverse as food, agriculture, labour, telecommunications, nuclear energy and industrial development, tends to encourage a sectoral approach to development. This inhibits the transition to sustainability. A sober appraisal of the restructuring that has been put in hand by the creation of the CSD would be, at best, sanguine. The UN structure is essentially feudal. It is more reminiscent of the weak authority of the sixteenth-century Scottish Stuart kings than it is of that of their English Tudor contemporaries, whose successful centralisation the UN only appears to mimic. In the UN, the centre (the king) is weak, while the agencies (the barons) are strong. Some barons, such as the World Bank, marshal ten times the resources of the centre.

Indeed, the entire United Nations system rests upon an inadequate financial base. The centrepiece funding proposal that emerged from Rio, namely the GEF, extends to barely $2 billion, at a time when post-Cold War military spending fell (in constant 1985 prices) from a 1985 peak of $770 billion to $582 billion in 1991 (IISS 1993: 218–21). The 1992 total of ODA extended by the OECD countries, namely $68 billion, is barely half of the target figure agreed two years ago in Agenda 21, namely $125 billion. (The South was required to contribute $475 billion of the $600-billion-per-annum budget of Agenda 21 (Agenda 21: 33, 18)). In 1992, Third World debt servicing ran at $148 billion, making a mockery of all attempts to fund sustainable development (OECD 1994: 62–4). Set against the ODA flow, the difference between aid payments to the South and debt repayments to the North ran at $80.8 billion in that year. Only by adding private investment flows and export credits totalling $91.9 billion did a positive transfer emerge. These statistics go some way to substantiating the assertion that the UN is an institutional bandage applied to a structural haemorrhage.

The political message that these figures convey is revealing. During the second Cold War (1979–89), the UN was denounced in certain quarters as politicised, overbudgeted and profligate (Moynihan 1979; Pines 1984). In the post-Cold War environment, the opportunity for the UN to be revived as an *arena* for North–South negotiation is in imminent danger of conceding to the alternative of its co-option as an *instrument* of those who would promote the marketised, globalised 'end of history'. The OECD countries, with notable Scandinavian and Dutch exceptions, will prove unwilling to fund the transition to sustainability, or to support the modest mechanisms of global governance which would assist that task.

Does this actually matter? In the UN's fiftieth-anniversary year, should we come to praise it or to bury it? Whilst it is true that the rhetoric of 'only one earth' suggests a need for the global governance of global environmental change, the cosmopolitan project of converting the UN into a supranational government is hardly credible, either now or in the foreseeable future. The imperfect prospect of an *inter*-national organisation of states, driven by 190 national administrations with varying levels of rhetorical commitment to sustainable development, does not set the heather on fire. Some environmental issues can be more readily managed on a regional level. Acid rain in North America and in Europe, international river systems such as the Zambezi, Nile and Niger systems in Africa, and water management in the Middle East are all examples of genuinely discreet, if not hermetically sealed, environmental problems. Despite the appeal of globalism, the obstacles to global consensus-building discussed above may actually *cause* delay and *excuse* inaction. This argument does not reduce the importance of pursuing UN mechanisms for the negotiation of genuinely global issues. Rather, it frees the UN from a bogus globalism which, anyway, is not consistent with the green imperative to 'think global, *act local*'. It would restore something of the flexibility formerly associated with the functionalist approach – 'binding together those interests which are common, where they are common and to the extent that they are common' (Mitrany 1966: 115–16). And it would free the UN to do what it can, as an arena or forum, to advance the normative and legal case for sustainable development. Rather than either vacuous praise or the cynical burial of the UN, the only politically realistic path is that of constant agitation for reform. There is no shortage of proposals for the democratisation of the UN, for the enlargement of the Security Council and for schemes to provide sources of independent finance (by levies on defence expenditure and international airline travel, by the taxation of transnational corporations, etc.). The test for the UN (and indeed for the functional or institutional paradigm) is whether *any* liberal project can overcome the arithmetic of the structural disadvantage revealed by the continuing impact of Third World poverty and debt. That cannot occur until the protection of the global commons and the large-scale relief of debt, funded by the scope for defence conversion that has already been shown to exist, are both recognised by the OECD countries as integral elements, rather than optional extras, in the definition of sustainable development.

## NOTES

1 The reader is directed to M. Thacher in Hurrell and Kingsbury 1992, and to Birnie in Roberts and Kingsbury 1993, for a comprehensive treatment of the UN's full institutional activities. A more comprehensive treatment of UNEP is contained in

McCormick 1989 and in Imber 1993a, 1993b and 1994. For more detailed reviews of the post-UNCED issues, see also Grubb *et al.* 1994, and Thomas 1992 and 1994.

2 For a more elaborate explanation of the prisoner's dilemma, see Axelrod 1990; and for 'free-riding' and externalities, see Imber 1992, 1994: 13–15. Both areas provide examples of conditions in which individually rational behaviour can create negative outcomes not just for society at large but also ultimately for *those individuals whose anti-social actions create the problem.* They are central to understanding the problems faced both by the public sector and by market forces in providing adequate levels of environmental protection. Public-sector provision will always tend to fall short of the level of service that voters claim to desire because actors (whether individual tax-payers, corporations or sovereign states) will seek to avoid bearing their full share of costs and regulation. On the other hand, by definition, the market can only detect and respond to changes in prices. As environmental quality (e.g. clean air) and the global commons (e.g. the climate system) and both mostly zero-priced, and many internal costs can be externalised (e.g. by pollution discharge), 'the market', in its Thatcherite form, is largely incapable of assigning prices and hence controlling environmental damage. This has led to many attempts to adapt taxation, permits and other devices in such a way as to allow the assignment of 'market values' to environmental quality. (See Pearce *et al.* 1989: *passim*; Grubb 1990: 67–89; Beckerman 1990.)

3 Functionalism is usually attributed to the writings of David Mitrany (1948, 1966 and 1975), but see also Taylor and Groom 1975, Claude 1964 and Imber 1984 and 1989. For an extensive criticism of Mitrany's scheme, see McLaren 1985. On the preferred vocabulary of 'institutionalism' and the case for the hegemonic origins of functional cooperation, see Keohane 1984: 8–9. See also chapters by Williams and by Paterson in this volume.

## BIBLIOGRAPHY

Archer, C. (1983) *International Organisations*, London: Unwin.

Axelrod, R. (1990) *The Evolution of International Cooperation*, London: Penguin.

Baylis, J. and Rengger, N. (eds) (1992) *Dilemmas of World Politics: International Issues in a Changing World*, Oxford: O.U.P.

Beckerman, W. (1990) *Pricing for Pollution*, London: Institute for Economic Affairs.

Bertrand, M. (1988) 'Some reflections on the reform of the United Nations', in Taylor, P. and Groom, A.J. (eds) *International Institutions at Work*, London: Pinter.

Brundtland, G. (1987) 'Report of the World Commission on Environment and Development', *Our Common Future*, Oxford: O.U.P.

Claude, I. (1964) *Swords into Plowshares*, New York: Random House.

Deudney, D. (1990) 'The case against linking environmental degradation and national security', *Millennium: Journal of International Studies* 19: 461–76.

Doran, P. (1993) 'The Earth Summit (UNCED): ecology as spectacle', *Paradigms* 7: 55–66.

George, S. (1992) *The Debt Boomerang*, Boulder, Col.: Westview.

—— (1990) 'The greenhouse effect: negotiating targets', *International Affairs* 66: 67–89.

Grubb, M. *et al.* (1994) *The Earth Summit Agreements*, London: RIIA.

Haas, E. (1964) *Beyond the Nation State*, Stanford, Cal.: Stanford U.P.

Hardin, G. (1968) 'The tragedy of the commons', *Science* 162: 1243–8.

Hurrell, A. and Kingsbury, B. (eds) (1992) *The International Politics of the Environment*, Oxford: Clarendon.

Imber, M.F. (1984) 'Re-reading Mitrany: a pragmatic assessment of sovereignty', *Review of International Studies* 10(2): 103–24.

—— (1989) *The USA, ILO, UNESCO and IAEA*, Basingstoke: Macmillan.

—— (1992) 'International Organisations', in Baylis, J. and Rengger, N. (eds) (1992) *Dilemmas of World Politics*, Oxford: O.U.P.

—— (1993a) 'Too many cooks? The post-Rio reform of the United Nations', *International Affairs* 69(1): 55–70.

—— (1993b) 'The UN role in sustainable development', *Environmental Politics* 2(4): 123–36.

—— (1994) *The Environment, Security and UN Reform*, Basingstoke: Macmillan.

International Institute of Strategic Studies (1993) *The Military Balance*, London: IISS.

Jacobson, H. (1979) *Networks of Interdependence*, New York: Alfred A. Knopf.

Keohane, R. (1984) *After Hegemony: Cooperation and Discord in the World Political Economy*, Princeton, NJ: Princeton U.P.

—— and Nye, J.S. (1977) *Power and Interdependence*, New York: Little, Brown.

McCormick, J. (1989) *The International Environmental Movement: Reclaiming Paradise*, London: Belhaven.

McLaren, R. (1985) 'Mitranian functionalism: possible or impossible?', *Review of International Studies* 11(2): 139–52.

Martell, L. (1994) *Ecology and Society*, Cambridge: Polity.

Meadows, D. *et al.* (1983) *The Limits to Growth*, London: Pan.

Middleton, N., O'Keefe, P. and Moyo, S. (1994) *Tears of the Crocodile: From Rio to Reality in the Developing World*, London: Pluto.

Miller, M. (1991) *Debt and the Environment*, New York: United Nations.

Mitrany, D. (1948) 'The functional approach to world organisation', *International Affairs* 24: 350–61.

—— (1966) *A Working Peace System*, Chicago: Quadrangle.

—— (1975) *The Functional Theory of Politics*, London: Martin Robertson.

Moynihan, D.P. (1979) *A Dangerous Place*, London: Secker & Warburg.

New Economics Foundation (NEF) (1994) *Indicators for Sustainable Development*, London: NEF and World Wide Fund for Nature.

OECD (1994) *Development Cooperation, Aid in Transition, 1993 Report*, Paris: OECD.

Paterson, M. and Grubb, M. (1992) 'The international politics of climate change', *International Affairs* 68: 293–310.

Pearce, D. *et al.* (1989) *Blueprint for a Green Economy*, London: Earthscan.

Pines, B.Y. (ed.) (1984) *A World Without the UN*, Washington, DC: Heritage Foundation.

Roberts, A. and Kingsbury, B. (eds) (1993) *United Nations, Divided World*, Oxford: Clarendon.

Roddick, J. (1993) 'UNCED, its stakeholders and the post-UNCED process', Glasgow: Institute of Latin American Studies.

—— and Dodds, F. (1993) 'Agenda 21's political strategy', *Environmental Politics* 2: 242–8.

Saetevik, S. (1988) *Environmental Cooperation Between North Sea States*, London: Belhaven.

Sanger, C. (1986) *Ordering the Oceans*, London: Zed.

Smith, S. (1993) 'Environment on the periphery of international relations: an explanation', *Environmental Politics* 2(4): 28–45.

Taylor, P. (1988) 'Reforming the system: getting the money to talk', in Taylor, P. and Groom, A.J. (eds) *International Institutions at Work*, London: Pinter.

—— and Groom, A.J. (eds) (1975) *Functionalism*, London: London U.P.

—— and Groom, A.J. (eds) (1988) *International Institutions at Work*, London: Pinter.

Thomas, C. (1992) *The Environment in International Relations*, London: Royal Institute of International Affairs.

—— (ed.) (1994) *Rio: Unravelling the Consequences*, London: Cass.

United Nations (1972) *Final Report of the Stockholm Conference*, New York: UN.

—— (1993) 'Agenda 21', The United Nations Programme of Action from Rio, New York: UN. (This combined volume includes the texts of Agenda 21, the Rio Declaration, and the Statement of Forestry Principles.)

United States General Accounting Office (USGAO) (1989) *US Participation in the Environment Program*, Washington, DC: USGAO.

Vallely, P. (1990) *Bad Samaritans*, London: Hodder & Stoughton.

von Weizsacker, E. (1994) *Earth Politics*, London: Zed Books.

# 9 Between the devil and the law of the sea

## The generation of global environmental norms

*Roderick Ogley*

Global environmental norms can be defined as changes made and constraints accepted in the behaviour, habits and practices of human actors – states, firms, individuals or others – as a result of beliefs as to the disadvantages that would otherwise follow for the (global) environment. We can think of such norms as commodities – abstract, invisible commodities like insurance. The likelihood of a given norm arising – being 'produced' – will, as with other commodities, depend on the interaction of supply and demand. The demand side is concerned with such questions as: what environmental consequences are we threatened with, and what changes or constraints are needed to avert them, either wholly or to any specified degree? And on the supply side, we ask: how are such norms generated – in other words, what circumstances, arrangements, etc., are conducive to the adoption, worldwide, of such behavioural restraints? This chapter concentrates on the analysis of the 'supply side'.

We are, then, concerned with how norms are produced. Given a willingness on the part of the relevant actor(s) to devote resources – money, attention, personnel – to the creation of norms in a certain field, and given that this has a cost, in that resources so devoted become unavailable for other uses to which they might have been put, we can delineate the choices that have to be made in the process of norm-generation, attempt to assess the productivity of each and ask whether there are critical points at which a small additional commitment of resources could have a major impact, either on whether a norm is generated at all or on how scrupulously this norm is observed.

Of course, every process of norm-generation is unique. The threat with which it purports to deal is likely to be in some respects different from any preceding threat. Again, and particularly at the global level, any given episode of attempted norm-generation will be approached with some awareness, differing for different actors, of the fate of previous attempts at norm generation, whether in the same or in different fields. Such actors' responses will be affected by what they have learnt, or think they have learnt, from these earlier instances, which again will differ for different actors.

All this creates formidable obstacles to the development of a solidly based discipline, let alone a science, of 'supply-side diplomatics', or norm-generation, particularly when we remember that, logically, the productivity we are concerned with is to be measured not in terms of legal commitments incurred but in terms of behaviour modifications – how much less 'polluting' of any given kind we actually do, in comparison with what we would have done. We also need to bear in mind how great a transformation may have occurred in the ease with which agreements might now be reached as a result of changes in the international political system such as the disintegration both of the USSR and of communism within its constituent, now independent, republics. Technical developments, too, like the invention of the fax, may be pertinent to comparisons over time in respect of the effectiveness of norm-generation, since agreements ought to be easier to reach when delegates can transmit proposals and other documents *immediately*, in full, to foreign offices.

Nevertheless, these considerations should not rule out an attempt both to understand the other options open to would-be norm-generators and to examine the assumptions on which each of these rests. Tentative though any conclusions will have to be, they may still be useful if they lead to a critical scrutiny of the rationale by which decision-makers tend to choose between these different options.

We shall begin by looking at some of the main options set out by scholars in the field. We will then briefly speculate about the processes involved in negotiations, applying a crucial distinction prompted by conflict theory. Next, we will speculate about some of the major factors in norm production, and see if we can trace their influence in recent attempts at the generation of global environmental norms. Finally, we will focus on the most conspicuous of these attempts, the United Nations Conference on Environment and Development (UNCED) at Rio in 1992, and assess how well it was designed for its purpose.

## THE OPTIONS: FRAMEWORK CONVENTIONS OR PACKAGE DEALS?

Hurrell and Kingsbury, in their introduction (1992: 18), sharply contrast the 'framework convention and protocols' format with the 'single package deal approach' by which, at the Third United Nations Conference on the Law of the Sea (UNCLOS III), the 1982 Law of the Sea Convention came to be adopted. The advantage, they clearly imply, lies with the former, and they invoke Elliot Richardson's chapter on climate change as supporting that judgement. Since Richardson led the US delegation to UNCLOS III throughout the Carter Administration, when US policy was at its most accommodating towards the developing countries, his opinion carries much weight, but on closer examination of his article it seems rather less clear-cut than the editors suggest, and, as they go on to remind us, one of the other contributions, by Lawrence Susskind and Connie Ozawa, emphasises some of the 'potential drawbacks to the convention-protocol approach', as currently practised. Relying on a study, not easily obtainable in the UK, of nine cases of international environmental negotiations, it offers nine recommendations for improving on that approach as it has been practised (Susskind and Ozawa 1992: 155–64).

In some contrast, another scholar, Douglas Johnston, argues that, at least within the field of marine pollution, the legislative side of norm-generation, though it has yielded forty separate 'clusters' of conventions and associated instruments, has been disappointing in its long-term results. Global agreements have proved particularly difficult, and 'the economic and technological assumptions underlying them are not infrequently open to question, if not clearly invalid' by the time they come into force. In his view, the 'success' of such diplomacy depends, above all, on the 'political skills of the relevant technical elites – *los tecnicos*', and what is now needed is not more agreements (except in one or two areas such as hazardous substances) but the integration of existing treaty-based arrangements at the regional level (Johnston 1988: 205) – a plea for a depoliticisation of issues in accordance with the best traditions of functionalism! These comments are valuable in reminding us that legislation is not the only important part of the process of norm-generation.

Nevertheless, global law-making (including the development of 'soft' law) *is* important in the environmental field, and the arguments of Hurrell and Kingsbury need to be understood and addressed. In proclaiming the superiority of the 'framework convention-protocol' approach over that of the 'package deal', they adduce UNCLOS III as the classic case of the latter and both the Geneva Convention on Long-Range Transboundary Air Pollution ('acid rain') of 1979 and – 'with certain improvements' – the 1985 Vienna Convention for the Protection of the Ozone Layer as exemplifying the former (Hurrell and Kingsbury 1992: 16–17).

Reviewing the account given of the ozone-layer negotiations by the chief US delegate (Benedick 1991), Fiona McConnell, who led the UK delegation, agrees that they were remarkable in the speed with which they produced a ratified treaty 'setting out concrete and legally-binding targets for reducing ozone-depleting chemicals'. In addition, the treaty enabled these targets to be made more stringent by subsequent 'meetings of the parties', allowed developing countries to be brought in on easy terms and with the prospect of financial compensation, and permitted sanctions to be taken by the parties to deter trade in the relevant substances with outsiders. It is now, McConnell says, 'being hailed as a model for new environmental treaties' (McConnell 1991: 320). Even allowing for parental pride, their enthusiasm seems well founded, although the problem it addresses is reportedly worse than was first thought – a 'demand-side' development outside the scope of this chapter.

Nor is it easy to dispute the implied characterisation of UNCLOS III as a diplomatic horror story. Far from being a model for subsequent global conferences, it led one commentator, generally sympathetic to its purposes, to assert:

> The General Assembly should *never again* convene a conference of the size and complexity of the Third Conference on the Law of the Sea. As a decision mechanism it is absurd and in its size and complexity imposes demands on delegates which in their totality are quite beyond the competence of human beings to manage.
>
> (Miles 1975: 40)

That comment came after only the first substantive session of UNCLOS III, at Caracas in 1974. It took ten such sessions to adopt a treaty, absorbing in all ninety-three weeks of diplomatic time, not counting a series of important, though informal, 'inter-sessionals'. There had, moreover, been six years of deliberations in the General Assembly, and its Sea-Bed Committee, between the inscription of the item that gave rise to the treaty on the Assembly's agenda in 1967 and the opening of UNCLOS III, formally in 1973 and substantively in 1974.

In the end, the Convention it produced was not accepted by three of the states whose support was most critical to the success of its most innovative and controversial feature, the regime to govern sea-bed mining. The three recalcitrant states were the USA, the UK and Germany. Though it eventually, on 16 November 1993, received the sixtieth ratification, that of Guyana, needed to bring it into force one year later, no states with sea-bed mining capacity were among its parties, and, after an initiative taken by the UN's then Secretary-General, Javier Pérez de Cuéllar, in 1990, involving 'informal consultations with key persons in both developed and developing countries' (Birnie 1994: 1), the UN General Assembly, on 28 July 1994, adopted, by 121 votes to none with seven abstentions including Russia, an Agreement whose effect was to transform the sea-bed mining provisions of the Convention virtually beyond recognition.[1]

If such 'informal consultations' in the early 1990s can produce workable agreement on all these issues, where UNCLOS III, with all its protracted sessions and procedural ingenuity, could not, the latter's futility, with respect to the creation of a regime to govern sea-bed mining in the interests of mankind – which was the purpose for which the whole process was ostensibly launched in 1967 – becomes even less disputable.

Susskind and Ozawa do not mention UNCLOS III. Their focus is on the 'convention-protocol' approach. They concede that this approach can create momentum. Governments initially unwilling or unable to commit themselves to specific pollution-reducing targets might be encouraged to 'sign on' if the initial commitment is only to monitoring and research, and might later be ready (or be persuaded by domestic opinion) to take such remedial action as the research suggests may be required. The two authors also allow that the very signing of a convention can boost the campaigns of the relevant environment-protection groups in the country (Susskind and Ozawa 1992: 146).

What, then, is wrong with this approach? It is, they say, a 'time-consuming process' (but so was UNCLOS III!). They also claim that it tends to be dominated by the most powerful states, and that, as a result, the conventions that flow from it are weakened to satisfy those most opposed to effective action, instancing, in this case more persuasively, the Basel Convention on the Control of Transboundary Movements of Hazardous Wastes. They also point to the danger that, at the 'framework' or 'convention' stage, decisions may be made on political grounds which are technically untenable, such as the exclusion of Romania and Bulgaria from the Barcelona Convention on the Mediterranean. They see flaws, too, in the Ozone Layer Convention of 1985, both because 'firm limits' (for reductions) were not set until the first of its protocols was adopted at Montreal in

1987 (which was perhaps not a defect at all but good diplomatic strategy!) and because of the inadequate incentives which even the Montreal Protocol offered large developing states, and particularly India and China, to induce them to associate themselves with the system, a defect they admit, however, to have been remedied by the London Amendments of 1990 (Susskind and Ozawa 1992: 148–52).

Their nine recommendations for improving on the convention-protocol approach were: first, 'empowering non-traditional clusters of countries' to caucus well ahead of formal negotiations; second, helping poorer countries to prepare for negotiations; third, encouraging the devising of multiple alternative proposals, not involving any official commitment, before getting down to treaty-drafting; fourth, expanding the role of non-governmental organisations (NGOs); fifth, recategorising countries to enhance the perception of fairness by not prescribing the same obligations for all (they do not explain the ends–means link here); sixth, ensuring the continued input of scientific research not tied to national purposes, and allowing for a variety of commitments, each predicated on a different future, so that the correction of policy appropriate to new knowledge can be built into the system; seventh, encouraging 'appropriate' linkages – for instance between subsidies on energy-efficient technologies and commitments to $CO_2$-emission reductions; eighth, encouraging unilateral actions by setting a baseline year from the beginning and agreeing to 'count' all action taken after that baseline towards whatever targets may in the end be negotiated; and finally, involving the mass media in negotiations, making data banks available to them, and honouring those journalists that make outstanding contributions to public enlightenment on the issues in question (Susskind and Ozawa 1992: 155–63).

Several of these recommendations have a whiff of UNCLOS III about them. That conference certainly fostered the spawning of 'non-traditional clusters of countries' (Recommendation 1), whose only point of unity was the common interest they had in some issue or set of issues before the conference. Among these were the groups of Land-Locked and Geographically-Disadvantaged States, of Archipelagic States, of Broad Shelf States and of Straits States. The building-in of sets of alternative responses to alternative futures (Recommendation 6) is found in at least two features of the sea-bed mining regime of the Law of the Sea Convention as adopted in 1982, one being the financial terms of contracts, mentioned earlier, and the other the criteria governing the imposition of a limit on sea-bed production. Both have now gone, so, sensible though this recommendation is, the case for it is not strengthened by the experience of UNCLOS III. The latter's leisurely, some would say glacial, pace also afforded plenty of scope for suggestions to be put to the conference (or to informal cross-cutting groupings within it, such as the Evensen Group) as *suggestions only*, rather than as proposed treaty clauses (Recommendation 3).

UNCLOS III may not be the only conference exhibiting these features. What makes the resemblance particularly striking – uncannily so if UNCLOS III is not one of the nine cases examined in their fuller study – is Recommendation 7, advocating linkages between different issues. Linkage in the example cited earlier would be logical, but a linkage between environmental negotiations and 'other international issues such as debt, trade and security', which they also advocate at one point (Susskind and Ozawa 1992: 153), must amount to something very like an UNCLOS III-style 'package deal'.

At UNCLOS III, it was agreed at the outset that only one convention would emerge from the conference, and that it would be comprehensive. Thus each party insisted ad nauseam that if it agreed to anything at all on any item or sub-item of the agenda, that was conditional on the convention that would eventually emerge being, as a whole, acceptable to it. So, supposedly, the overall package was absolutely indispensable if UNCLOS III were to yield any fruits at all.

The implicit overall package was this: maritime powers – those, broadly, that tended to use the seas adjacent to other states' coasts – faced with a revolutionary trend, initiated by the Latin Americans, to deny them almost all their traditional rights for at least 200 miles from land, sought a modus vivendi, a way of preserving their right to use these newly coastal seas, if not to fish in them. In return, in their capacity as potential sea-bed-mining states – a category which almost coincided, in its membership, with that of 'maritime powers' – they agreed in principle that, were they to be assured of access to sites of their choice, they would conduct their sea-bed-mining operations under global management, in such a way as to yield revenues for the global community, and even enable the proposed international sea bed authority to go into the mining business itself, on suitable sites and with appropriate technology afforded by private (and state) sea-bed miners. They acknowledged, in other words, that the minerals of the *international* area of the sea bed belonged to 'mankind' as a whole; they were not just free for anyone to take without payment in any manner they chose. Regulation, inspection and taxation by the international sea-bed authority were seen as the price to be paid for the benefits that the parties involved would reap from the more orderly world that a generally accepted convention would tend to promote.

As UNCLOS III went on, however, some mini-packages began to emerge. In theory, their acceptability depended on that of the convention in which they were embodied; in practice, however, it did not, and, as it was controversially claimed, they became 'instant customary law'. In this way the USA, though rejecting the convention, was not thereby inhibited from claiming rights it would have enjoyed under it. UNCLOS III, even before it came into force, may thus be said to have generated effective norms; but the unacknowledged nature of this process not only helped to protract the conference into the inhospitality of the Reagan era but also left a legacy of frustration and resentment in those whose valiant attempts to reach consensus on the comprehensive convention to which it was officially dedicated were thus seemingly nullified.

Susskind and Ozawa, therefore, seem to be arguing, it appears unconsciously, for a rehabilitation of UNCLOS III as a model for global norm-generation. Elliot Richardson, too, is far less dismissive than his editors imply of the conference in which he was so heavily involved, acknowledging that it 'pioneered negotiating procedures that will serve the environment no less well than they served the oceans', and mentioning both the 'single negotiating text' procedure that it 'so successfully' employed and the provisions of the convention that obliges parties to observe 'generally-accepted international environmental rules, regulations and standards adopted through the competent international organisation' (Richardson 1992: 169–72).[2]

To summarise, UNCLOS III differed from the framework convention-protocol approach, exemplified by the ozone-layer negotiations, in at least eight ways. It was launched by the UN General Assembly, not by a technical body like UNEP; it had an extremely broad agenda; it was committed to arriving at a single comprehensive convention; it included, from its inception *as a conference*,[3] practically every state in the world; among its many tasks was the complicated and recalcitrant one of setting up a new and innovative global body, the international sea-bed authority; it punctuated its 'informal' sessions with fairly regular public debates; it contained elaborate provisions, never as such used, to ensure that no votes were taken before every effort had been made to achieve consensus; and it relied, for the drafting of compromise texts, on committee chairmen, appointed on political and geographical grounds, rather than on international civil servants.

## NEGOTIATIONS – GAMES OR DEBATES?

It is at this point that conflict theory can contribute to the analysis. In an earlier book (Ogley 1991), the author elaborated on Rapoport's distinction between 'games' and 'debates' (Rapoport 1960). In a 'game', each party is trying to maximise its own payoff in terms of its interests and preferences, and does not expect the other party's interests or preferences to change. In a 'debate', each party believes its policy to be based on some important truth which it must make others see and act on, because it is, or should be, a truth for them as well as for itself. In a game, the question is: what incentives – carrots and sticks – can you devise for others so that it becomes rational for them, in terms of their original preferences, to do what you want them to do? In a debate, it is: how can you induce others to see the world as you see it?

Susskind and Ozawa tend to talk about international environmental diplomacy as if it were essentially a debate, *except* when they discuss 'linkages'. Linkages imply bargains, and thus games. If you agree to my getting X, which I want and you would rather not concede to me but are prepared to if necessary, I will agree to your getting Y, which you want and which I am prepared to let you have, though I would have preferred not to. In negotiations conceived of as games, it makes no sense to provide assistance for other parties with whom one expects to be bargaining, since it will merely help them to drive a harder bargain; in those conceived of as debates, however, this would be useful, because it would help other parties to understand the truths that you have discovered. Also, like legal aid for a defendant, it would ensure that, by presenting aspects both of the situation and of the needs of the other party that might not have come out had it not been properly advised, the body that has to decide the issue is in a better position to reach an appropriate conclusion. In contrast, Susskind and Ozawa claim:

> Convention writing and protocol writing are usually treated as zero-sum games. By the time countries come together to negotiate treaty language, they have usually locked into certain fixed positions. Little if any creative problem-solving is possible. When agreements do emerge, they are usually the result of compromise by the most powerful parties rather than the result of the creative resolution of differences.
>
> (Susskind and Ozawa 1992: 151)

The term 'zero-sum game' is here, as so often, used inaccurately. In a truly zero-sum game, there could be no point in negotiations. What they mean is that the parties are usually assumed to be on the 'contract curve', that is, in a situation where there is no way that the proposals under discussion could be improved for all parties. Each party, they allege, imagines that any amendment to its own proposal which would benefit some other party must impose some cost, or reduction of benefit, to itself – a very closed-minded stance, which seems unlikely to hold literally for any category of genuine negotiations. Certainly, in negotiations about aspects of the environment, where the facts are often novel and not easy to appraise, one would expect to find a 'debate' element. But can such negotiations ever be *pure* debate? Is there not always also an element of 'game', because at least some countries' interests are opposed to those of other countries? Can one really believe that, if environmental negotiations are treated as debates, the game element will go away?

The 'acid rain' negotiations would provide a good test of this. Game theory would lead one to expect that, since some states allegedly 'export' acid rain, while others suffer from 'importing' it, effective norm-creation would be unlikely since the former, who need to act on it, would have no incentive to. Regarded as a 'debate', and bearing in mind that, for the most part, 'victim' countries are democracies with outlooks and values similar to those of the allegedly emitting countries, the acid-rain issue ought to be relatively easy to resolve. It is surely possible to determine whether such transboundary pollution does occur; and if it does, how could there be any serious objection to stopping it?

Assessments of the current state of play on this issue differ. Porter and Brown report an unsatisfactory situation where the chief alleged emitters, the USA in North America and the UK in Europe, have successfully resisted the adoption of effective remedies (Porter and Brown 1991). Nigel Haigh, on the other hand, commends the outcome of the process initiated by the change in German policy in 1982 (itself a subject worthy of further study in the context of this chapter), reporting that differentiated percentage reductions have been agreed for different members which will, by 2003, reduce aggregate emissions from EC countries by 58 per cent, and claiming that this agreement on a differentiated reduction could be 'a better model for the global warming issue across the world than the uniform reduction agreed for ozone-depleting substances', thus echoing Susskind and Ozawa's Recommendation 5 (Haigh 1992: 238).[4] Another case of a change of heart, where interests were sharply opposed, occurred on the question of mining Antarctica. Susskind and Ozawa seem to be saying that the convention-protocol approach is less conducive than others to the transcendence of 'games' and the flowering of the 'debate' element, a contention which needs more support, both in theory and in historical observation, than they give it in their Hurrell and Kingsbury chapter.

## FACTORS IN THE GENERATION OF GLOBAL ENVIRONMENTAL NORMS

Let us now list what seem to be the 'factors of production' involved both in the global norm-producing industry and, in particular, in the generation of *environmental* norms.

One is generality of participation. Those whose policies or behaviour the norm is to change or at least constrain must have their say – not necessarily a veto – in the process of articulating it.

A second is external legitimacy: the extent to which a proposed norm can be seen as governed by some internationally accepted principle such as 'the common heritage of mankind' (in the case of the sea-bed negotiations) or the 'precautionary principle' (in the case of serious but as yet only hypothetical climatic or atmospheric hazards).

Third, there is *internal* legitimacy: the extent to which conformity with the norm is likely to be reinforced – or resisted – by the pressures of domestic opinion groups.

Fourth, there is flexibility, including responsiveness to feedback. Norms whose precise content can be adjusted in the light of new knowledge and new situations will tend to command more respect.

Finally, specificity seems important, since the actors concerned must, surely, know what their obligations are before they can meet them, but this is not always either sufficient or necessary. There could hardly be a more specific (indirect) norm than that set out in Article 25 of the United Nations Charter, obliging all members to accept and carry out the decisions of the Security Council; but who could claim that it has been effective? By contrast, the vaguely sub-Keynesian, but market-oriented, norms developed by the Organisation for Economic Co-operation and Development (OECD) in its early years, and by its predecessor the OEEC, buttressed by expert critiques – coming from inside the organisation and from other members – of each state's policies, seem to have acquired considerable influence and effectiveness. We should not rule out a role for Johnston's *los tecnicos* in the development of environmental norms.

These factors may often point in opposing directions. For instance, if (in the tradition of Woodrow Wilson) we are to rely on public opinion to put the brakes on norm violations by governments, citizens need to be able to identify with the norm in question and to be able to see when it is being broken. We need simple, appealing and lasting norms. Scientific advances, however, may require norms to be complicated and to change rapidly. There is a parallel here with the dilemmas posed by global norms in the field of health.

There do indeed, then, seem to be two fairly distinct formulae for norm-generation in the realm of the environment. One operates through networks of *los tecnicos*, aiming at technically workable agreements, responsiveness (which need not be uncritical!) to new scientific findings, effective monitoring and only a minimum degree of inclusiveness (since the smaller the number of participants, the smoother these processes will operate). The other works through quasi-universal political commitment, induced by well-publicised global conferences like UNCLOS III and UNCED; however, it may be that what gives a given deliberation salience is neither its venue nor the institution promoting it but the *issue* with which it deals.

Among recent cases, the two most notable successes for environmental norm-generation, other than that concerned with the ozone layer, appear to have been the adoption of a fifty-year moratorium on mining in Antarctica in 1991 and the transformation of the International Whaling Commission (IWC) from an associ-ation of whaling states supposedly dedicated to determining and sharing out the sustainable catch into one attempting to institute a complete ban on the activity. The first of these developments seems attributable to the persistence with which Australia opposed American proposals to open up the continent for mining. Since the agreement of all the Consultative Parties is required before any decision can be taken under the Antarctica Treaty, each has a veto. Australia's use of hers, combined with the success of America's environmental groups in alerting American public opinion to what was being proposed in their name, managed to bring about what amounted to virtually a total reversal of the latter country's policy. The second followed the simple device of an influx of non-whaling states, under US leadership, into the International Whaling Commission, until its policy, determined by a majority vote, became anti-whaling instead of the opposite. In both cases, as well as in that of aerosols within the ozone-layer negotiations, the state leading the campaign to ban an activity first unilaterally renounced it for itself. In the case of whaling, the USA backed up this ban by unilaterally imposing trade sanctions on states that objected to the IWC's ban on commercial whaling, at a time when such objections were perfectly legal (Birnie 1992: 74).[5]

Another feature of both the Antarctica and the whaling cases is what might be called institutional opportunism. Here, the existing procedures of an organisation are used in ways not contemplated at its initiation. The joint World Health Organisation/United Nations Children's Fund (WHO/UNICEF) code of conduct on baby milk of 1981, though hardly qualifying as an environmental issue, exhibits a similar pattern. After three years unavailing resistance to powerful consumer pressure, Nestlé, its main target, agreed to comply with the code (Sikkink 1986: 815). This potent norm-generating decision was adopted by WHO as a 'recommendation', with no legal force. At the International Health Conference of 1946 which set up WHO, although considerable time was spent on debating by what modes, and in what fields, WHO could make regulations that could become legally binding on members, the seemingly innocuous capacity to make 'recommendations' went through practically on the nod. These three cases remind us that organisations, including the very rudimentary 'consultations' and 'meetings of the parties' associated with some treaties like that for Antarctica, are liable to have a life of their own. UNEP, as we have seen, also played a part in the ozone-layer negotiations that was probably critical, though more straightforward than in the three preceding cases. The fact that UNEP's Executive Director, Mostafa Tolba, seems to have been able to present the negotiators with texts that made good scientific sense as well as being attuned to the diplomatic possibilities of the moment, is one reason why these negotiations were more productive than those in UNCLOS III, where the need to allocate committee chairmanships among the regional groups in the name of 'equitable geographical representation' produced at least one chairman seemingly incapable of performing this innovative role reliably and uncontroversially (Ogley 1984: 72–4).

Are we, then, left between the devil and the law of the sea in seeking to generate global norms? Not quite. The major international conference might work, provided that it is not organised on the principle of a package deal – not committed, that is, to arriving at a single convention whose benefits are supposedly confined to its parties. In any case, constructing a convention whose benefits are reserved only for those party to it is quite hard for environmental questions, since environmental improvement tends to be a 'public good'.

## RIO – AN ASSESSMENT

The Rio 'Earth Summit' of June 1992 at least avoided the 'package deal' hazard. Stanley Johnson describes the 'global bargain' which it 'failed, some would say failed dismally, to strike' as 'certainly one of [its] underlying objectives', though an unrealistic one which was far from 'ever being on the table at Rio' (Johnson 1993: 5). If the 'global bargain' *was* such an objective, at least the failure to achieve it did not condemn Rio's other fruits to the fate of either withering or being plucked illegally. The Framework Convention on Climate Change, the Biodiversity Convention, the Rio Declaration, the Authoritative Statement of Forest Principles and Agenda 21 are not linked extraneously in the sense that a state that supports one is required to support the others. One striking feature of UNCED, indeed, was the fact that these fruits, such as they were, had grown on three different trees: the Climate Change Convention emerged from the Intergovernmental Negotiating Committee (INC) which was appointed by the General Assembly in 1990 and whose work was grafted onto the work of the Intergovernmental Panel on Climate Change created, with US support, at the insistence of the World Meteorological Organisation (WMO) rather than UNEP, although with input from the latter – and from the International Council of Scientific Unions (ICSU); the Biodiversity Convention sprang from another Intergovernmental Negotiating Committee (INC), this time set up by UNEP originally as an 'Ad Hoc Working Group of Legal and Technical Experts' following a US call, in 1987, for a comprehensive convention on the subject (Grubb *et al.* 1993: 75). The Rio Declaration, Agenda 21 and the Forest Principles came out of UNCED itself and its Preparatory Committee, both created by the UN General Assembly's Resolution 44/228 of 22 December 1989. This diplomatic biodiversity perhaps in itself merits conservation.

Four desiderata might be posited for any major international conference designed to generate global environmental norms.

First, the lead time between the commitment to such a conference and its actually being held should be carefully calculated. It should be long enough to permit the negotiation of such conventions and other statements of global policy as the major states can be induced to agree to; and while the fruits of these negotiations would need to be subjected to public scrutiny at the conference itself, and while all states would need to be able to have their say in them, it should allow the negotiations themselves to be pursued away from the limelight. On the other hand, the lead time should not be so great that such initial enthusiasm for agreement as there may be is dissipated or diverted into appealing side-issues.[6]

For all three sets of negotiations, UNCED provided a deadline. The allegedly 'extremely bad-tempered and confused' final Nairobi meeting of the Biodiversity INC (Brenton 1994: 203), denied the bromides of barbecues and square-dancing with which any potential for excitability in the ozone-layer negotiations was sedated (Benedick 1991: 49), suggests that in this case the timing was about right. At any rate, an agreed text was adopted, in time for the conference, on 22 May 1992. The Climate Change Convention negotiations, on the other hand, seem to have gone backwards. The first session of its INC, in February 1991, met in Washington – the fact that it had been invited there being itself an indicator of American support – and heard the US delegate, Michael Deland, promise that his country *would* stabilise 'greenhouse-gas' emissions (which include, but of course are not confined to, carbon-dioxide emissions) at or below 1987 levels by 2000. At Rio, the USA made it a condition of signing the Climate Change Convention that no target dates were set for the stabilisation of carbon-dioxide emissions. Here, the lead time may well have been too long.

Second, the conference should attract the attention, however briefly, of the world's political leaders. That might help to give 'external legitimacy' to its proceedings. Their actual attendance would make it possible, if not likely, that something they see or hear there, informally or formally, would sow the seeds in some of them of an enhanced hospitality towards environmental considerations.

Third, there should be some institutional follow-up, to monitor the extent to which the conference's conventions and other declarations of intent have been translated into changes in habits and practices. In this respect, UNCED itself must be judged in terms of the Sustainable Development Commission (SDC), but it should also be borne in mind that the two conventions each provide a conference for the parties to meet regularly. These conferences, among other things, are given the power to adopt amendments to the convention, or to any protocol agreed in connection with it, by consensus if possible, but 'in the last resort' by a majority – three-quarters in the case of the Climate Change Convention, two-thirds in the case of the Biodiversity one. This is a significant power – or could be – but the parties to the original convention or protocol are not bound by such amendments unless they go on to deposit instruments of approval.

Fourth, the conference should foster a global network of non-governmental organisations. The existence of a meeting point for such NGOs can have at least three functions: NGOs can influence the decisions of the conference; the conference can assist them in their domestic task of enhancing the internal legitimacy of such norms as flow from those decisions; and it can also facilitate the domestic pressure for commitments that go beyond those decisions.

Judged by these standards, UNCED looks to have been well designed. Both its conventions have now received the ratifications needed to bring them into force. Though the Climate Change Convention was ratified under the Bush Administration, Clinton has gone further than his predecessor and committed the USA to reducing carbon-dioxide emissions to 1990 levels by 2000. He has also signed the Biodiversity Convention, though ratification has not so far followed (Brenton 1994: 193). This more favourable attitude no doubt in part reflects the substantial differences in political philosophy between Bush and Clinton, but that is by no means the whole story. As is noted by the authors of a House of Commons Library Research Paper, 'The Earth Summit: one year on', other nations as well as the USA, such as India and Malaysia 'which refused in Rio to have the ecological friendliness of their policies judged by the international community have now conceded to do this, and provide progress reports to the SDC' (Hughes and Lea 1993: 4). This trend must at least in part be attributed to the existence of high-profile international norms and instruments to which a favourably inclined leader could affiliate.

Effective norm-generation is about changing human behaviour, practices, operations. How far the UNCED process has contributed to that remains to be seen. It is difficult to resist the impression that the world *is* gradually becoming more conscious of the hazards facing its environment, for which UNCED deserves a share of the credit. Translating that consciousness into the necessary global constraints on how we live (whatever these may in the end turn out to be) is another matter. The techniques by which such a translation can be accomplished will be diverse. We should not expect to discover a single, universally applicable formula. It does seem, though, that the world has learnt to avoid some of the more glaring procedural misjudgements of the Third United Nations Conference on the Law of the Sea.

## NOTES

1 The original Convention had given applicants (states, companies or combinations of both) assured access to sites subject to specific conditions in a number of areas, of which three, where the text represented arduously negotiated solutions to seemingly intractable problems, were particularly important.

The first such area was that of the 'system of exploitation' which was to facilitate the development of a 'parallel system' in which an arm of the International Sea-bed Authority, the Enterprise, would also engage in mining. Applicants would offer the Authority two sites of equal value, one of which it would 'reserve' on behalf of the

Enterprise which could then, subject to the Authority's general rules, exploit it as it thought best. It would be helped in this by being provided from the start with enough funds to exploit one site, and by being authorised, for an initial period, to buy from private and state contractors, at internationally arbitrated prices, technology that it needed and could not obtain elsewhere. Under the new Agreement, the Enterprise loses these rights both to initial funding and to the compulsory purchase of technology (Article 5.2), and is confined, in its initial operations, to joint ventures, with the applicant who had originally submitted the reserved site in question having the right of first refusal (Article 5).

Another key area where the Convention's sea-bed-mining regime was the fruit of protracted haggling was that of the protection of land-based producers of the same minerals. The Convention imposed, for an initial period, a limit on sea-bed production, and a compensation scheme to assist developing countries adversely affected by such production (Article 151). It is now agreed that Article 151 will not apply, and all that is left of the protection it offered is a vague obligation on the part of the Authority to help developing countries whose exports have been hit.

Third, the specific financial obligations of contractors (Annex III, Article 13), based either wholly on percentage 'production charges' (i.e. royalties) or partly on these and partly on a progressive tax on profits ranging from 35 to 70 per cent, were scrapped. They had been a rare feature of the 1980 draft on which (with the aid of computer models) so persuasive a consensus had been reached that even the 'Reagan Review' of 1982, whose brusque demands for wholesale changes had wrecked hopes that UNCLOS III might achieve unanimity in adopting its convention, had left it undisturbed. By the Agreement, contractors are to pay something, but exactly what has been left quite vague.

Further changes made by the Agreement include the dropping of the requirement that a Review Conference be held not more than fifteen years after commercial production has begun, and considerable modification of the Authority's structure and voting rules.

The process by which this Agreement has been negotiated has been kept secret, but the outcome looks very much like dictation by the rich, potential sea-bed-mining states. By early December 1984, the Agreement had received seventy signatures but only seven ratifications or expressions of intentions to be bound by it. Others, including the UK, had also indicated their intention to ratify.

2  In other words, to accept the substance of conventions adopted by the International Maritime Organisation (IMO) even if they had not otherwise acceded to them, and indeed even if they were not members of the IMO. This is indeed a far-reaching commitment.

3  Its predecessor, the Sea-Bed Committee, had only thirty-five members initially, growing eventually to ninety-one, but since it reported annually to the General Assembly, its selective character had less impact.

4  In fairness to the ozone-layer agreements, though, it should be remembered that under it, developing-country parties are exempted from this uniform percentage reduction requirement.

5  Apparently, the Packwood-Magnuson Amendment to the Fishery Conservation and Management Act of 1978 provides for a ban on the import or export of fish or fish products, or a denial of access to the USA's Exclusive Economic Zone, in respect of states which the US Secretary of State determines and certifies to have undermined those conservation treaties to which the USA is a party.

6  The delay in launching UNCLOS III allowed coastal states to effect a drastic extension of the limits of their jurisdiction, and thus correspondingly diminish the dimensions of the 'common heritage of mankind' whose definition, preservation and management were, supposedly, the *raison d'être* of the process from which the conference had sprung.

# BIBLIOGRAPHY

Benedick, R. (1991) *Ozone Diplomacy*, London: Harvard U.P.
Birnie, P. (1992) 'International environmental law: its adequacy for present and future needs', in Hurrell, A. and Kingsbury, B. (eds) *The International Politics of the Environment*, Oxford: Clarendon.
—— (1994) 'Law of the Sea to come into force', *New World* April–June 1994: 1.
Boehmer-Christiansen, S. (1994a) 'Global climate protection policy: the limits of scientific advice – Part 1', *Global Environmental Change* 4(2): 140–59.
—— (1994b) 'Global climate protection policy: the limits of scientific advice – Part 2', *Global Environmental Change* 4(3): 185–200.
Brenton, T. (1994) *The Greening of Machiavelli*, London: Earthscan/Royal Institute of International Affairs.
Choucri, N. (1993) *Global Accords*, Cambridge, Mass.: MIT Press.
Gardner, R. (1993) *Negotiating Survival: Four Priorities after Rio*, New York: Council on Foreign Relations Press.
Grubb, M., Koch, M., Munson, A., Sullivan, F. and Thomson, K. (1993) *The Earth Summit Agreements: a Guide and Assessment*, London: Earthscan/Royal Institute of International Affairs.
Haigh, N. (1992) 'The European Community and international environmental policy', in Hurrell, A. and Kingsbury, B. (eds) *The International Politics of the Environ- ment*, Oxford: Clarendon.
Hughes, P. and Lea, W. (1993) 'The Earth Summit: one year on', London: House of Commons (Library Research Paper 93/71).
Hurrell, A. and Kingsbury, B. (eds) (1992) *The International Politics of the Environment*, Oxford: Clarendon.
Johnson, S.P. (1993) *The Earth Summit: the United Nations Conference on Environment and Development (UNCED)*, London: Graham & Trotman.
Johnston, D.M. (1988) 'Marine pollution agreements: successes and problems', in Carroll, J.E. (ed.) *International Environmental Diplomacy*, Cambridge: C.U.P.
McConnell, F. (1991) Review of Benedick, *International Environmental Affairs* 3(4): 318–20.
Miles, E. (1975) 'An interpretation of the Caracas proceedings', in Christy, F.T., Clingan, T.A., Gamble, J.K., Knight, G.H. and Miles, E. (eds) *Law of the Sea: Caracas and Beyond*, Cambridge, Mass.: Ballinger.
Ogley, R.C. (1984) *Internationalizing the Seabed*, Aldershot: Gower.
—— (1991) *Conflict Under the Microscope*, Aldershot: Avebury.
Paterson, M. (1993) 'The politics of climate change after UNCED', in Thomas, C. (ed.) *Rio: Unravelling the Consequences*, London: Frank Cass.
Porter, G. and Brown, J.W. (1991) *Global Environmental Politics*, Boulder, Col.: Westview.
Rapoport, A. (1960) *Fights, Games and Debates*, Ann Arbor: University of Michigan Press.
Richardson, E.L. (1992) 'Climate change: problems of law-making', in Hurrell, A. and Kingsbury, B. (eds) *The International Politics of the Environment*, Oxford: Clarendon.
Roddick, J. (1992) 'The results of the Rio Earth Summit', *Science, Technology and Development* 10(3): 347–63.
Sachs, W. (1993) *Global Ecology*, London: Zed Books.
Sands, P. (ed.) (1993) *Greening International Law*, London: Earthscan.
Sikkink, K. (1986) 'Codes of conduct for TNCs – the case of the WHO/UNICEF code', *International Organization* 40(4): 815–40.
Skjaerseth, J.B. (1992) 'The "successful" ozone-layer negotiations', *Global Environmental Change* 2(4): 292–300.

Susskind, L. and Ozawa, C. (1992) 'Negotiating more effective international agreements', in Hurrell, A. and Kingsbury, B. (eds) *The International Politics of the Environ- ment*, Oxford: Clarendon.

Thacher, P.S. (1992) 'The Earth Summit – an institutional perspective', *Security Dialogue* 23(3): 117–26.

Thomas, C. (1992) *The Environment in International Relations*, London: Royal Institute of International Affairs.

Woods, L.T. (1993) 'Nongovernmental organizations and the United Nations system: reflecting upon the Earth Summit experience', *International Studies Notes* 18(1): 9–15.

# 10 The international research enterprise and global environmental change

## Climate-change policy as a research process

*Sonja Boehmer-Christiansen*

The question addressed here is how the scientific community, described as the global research enterprise, raised the issue of global environmental change and shaped political responses to it, in particular the Framework Convention on Climate Change (FCCC).[1] Research in the natural sciences related to climate, energy and ecology are all considered parts of the same enterprise because they rely on the same global data sets and modelling capacities and are well organised internationally (Boehmer-Christiansen 1994a). Did this enterprise by the scientific community (as it likes to describe itself) effectively influence international policy on global environmental change, as is widely assumed and even predicted (Haas, P. 1990)? Or did it primarily act to create both future markets for its products and new findings using new space and information technologies? Another way of posing the question is to enquire to what extent international agreements commit governments to do more than engage in further research and data collection, especially more than they would have done anyway. If it is likely that they did not do so, then doubts may be raised both about the benign role of epistemic communities and about the impact and function of international environmental regimes (Young 1989). Attention is drawn to wider problems which may arise for environmental policy and society if purely science-based international environmental agreements are adopted.

A tacit alliance between scientific institutions, intergovernmental bureaucracies, Northern environmentalists and assorted commercial interests took the issue of global warming to the Rio Earth Summit in 1992, but apart from issuing many exhortations, it could persuade governments to do little more than make commitments to further research and data collection in order to learn more about global environmental change (Boehmer-Christiansen 1994a, b). This served the interests of the research enterprise, and it may well be rational international politics were it not for its impacts on national research priorities (Boehmer-Christiansen 1995). Scientific institutions as one home of the 'epistemic community' are widely seen as a benign influence on environmental regimes and policy formulation. However, as the scientific community and its allies in international bureaucracies are primarily concerned with the solution of scientific and technological problems as defined by themselves, their advice cannot but reflect these priorities which, once turned into policy advice, tend to be impossible to implement because of their limited perspectives, narrow knowledge base and simplistic theories of government and human behaviour.

Once researchable uncertainties become objectives of international treaties, existing problems, including environmental ones, may be ignored and power differentials widened further as global information is collected, stored and made accessible to only a very few countries. Even worse, if non-environmental problems (such as poverty or lack of 'development') are disguised as environmental issues, then the failure of science to provide 'proof', so easily achieved at the frontiers of knowledge, may undermine worthwhile responses. It is therefore argued that in the current world political context, the global research enterprise has not only become a significant political actor, promoting the globalisation of information collection and 'business-as-usual' research, but has also done so with reference to specific global environmental concerns that were exaggerated (not necessarily by all scientists but certainly by many users of their ambiguous scientific advice) for this purpose. This hypothesis will be developed with reference to the Intergovernmental Panel on Climate Change (IPCC), the scientific body formally appointed by a small number of countries at the advice of the World Meteorological Organisation (WMO) in 1988.

## IN SEARCH OF ENERGY AND INFORMATION MARKETS: THE CONTEXT OF IPCC ADVICE

The efforts of the International Panel on Climate Change and its predecessors in shaping climate policy need to be analysed, and to do this, the role of these panels not only as providers of knowledge but also as political actors with deliberate policy goals – including the advancement of research agendas – needs to be considered. Such strategic behaviour on the part of these panels is necessary because knowledge is now a commodity which must be marketed to users and must attract public funding in highly competitive conditions. The IPCC reflects this requirement by primarily serving two global programmes, the 'private' International Geosphere Biosphere Programme (IGBP),[2] coordinated by the International Council of Scientific Unions (ICSU) based in Sweden, and the 'public' World Climate Research Programme (WCRP), coordinated by the WMO and the United Nations Environment Programme (UNEP) but largely implemented by the research sections of national meteorological offices. In the end, of course, most of this research is paid for by taxes. In 1994/5, the USA alone will spend $1.6 billion on global change, and Europe probably more (see Figure 10.1).

The 'mission' of these research programmes is the full understanding – already dreamt of by American scientists in the 1950s – of the physical systems of the planet Earth (including their complete visibility via remote sensing by satellites) as increasingly affected by the human species. To the scientific uncertainties which so clearly afflict the human understanding of the natural system (in spite of growing attention to 'biotic feedbacks' and advances in modelling capacity), additional 'socioeconomic' uncertainties are added. The global-warming threat was in fact produced by a combination of these two sets of

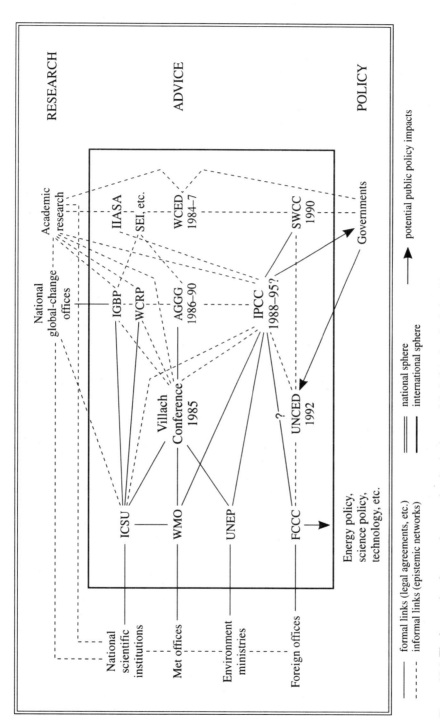

RESEARCH

ADVICE

POLICY

Academic research

National global-change offices

IIASA

SEI, etc.

WCED 1984–7

SWCC 1990

Governments

IGBP

WCRP

AGGG 1986–90

IPCC 1988–95?

Villach Conference 1985

UNCED 1992

?

ICSU

WMO

UNEP

FCCC

Energy policy, science policy, technology, etc.

National scientific institutions

Met offices

Environment ministries

Foreign offices

——— formal links (legal agreements, etc.)

- - - - informal links (epistemic networks)

═══ national sphere

——— international sphere

——▶ potential public policy impacts

*Figure 10.1* The international research enterprise: institutions and their functional relationships

factors: changes in the energy balance brought about by past changes in the chemical composition of the atmosphere (which have produced very little warming), and rapid increases in future emissions based on socioeconomic assumptions and predicted, by mathematical models, to lead to rapid warming in the next century.

Behind this mission are a small number of governments with strong atmospheric-science/climatology research capacities and space lobbies: the USA, the UK, Sweden, Canada, Japan, Germany and Australia, all major actors in the IPCC process.[3] This Panel and its predecessor, the Advisory Group on Greenhouse Gases (AGGG), stressed the need for more knowledge, and advocated changes in energy use and technology requiring vast investments. This created a major debate of which demands for more science were the major outcome. Once the scientists and scientific institutions involved had begun to disseminate their message both to the general public and to industries and governments, worldwide political processes were set in motion – and were also studied, in as far as they impinged upon energy-policy debates. Scientific advice did indeed become an independent policy influence, but it did so through its interpretation and use by other major stakeholders: the scientific institutions themselves withdrew into neutrality.

The Panel's motivation, fate and impacts were examined with the help of internal files, official reports, a questionnaire returned by over 100 IPCC participants and more than sixty interviews with scientists, users and observers. To contextualise the argument, a brief explanation is needed of why the 'Rio' alliance failed to achieve its apparent 1990 global goal of initiating the rapid reduction of carbon-dioxide emissions (Boehmer-Christiansen 1994c; Boehmer-Christiansen and Skea 1991).

The analysis of this material from national, international and scientific – as well as business – sources allowed some testing of the anti-Realist vision of international relations so fashionable in the study of environmental issues, and especially as understood by supporters both of the concept of 'epistemic communities' (Haas, P. 1990, 1993) and of the view that changing knowledge leads to a redefinition of interest (Haas, E.B. 1990). Both approaches tend to view the international political process as involving 'social learning', and both use models of international relations which assume a shared interest among all nations in keeping 'the environment' in a scientifically defined condition of 'health'.[4] The action of such communities, defined as involving operationalised scientific knowledge or transnational networks of specialists, is seen to lead to managed interdependence 'where new threats or problems are identified and collective understanding evolves and is mobilised to respond to and collectively manage the newly apparent risks' (Haas, P. 1993: 1). While rightly emphasising that knowledge and ideas play an innovative role here by shaping perceptions and expectations, and therefore contribute to definitions of 'preferences' or interest, the research reported also suggests that the epistemic approach tends seriously to exaggerate the independence of expert communities from the political process. Indeed, such communities in fact emerge as interested parties in the regime-building process in a quite unexpected manner. However, overconfident of their influence, epistemic communities may actually be able to achieve little more than a protection of their own interests in the genuine belief that 'more knowledge' will automatically benefit all mankind. Indeed, it is argued that the creation of consensual, problem-solving knowledge is alien to science and tends to be a strategy which does *not* serve the interests of research communities. Scientific consensus, as marketed by epistemic communities, may well be fundamentally unreliable for policy purposes. Rather than knowledge redefining interest and power, it is suggested that power and interest select areas of new knowledge – that is, define research agendas in collaboration with 'apolitical' epistemic communities, in other words, with areas of expertise which do not challenge but confirm existing patterns of power. The epistemic approach is therefore questionable in that it is likely both to raise unrealistic expectations and to undervalue the role of informed politicians and administrators; and it is also dangerously elitist.

The innovative capacity attributed to international organisations as transnational actors may suffer from the same fault: rather than being able to create consensual, cooperative, problem-solving environmental 'regimes', epistemic communities may instead capture these regimes and use them to serve the research enterprise. The exaggeration of the benign role of both expert networks and certain intergovernmental organisations may in turn mislead other intergovernmental organisations who may be persuaded by theory to allocate their own scarce political resources to the least effectual level of governance and innovative action. While empirical research does not question the claim that international negotiations may be an effective process for reducing uncertainty (Winham 1977), the very definition of epistemic communities 'as networks of knowledge-based communities with an authoritative claim to policy-relevant knowledge' raises questions, if the implication is that experts are, or should be, above politics. Research networks, or rather the global-knowledge-producing enterprise itself, may have been given dangerous advice by the epistemic model. The very persistence of their influence at the domestic level, believed by Peter Haas to be due to their capture of important bureaucratic positions (and hence of future funding), is 'subject to their ability to avoid widespread internal disagreement' (Haas, P. 1993: 9). (See Figure 10.2 for international research enterprise list of acronyms.)

The political forces at work behind the scenes and, de facto, acting as implicit allies of research can be identified from responses to the FCCC. Fossil-fuel interests are fairly content with the treaty, while recognising that the battle is not yet won. Bureaucracies are also content, as they are extremely busy drafting reports to international bodies and preparing, *inter alia*, national emission plans, while also engaging in interdepartmental battles over new competencies. Major interventions in national energy and land-use policies remain a possibility, but little has as yet happened, as more scientific verdicts are awaited. The implementation of global research programmes linked to the IPCC, on the other hand, is prospering well (Royal Swedish Academy of Sciences 1994: IGBP newsletters). Coordinated by the WMO, UNEP and the ICSU, these programmes

| AGGG | Advisory Group on Greenhouse Gases |
|------|-----------------------------------|
| BAHC | Biosphere Aspects of the Hydrological Cycle |
| CCCO | Committee on Climate Changes and the Ocean (SCOR/IOC) |
| CMP | Climate Modelling Project (WMO) |
| CSIRO | Commonwealth Scientific and Industrial Research Organisation |
| EDF | Environmental Defence Fund (US) |
| FCCC | Framework Convention on Climate Change |
| GAIM | IGBP Task Force on Global Analysis, Interpretation and Modelling |
| GARP | Global Atmospheric Research Programme (WMO/ICSU) |
| GCTE | Global Change and Terrestrial Ecosystems (IGBP) |
| GEMS | Global Environmental Monitoring System (UNEP) |
| GEWEX | Global Energy and Water Cycle Experiment |
| HDP | Human Dimension on Global Environmental Change Programme |
| ICSU | International Council of Scientific Unions |
| IGAC | International Global Atmospheric Chemistry Programme (MIT/ICSU) |
| IGBP | International Geosphere Biosphere Programme |
| IGOSS | Integrated Global Ocean Services System (WMO/IOC) |
| IHP | International Hydrological Program (Unesco) |
| IIASA | International Institute for Applied Systems Analysis |
| INC | International Negotiating Committee |
| IOC | Intergovernmental Oceanographic Commission (of Unesco) |
| IPCC | Intergovernmental Panel on Climate Change |
| ISCCP | International Satellite Cloud Climatology Project |
| ISLSCP | International Satellite Land Surface Climatology Project |
| JGOFS | Joint Global Ocean Flux Study |
| LOICZ | Land–Ocean Interactions in the Coastal Zone |
| MAB | Man and Biosphere Programme |
| MIT | Massachusetts Institute of Technology |
| NASA | National Aeronautics and Space Administration |
| NCAR | National Corporation for Atmospheric Research |
| NERC | Natural Environment Research Council |
| OECD | Organisation for Economic Cooperation and Development |
| PAGES | Past Global Changes (IGBP) |
| SCAR | Scientific Committee on Antarctic Research (ICSU) |
| SCOPE | Scientific Committee on Problems of the Environment |
| SCOR | Scientific Committee on Oceanic Research (ICSU) |
| SEI | Stockholm Environment Institute |
| SPARC | Stratospheric Processes and their Role in Climate (WMO) |
| START | System for Analysis, Research and Training |
| TOGA | Tropical Ocean and Global Atmosphere Programme |
| UN | United Nations |
| UNCED | United Nations Conference on Environment and Development |
| UNEP | United Nations Environment Programme |
| Unesco | United Nations Educational, Scientific and Cultural Organisation |
| UNGA | United Nations General Assembly |
| USDoE | United States Department of the Environment |
| WCED | World Commission on Environment and Development |
| WCP | World Climate Programme |
| WCRP | World Climate Research Programme (WMO) |
| WG | Working Group (IPCC) |
| WMO | World Meteorological Organisation |
| WOCE | World Ocean Circulation Experiment (WMO) |
| WRI | World Resources Institute (US) |

*Figure 10.2* The international research enterprise: list of acronyms

completed their planning stage during the mid-1980s (ICSU/IGBP 1992). They are the major market for data gathered from remote sensing, that is, for the increasingly privatised earth-observation industry, an industry characterised by rapid innovation and limited competition but in need of public subsidies (Mansell and Paltridge 1993).

Less directly, but more significantly, the energy industries, also, were deeply involved – though not united. While the FCCC, as finally negotiated, made no commitments against coal and cheap energy, these two areas of industry felt most threatened, for much was made in the late 1980s of the alleged IPCC advice that a 60-per-cent reduction in carbon-dioxide emissions was needed soon in order to prevent catastrophe. Official responses by believers were strong: as recently as 1988, a division of the UK Department of the Environment (DoE) believed that a hierarchy of energy-policy responses (including increasing the price of coal, expanding nuclear energy, improving energy efficiency and eventually removing carbon dioxide from flue gases) could not be defined in accordance with the timetable of expected findings from government-financed research over the next five to twenty-five years (a timetable which also made use of reliable regional predictions). Energy-policy goals would be defined by scientific progress, and research would directly serve policy. Other governments felt much less able to transform their energy economies (Grubb 1991), and were relieved when the FCCC remained as vague as the USA (with UK Treasury support) wanted. The US and UK governments were by far the best informed on the status of climate science, a subject that they were and still are funding generously.

In its 1990 report and advice, the IPCC had indeed confirmed the concern of 'independent' scientists. After the assumption had been made of a doubling of carbon-dioxide ($CO_2$) concentrations in the atmosphere at certain prescribed dates early next century, energy-policy scenarios, at the request of the USA and the Netherlands, were adjusted to suit these dates and then fed into equilibrium models which, as expected, predicted rapid and disturbing increases in the average global temperature. This emission-scenario methodology and type of model have since been improved upon, and a greater range of scenarios has now been produced. These are highly speculative experiments and even their creators still consider them to be improper policy tools. However, the assumptions built into the 1990 climate models – and hence their predictions also – were not widely debated at the time. This was intentional. The 'climate community' had also advocated, from the very beginning, technical solutions directed against the burning of coal, a very expensive fuel in Europe (but not elsewhere). Alternatives would divide the believers, however, between support for nuclear expansion and a switch to natural gas, on the one hand, and the advocacy of 'soft' energies (wind, waves, solar) and energy saving on the other hand. As most of these solutions were a long way off commercially or less attractive to governments since fossil-fuel prices were falling (oil prices collapsed in 1986 and have recovered but little), government subsidisation was called for in the name of preventing global warming. The 'new' technologies that had been developed in response to the oil-price shocks of the 1970s are thus in need of markets.

The market and the oil companies (as the owners) were ready for one change only, and had been waiting for it for some time: the use of gas as a replacement for coal or uranium – or both – in electricity generation. Both the UK and US plans for stabilising emissions under the FCCC rely on fuel-switching from coal to oil, something which would have happened any way in the UK if only for reasons of competition. Not all countries could or would avail themselves of this opportunity, but in Europe, Siberian and Norwegian gas was beckoning, and the nuclear industry remained hopeful for a while. The inability of the global – as distinct from European – energy system to stabilise emissions was well known. The International Energy Agency (IEA) warned in 1990 that for the whole world economy, stabilisation, let alone a 60-per-cent reduction, within two decades would require impossible efforts. The World Bank argued in 1992 that global energy use and production could only be changed at the margin over the next thirty years because of weak administrative and institutional structures (WEC 1993: 20). In 1993, the Intergovernmental Negotiating Committee (INC) could not agree on the proposed joint implementation strategy which would allow companies to reduce $CO_2$ anywhere in the world because it would mean outflows of investments and loss of jobs. The European Community's efforts to introduce a European carbon/energy tax will almost certainly experience the same fate. Coal, the world's cheapest, most widely distributed and most labour-intensive fuel, will not be wiped out globally, though this was the British Government's aim quite irrespective of global warming – an issue which merely served to green-wash its unpopular policy. Coal's competitors, however, after Chernobyl and the collapse of oil prices, had supported the perception of a strong warming threat. When Bolin (the IPCC's Chairman) and Houghton (the Chairman of the IPCC's Working Group I (WG I)) addressed the World Energy Congress in 1993, both spoke to the World Energy Council, a Non-Governmental Organisation and a major funder of environmental-energy research, in support of higher energy prices, energy efficiency and renewables (World Energy Council 1993). Bolin has been a vocal advocate of changes in energy-policy technologies for over a decade (Bolin 1977).

## A BRIEF HISTORY OF SCIENTIFIC ADVICE ON CLIMATE CHANGE

The threat of global warming was constructed in research institutions a decade or so ago and widely disseminated with the help of environmentalists and international bureaucracies. It gained world political salience in the second half of the 1980s shortly after scientific institutions began to seek active involvement in policy-making. This development is attributed less to the influence of new knowledge than to the combination of a powerful threat image and the open advocacy of anti-fossil-fuel policies at a time when this was welcome to a number of energy interests. The dissemination of the threat was achieved most effectively by the UN system with the assistance of Northern environmental networks, each soon to use the IPCC as a mouthpiece for diverging policy goals. The intellectual debate on which subsequent politics was based, and which resulted in the FCCC, can be traced back much further.

In 1827 Fourier raised the global-warming issue on the basis of a number of calculations, in 1896 Arrhenius predicted an increase in air temperature of between 4°C and 6°C on the basis of laboratory tests, and in 1938 a British steam technologist, Callendar, also calculated that the planet was getting warmer because of carbon-dioxide emissions. The latter added, however, that there was no need for concern as this meant that another ice age would be prevented. Forecasting weather and climatology remained little-respected sciences for several more decades as the splitting of the nucleus and nuclear technology rather than the complexity of nature occupied the brightest minds (Weart 1992). The climate-change research debate began in earnest in the late 1950s with reference to weather modification, with the USA, Germany and Sweden most deeply involved. In 1957 two American scientists pointed out that human beings were carrying out a large-scale geophysical experiment which might yield far-reaching insights into the processes determining weather and climate. In 1961 Charles Keeling proved the increase in carbon-dioxide concentration in the atmosphere by measurement, and warnings in the media began shortly afterwards.

The study of man's potential influence on the climate then advanced rapidly during the 1970s as research institutions learned to relate their search for knowledge to human concerns like the fears associated both with the limits-to-growth debate and with the idea of a 'nuclear winter' (Hart and Victor 1993). Climate modelling was now making rapid progress, and the US President's Science Advisory Council argued in 1965 that supercomputers would allow useful predictions, down to the regional level, to be made within two or three years. Almost thirty years later, no such detail is possible, and there is some doubt that it ever will be (McCracken 1992: 13). In 1970 the Massachusetts Institute of Technology, always at the forefront of research, convened a 'Study of Critical Environmental Problems' which concluded that global warming was a serious possibility. It advocated the aggressive expansion of climate research, combined with population control and protection of the food system – science was ready to solve a new problem with the help of the pill and the Green Revolution.

The 1972 Stockholm Conference recommended more climate-change research, as suggested by the First International Conference on Environmental Futures. This had proposed a UN institute for planetary survival, and in a keynote paper on 'Climatic modification by air pollution', the American climatologist Bryson discussed the matter of aerosols and the ozone layer. Atmospheric dust was feared to be the causal agent, though Bryson, in discussion, admitted to a 'sneaking' suspicion that the demands for more monitoring were 'mostly for the care and feeding of big computers' rather than for the welfare of man (Bryson 1972). Others argued that the development of numerical general-circulation models which successfully simulate both the present climate and the behaviour of the atmosphere in long time runs was the first step in attempts to predict what happens to the atmosphere as a result of man's activities, then considered to be the ultimate goal of the Global Atmospheric Research Programme (GARP), the project managed by Bert Bolin when he was a young man (Polunin 1972: 168). GARP is the predecessor to IGBP, and was never fully completed.

The executive of the WMO began to include climate change into its research portfolio, and the environmental lobby, growing in strength, would be on the look-out for new problems. By the end of the 1970s, UNEP, still a rather weak intergovernmental body in search of a function, had made climate both a research and a development issue, sharing the former interest with the WMO. UNEP's Executive Director had mentioned both energy and the need for better climate forecasting in 1974 without any reference to global warming, but when addressing the First World Climate Conference in 1979, he referred to climate change as the process of carrying out an uncontrolled experiment on the earth's atmosphere, and assured his audience that UNEP was ready to assess the environmental impacts of increased levels of carbon dioxide (Tolba 1982). The worlds of politics and energy remained unimpressed. Energy-demand forecasters, on the other hand, became interested in the subject as American, German, Canadian, Swedish and British research groups began collaborating on integrating energy forecasting and environmental futures. The nuclear lobby in particular was attracted to the subject. The more specific threat of global warming was now firmly tied to an advocacy of new energy technologies and to the frightening 'predictions' of energy-demand forecasters.

The estimated temperature changes put forward in the late 1970s in relation to the doubling of carbon-dioxide concentration differed surprisingly little from those put forward a decade later by the IPCC (Kellogg and Schware 1981).[5] The number of academic books on the subject soared, but the global political system still took no notice. The energy industries, still either largely in public hands or well supported by public R&D expenditure – or both – provided for the development and use of technologies and fuels which were generating, or promised to generate, less rather than more carbon dioxide. Climatic variability as a cause of damage to food production became the issue which justified the World Climate Research Programme (WCRP) which the WMO initiated in 1979 at the First World Climate Conference, but which remained poorly funded. The Paris-based International Council of Scientific Unions (ICSU), among them its Scientific Committee on Problems of the Environment (SCOPE), had already shown a growing interest in environmental subjects and global atmospheric modelling (ICSU/IGBP 1992). SCOPE had been set up in 1970 to assess environmental problems, and in the early 1980s contributed to the study of nuclear winter. The ICSU and UNEP were as concerned as the WMO about the growing inability of developing countries to contribute to data collection and monitoring. They eventually pooled their efforts and organised the 1985 Villach Conference, the second conference on the subject of the carbon cycle and climatic change, held in Austria.

# THE ADVISORY GROUP ON GREENHOUSE GASES AND THE EMERGENCE OF THE IPCC

A small group of environmental scientists and research managers working on energy and the climate was set up in 1985 at a UNEP/WMO/ICSU-sponsored meeting with an agenda revealingly described as 'the second joint UNEP/ICSU/ WMO international assessment of the role of carbon dioxide and other greenhouse gases in climate variations and associated impacts'. This group called itself the Advisory Group on Greenhouse Gases (AGGG), and held its first meeting in 1986. It was to become astonishingly active and influential until 1990. As an advisor to governments, it was replaced by the IPCC.

The Villach Conference was organised both by the Swedish International Meteorological Institute (IMI) (the home of Bert Bolin) and by the Beijer Institute (now the Stockholm Environment Institute – SEI) which has close research links with British institutions. The Conference concluded that 'it is now believed that in the first half of the next century a rise of global mean temperature could occur which is greater than any in man's history', and recommended that science-based emission or concentration targets should be worked out to limit the rate of change in the global mean temperature to a maximum of 0.1°C (WMO 1986). The meeting was attended mainly by non-governmental researchers, including three researchers from the Climate Research Unit at the University of East Anglia, one from the UK Meteorological Office (UKMO), and one scientist from the US Department of Energy's Carbon Dioxide Research Division. The proceedings were dominated by participants from Harvard University and the Vienna International Institute for System Analysis (IIASA), who already saw the responses to the climate threat as part of 'sustainable development'.

The Villach meeting was more cautious about science than the IPCC appeared to be in 1990. Another ten-to-twenty years of observation would be needed before the detection of global warming was likely, and the ecologist William Clark from Harvard stated that uncertainties dominated the greenhouse-gas question, from emission rates through environmental consequences to socioeconomic impacts (WMO 1986: 24). The Conference felt that refining estimates was 'a matter of urgency', and recommended a list of actions which remained vague with respect to policy but were very specific for research. The analysis of decision-making rules under specific kinds of risks, the determination of damage costs resulting from greenhouse warming and the analysis of the behaviour of policy-makers were all to be researched – an agenda for rational, technocratic decision-making. The Conference went beyond advocating more research but suggested that a small task force should be set up jointly by the ICSU, UNEP and the WMO to ensure that periodic assessments both of the current state of scientific understanding and of its practical applications would be undertaken. A global convention was to be considered, and a small group of advisors was to be set up that would suggest what needed to be done at the national and international levels. The small group, in fact, already existed – it had organised the Conference and provided the backbone of the AGGG. There was no need for consensus-generating procedures as only those in agreement with the aims of the group had been asked to join in the first place. The Conference largely approved the broader, political brief urged by Tolba for UNEP under an 'agenda of action'. A non-governmental International Greenhouse-Gas Coordinating Committee was to:

- promote and coordinate research, monitoring and assessment;
- promote the exchange of information related to climate warming;
- prepare and disseminate educational material; and
- approve the possible advantages of an intergovernmental agreement on global convention.

While the AGGG succeeded in taking the policy debate into the world of politics, its institutional base proved too poor to keep the issue out of the hands of big, responsible institutions, governments and the WMO, which all had the ability to fund the global-change experiment. Its publications, all the same, would be more influential. The scientific papers read at Villach and commissioned and peer-reviewed by its organisers were published jointly by the WMO/ICSU and UNEP (Bolin *et al.* 1988). In a 1992 interview, a British coordinator of the IPCC WG I called this Scope 29 report 'the IPCC bible'. AGGG members subsequently organised the 1988 Toronto NGO Conference on the Changing Atmosphere Implications for Global Security which called for a 20-per-cent reduction in $CO_2$ emissions and caused considerable unease among governments, industry and government scientists. They also organised the Second World Climate Conference in 1990. This Conference failed to agree on $CO_2$-reduction targets, but its results were disseminated nonetheless (Jager and Ferguson 1991: 473). The AGGG had drafted a recommendation which not only reflected a degree of policy ambition which was subsequently disputed but also added to the pressures for the setting-up of an intergovernmental group. The AGGG also prepared the Meeting of Legal and Policy Experts held in February 1989 in Ottawa which recommended an 'umbrella' consortium, to protect the atmosphere, which was to be implemented through subsequent protocols. And it further proposed both a World Atmosphere Trust Fund and a Convention that should be served by a panel of independent experts (Churchill and Freestone 1992: 375). There was therefore considerable bitterness when the AGGG was replaced by the IPCC under pressure from the US State Department exerted through the Executive Committee of the WMO. The IPCC was also supported by many developing countries who felt excluded from the whole process. The US State Department, presumably with the support of the US Department of Energy (a major sponsor of carbon-dioxide research), wanted the scientific assessment to stay in governmental hands, not in those 'of free-wheeling academics' (a WMO source).

By 1985, therefore, a community of scientists had formed which included people deeply involved in energy and policy research and was determined to initiate a dialogue with 'policy-makers', a selected few of whom they invited to a 1986 meeting. The IPCC is best understood as a response both to this initiative and to the policy advocacy which emerged from Villach. Governmental scientific interests closer to meteorological offices and the hearts of governments would take over the research agenda. By the absorption and rejection of groups and individuals, this led, in 1988, to a gathering of individuals that would form the IPCC. The overlap of individuals and institutions attending the Villach Conference and later supporting the IPCC and IGBP is considerable, and provides evidence for the ability of the research enterprise to attract attention to its programmes by making its problems those of mankind (Boehmer-Christiansen 1993, 1994c). The links between the IPCC and IGBP are strong. The US Committee on Global Change and the US National Committee for the IGBP of the Commission on Geosciences, Environment and Resources of the National Research Council have stated that the IGBP was developed as a step in the evolving process of defining the scientific needs involved in understanding those changes in the global environment which are of great concern. One chapter out of nine in this report deals with humanity (US National Research Council 1990), and a small section of the Global Change research agenda is also now devoted to the human dimension, primarily because of the impacts of land-use changes on physical variables (Price 1992). This, too, primarily reflects US research needs.[6] The importance of 'Global Change' to the US research community is enormous, as is the need to ensure policy relevance. Neither science nor vested energy interests had much to gain from a global advisory body that would hurry along the policy process by recommending action rather than further decades of research. IGBP representatives addressed the eighth plenary session of the IPCC in connection with the IGBP's START (System for Analysis, Research and Training) programme, which works closely with the International Group of Funding Agencies for Global Change Research (IGBP 1994). START aims to strengthen the scientific capacity of developing countries (an interest it shares with the IPCC), and it is already being funded by the Global Environment Facility.[7] START's secretariat is in Washington, and is guided by the IGBP Standing Committee – at which the WCRP is also represented. The November-1992 START workshop in Niger was attended by the Chairman of the 1985 Villach Conference who now chairs the new IPCC WG III. Space science and technology are deeply involved in all these bodies.[8]

## THE INSTITUTIONAL NATURE OF THE IPCC

By the time the WMO and UNEP had been invited by the General Assembly (UNGA) in 1988 to jointly prepare a Framework Convention on Climate Change which was to contain commitments for actions, to combat climate change, 'taking into account the most up-to-date sound scientific knowledge and any existing uncertainties' (Churchill and Freestone 1992: 249), the IPCC had already been set up. The sound knowledge (what is unsound knowledge?) and uncertainties in question were both to be supplied by a group of research managers, science-policy leaders and government officials that had formally been set up a few months earlier in response to statements and claims, about the approaching risk of global warming, made by 'independent' scientists under the auspices of the ICSU, the WMO and UNEP. Such claims had been made for decades, but had been rejected by the WMO as too speculative until 1986 when the task of scientific assessment passed into the more responsible hands (with deeper pockets) of government laboratories and meteorological offices in the UK, the USA, Canada and Australia. The independent research sector was not excluded, but it would now work as funded and instructed. The IGBP, in preparation since the early 1980s, was also adopted by the ICSU in 1986.

As had happened for the protection of the ozone layer, UNEP expected the climate convention to be negotiated under its own auspices, but in late 1990 UNGA decided otherwise. Too many agendas, fears and doubts had by then attached themselves to the climate threat for the issue to be left to environmental scientists alone. Negotiations would be undertaken not by the IPCC but by the International Negotiating Committee (INC). Politicians took the task away from the research enterprise, but had meanwhile become dependent on it for authority. Science is an unreliable ally. By 1992, with funding ensured, researchers wanted not to give 'new' advice but instead to be left alone to get on with data collection and the testing of global models in order to assess and reduce a growing number of uncertainties. There was not much that was 'new' anyway. The scientific perspective is not that of the policy-makers; rather, 'it is important that we are able to predict the effects of global environmental changes on the long-term climate, but our present understanding of the problem is far from complete and our ocean-climate models are not sophisticated enough, nor is present computing power sufficient' (Smithon 1994: 9).

The IPCC consists of a small secretariat and bureau of about thirty people, the former based in Geneva inside the WMO's headquarters. Its budget in 1992/3 was under 2 million French francs. Biannual plenary sessions bring together leading government scientists and research managers, plus mainly junior government officials in charge of designing national climate policy or preparing international negotiations – or both. While formal decisions are taken at these plenaries, most of the real work of the Panel – collecting and assessing scientific evidence and theories – takes place in Working Groups whose subdivisions act as writing teams for individual chapters. The structure of these chapters has been decided both by small groups of lead authors and by the WG (Working Group) Chairman, who together also condense the findings of these chapters into 'policy-makers' summaries' for general consumption. Each Working Group represents a more or less stable research network which operates in a symbiotic relationship with the writing teams. The networks provide data and ideas for the authors, and the IPCC management structure brings research results and needs to the attention of governments and other interested parties, including UN agencies.

The IPCC Bureau and the bureaux of its WGs are able to function as the decision-makers, selecting authors and reviewers for reports (in consultation with governments), negotiating consensus and transmitting research needs to governments. Three WGs were set up to deal with knowledge issues. The most coherent and basic WG dealt with scientific assessment (WG I, Science), and is coordinated from the Hadley Centre of Climate Prediction and Research in the UK Meteorological Office (UKMO). It has had a major impact on UK research policy and environmental diplomacy. WG I as a whole reflects the existing research interests of the WMO, coordinated as the WCRP, while WG II, dealing with climate-change impacts, reflects those of UNEP. As part of the WRCP, UNEP's research programme also complements the more ambitious IGBP (ICSU/IGBP 1992). WG III attracted most countries, but was attended by government officials and NGO lobbyists rather than scientists. The purpose of WG III was to define 'realistic' response strategies, but it was also, de facto, the meeting place for those people with whom scientists did not want to mix.[9] From both IPCC reports and especially their more controversial policy-makers' summaries, actors in the world of politics and commerce would develop threat images, select options and define positions based on particular interests. Bureaucratic empire-builders, NGOs driving for new members and party-political and commercial competitors all quickly took up 'global warming' prevention as a goal to suit themselves.

The main achievement of the IPCC so far has been its reports, which are addressed both to policy-makers and to the UN. The first science assessment was published in 1990 (Houghton *et al.* 1990) and updated for UNCED in 1992. A Second Assessment is under way for 1995, but will not become available in time to assist in the preparations of the first meeting of the parties of the FCCC, as scientists refuse to be hurried by political timetables (Pearce 1994: 5). These same scientists had, however, helped to define these timetables by promises made when the research programmes were marketed as strategic knowledge needed by policy-makers.

The WG structure, as it turned out, proved highly unsuitable for policy-making, as the producers and users of knowledge hardly ever met. It reflected a highly linear conception of policy-making in which scientists think and recommend, while politicians merely add values and implement (Bolin 1994; Boehmer-Christiansen 1994b).

## IPCC ADVICE, OR THE ART OF AMBIGUITY

The IPCC first met in the Autumn of 1988. By 1990 the first stage of funding for global systems research had been achieved, and experts began to talk (as those opposed to rapid-abatement action had already done for some time) more about those uncertainties that needed studying than about confirming the predicted warming range (namely, a rate of increase in the global mean temperature, during the next century, of about 0.3°C per decade, with an uncertainty range of between 0.2 and 0.5). Environmentalists responded with that one version of the precautionary principle which proved attractive to those in favour both of higher energy prices and of regulation for non-environmental reasons.

Like all lobbies, the research lobby speaks with more than one voice. For example, two climatologists who had attended the 1985 Villach Conference and contributed to the work of the IPCC (and therefore added their voice to what appeared to many to be calls for immediate action) argued shortly afterwards, when addressing the science-policy community, that the range of scientific uncertainty was still so large that neither the 'do nothing' option nor the 'prevent emissions' option could be excluded from consideration (Warrick and Jones 1988: 48–62). Full support for a research effort which would narrow the range of scientific uncertainty, and which would indicate how socioeconomic and environmental (but not political) systems were likely to be affected, was needed. The IPCC follows this example. While much has been made of its scientific consensus, especially in the UK, this consensus includes clear statements on uncertainty, and, if read closely, remains highly ambiguous, especially as far as the Executive Summaries go (Houghton, Jenkins and Ephraums 1990: xi–xxiii). Instead of using the terms 'model' and 'prediction' (as injected into the 1990 policy debate), scientists might have used more neutral terms such as 'numerical experimentation' and 'scenario-building'. Ambiguity and its political utility are readily documented. In 1990, IPCC lead authors had agreed that they could calculate with confidence – not measure – average global temperature increases from models which a few pages later were admitted to be 'comparatively crude', and from which two important greenhouse gases, water vapour and ozone, as well as aerosols and processes involving the biosphere, had been omitted.[10] The Executive Summary combined the phrase 'will result' with the phrase 'a likely increase' – a grammatical device to create both certainty *and* uncertainty simultaneously. It was not stated that the predicted rate of temperature increase was likely only in association with specific emission scenarios. Given these assumptions, the prediction was

> a rate of increase of global mean temperature during the next century of about 0.3 degree C per decade (with an uncertainty range of 0.2 to 0.5 degree C per decade) .... (T)his will result in a likely increase in global mean temperature of about 1 degree C above the present value by 2025 and 3 degrees C before the end of next century.
>
> (Houghton, Jenkins and Ephraums 1990: xi)

This uncertainty range is huge, and ensured that most researchers, but not all, could support the consensus. The real source of friction, as already mentioned, was the prescribed emission scenarios. The IPCC has always admitted in its fuller reports that its understanding of the links between greenhouse-gas concentrations and 'climate sensitivity', involving a consideration of the actual changes produced by their accumulation and interaction in the air, remained poor. While some may well decide that increased greenhouse-gas concentrations provide sufficient reason for mitigation and adaptation strategies, the IPCC has never explicitly said so. To have decided this would have been against the interests of research. Both environmentalists and the promoters of advanced energy technologies could, however, select phrases which would allow them to claim that the IPCC supported their policy proposals.

Like many other environmentalists, a former director of UK Friends of the Earth could claim that 'the consensus view of the IPCC' was that a 60-per-cent reduction in $CO_2$ is needed to stabilise the climate at an acceptable temperature (Gee 1994: 17), and Greenpeace continues to campaign in the belief that the climate is 'in danger of catastrophic destabilisation' (Greenpeace, undated). The

UK Treasury, also bowing to the 'authoritative IPCC assessment by several hundred scientists', emphasised 'huge uncertainties' instead, and concluded that another decade of research would be needed before any policy could be made in response to man-made changes, adding that there should not be excessive costs for the world economy (Her Majesty's Treasury 1992), a view privately supported by some IPCC leaders. The IPCC had wisely 'calculated with confidence' that an immediate 60-per-cent reduction in emissions would have to take place if the stabilisation of current concentrations were to be the goal, but this was not advocated, and the difficulties of linking calculated temperature rises with real temperatures were pointed out. When addressing the World Energy Council, Houghton discarded the idea of certainty altogether, explaining that 'IPCC publications explain the degree of scientific uncertainty regarding future climate change . . . . Research therefore needs urgently to be undertaken in order to reduce scientific uncertainty' (WEC 1993: 47). And Bolin, in turn, supported the statement that 'as long as we do not know the natural carbon cycle adequately the prediction of atmospheric concentrations due to future emissions remains uncertain' (ibid.: 43). The uncertainty of uncertainties is worrying scientists.

Some sections of government and a growing number of scientific 'sceptics' have rejected not the idea of *some* level of warming but the idea of a *dangerous* level of warming, and hence have challenged not so much science but more some of the policy responses it has given rise to (Lindzen 1992; Michaels 1992). The debate clearly continues, and it is my judgement that the uncertainty involved will increase for quite some time yet. The coal industry is now supporting research into global greening (carbon dioxide stimulates plant growth), thereby recalling Russian claims made during the 1970s that global warming should be encouraged.[11] Little significant consensus was reached on this subject in the other, subsidiary WGs. And to the extent that the findings of these WGs would depend on WG I, their results must remain irrelevant to policy as long as WG I is largely reporting research needs – as is now admitted by the academic group making assessments using emission scenarios. Had it not been for opposition on the part of US and UK policy advisors fully aware of the scientific base, an international climate regime reflecting the demands of environmentalists and European energy interests might have committed other countries to considerable policy changes and possibly created disaster for the poorest and most dependent on cheap energy. The political pressures to reduce fossil-fuel use in favour of more expensive options may yet turn out to be unstoppable unless 'science' is used to reverse these pressures. Having said this, however, scientific messages can themselves be reversed, science being by nature self-correcting.

## THE WMO AS A RESEARCH COORDINATOR AND SCIENCE-POLICY ADVISOR

The decision to establish a panel on climate change was made at the WMO's 1987 Congress where, after extensive briefing by the Secretary of the Brundtland Commission, the WMO also made a strong bid for a consideration of the socioeconomic implications of climate change, as suggested by the AGGG. The WMO had become concerned that UNEP might 'run with' the global-warming issue without proper scientific advice (WMO interview 1992). The WMO invited governments to join the IPCC by appointing their WMO representatives. About thirty countries did so and thus gave their blessings to what can be called the largest international exercise of scientific-advice-giving.[12] The panel, as envisaged in 1987, was 'to provide the international assessment that would enable the Directors of National Meteorological Services to advise their governments on the evidence for and nature of the climate threat and what they might do about it' (McTegart and Zillman 1990: 10). It was to be small, involving experts from no more than fifteen to twenty-nine countries active in climate-change research, and including both a few other nations and those main scientific bodies responsible for international leadership in climate research.

The IPCC was set up jointly with UNEP, but with the WMO very much in control. And the political response to the WMO's proposal surprised the research community not involved in the AGGG, for

> almost overnight, greenhouse-induced climate change moved from being the business of specialised bodies . . . to become the centrepiece of a major political happening . . . an impressive array of world leaders, mostly unaware of what had been going on in national scientific laboratories and the UN system over the preceding decades, immediately seized on the need for drastic action.
>
> (McTegart and Zillman 1990: 8)[13]

In 1988, the WMO Executive Council agreed the brief of the IPCC after considerable debate. It was agreed that uncertainties and gaps in present knowledge with regard to climate change and its potential impacts needed to be identified. And links both with existing research programmes and with the IGBP were also stressed.

The choice of the WMO by the global research enterprise as the organisation most fitted for the task of promoting global research and advice-giving has surely been wise. The WMO is by far the most effective organisation for advancing the interests of interdisciplinary research. With a world-wide network of meteorological offices and a senior scientific elite deeply involved in atmospheric and oceanographic research, it has provided the essential national–international linkage for effective policy-making and research implementation. These WMO links were particularly important for the IPCC because they brought informal contacts not only with the ICSU and national research bodies but also with national meteorological offices and government departments. Since 1987 the research agenda underlying the IPCC has grown enormously, and the WMO appears to be laying claim to it (WMO 1992).

## THE FRAMEWORK TREATY ON CLIMATE CHANGE

The negotiation of a treaty (albeit an ambiguous one) on climate change had become unstoppable by the end of the 1980s. In 1992, the treaty emerged rich in exhortations and good advice, but weak on commitments on the energy-policy side. Rather, it codifies enormous data-collection needs and research commitments, serving both the natural sciences, the earth-observation industry and assorted bureaucracies. Tough international policy decisions dealing with immediate problems were postponed, or left to the national level to be decided on the basis of sovereignty. The process of scientific advice-giving can here therefore, in retrospect, be analysed as a dimension of 'power' politics, power referring both to energy and to the capacity of nations, official stakeholders and other interests to shape outcomes.

The negotiations were formally based on scientific evidence and its interpretation, and for this reason, very few countries could genuinely participate, though efforts were made to include delegates from other countries as learners.[14] Less openly, the Convention also reflected expectations about future energy demands, fuel choice and energy technologies, as well as creating new markets for the earth-observation industry and hence space agencies and their suppliers. Most importantly from the perspective adopted here, the climate treaty provided the rapidly expanding and encroaching field of environmental science with an almost permanent research agenda at the very heart of the IGBP and WCRP, with a small human dimensions component more recently added by the International Social Science Council (Boehmer-Christiansen 1994a, b; Price 1992). The data needs are enormous. The very objective of the FCCC depends on further scientific evidence. The objective of the treaty is the

> stabilisation of greenhouse gas concentrations . . . at a level that would prevent dangerous anthropogenic interference with the climate system. Such a level should be achieved within a time frame sufficient to allow ecosystems to adapt naturally to climate change, to ensure that food supply is not threatened and to enable economic development to proceed in a sustainable manner.
>
> (IUCC (undated) *UNFCCC*)

A tall order indeed. How and by whom will 'dangerous' be defined? The IPCC has already claimed that defining this objective should be its task. Two 'subsidiary bodies' are to be set up by the Parties of the Convention in order to provide 'scientific-technical' information. The precise link between the IPCC and these bodies is not yet clear. Information will be needed on four subjects:

- the stabilisation of concentrations
- emission stabilisation
- the ecological limits or levels of tolerance
- emission inventories and reduction programmes.

The emission-reduction commitments that governments have accepted so far, apart from being very easy ones (the EU as a whole has already stabilised its carbon-dioxide emissions), consist of major data-collection and planning efforts. This obligation, too, is very research-intensive and requires much national expertise. Governments are required to make national inventories of all their greenhouse-gas emissions (other than CFCs controlled under the Montreal Protocol) using comparable methodologies. (The methodologies in question have been defined by the IPCC with help from the OECD/IEA.) This information concerning implementation must then be communicated to the Conference of the Parties. Countries shall also

> formulate, implement, publish and regularly update national and, where appropriate, regional programmes containing measures to mitigate climate change by addressing anthropogenic emissions by sources and removals by sinks of all greenhouse gases not controlled by the Montreal Protocol, and measures to facilitate adequate adaptation to climate change; and promote and cooperate in the development, application and diffusion, including transfer, of technologies, practices and processes that control, reduce or prevent anthropogenic emissions.
>
> > (IUCC (undated) *UNFCCC*, p. 8, para. 2)

The relevant sectors specifically referred to are energy, transport, industry, agriculture, forestry and waste management. Other paragraphs of the same article mention sustainable management and coastal zone management, water resources and agriculture, impact assessment and research collaboration, and even training and education. Remote sensing will be essential, and the global-change research enterprise will provide the major market for this heavily subsidised activity (Mansell and Paltridge 1993). If knowledge is a public good, then the public should be involved in deciding what knowledge, and technologies, it wants to finance, raising another hornets' nest of issues.

The Convention goes to considerable lengths to ensure that the parties will be provided with abundant technical advice. Two subsidiary bodies will be set up, one to give 'scientific and technological advice' and the other to assist the Parties with the implementation of the Convention. This former would provide the kind of knowledge that the IPCC's WGs have been gathering and assessing since 1988. Its functions and terms of reference may be further elaborated in future, but the range of expertise is generally defined as 'scientific'. Its duties remain firmly linked to the natural and technical sciences, but will also include the identification of innovative and efficient technologies. The implementation experts of the second subsidiary body will not, it seems, be asked to advise on implementation as such, but rather on its measurement. A main task of this body will be to help countries with their inventories of emissions and sinks – a rather fundamental inquiry, in the nature of economic activities under national jurisdictions, which is already under way. This knowledge will become widely available. The Earth's surface has been made transparent.

## CONCLUSIONS: THE ROLE OF SCIENTIFIC ADVICE IN INTERNATIONAL RELATIONS

The climate-change threat rose to the top of the agenda in international political and diplomatic debates not so much because science meekly responded to public concern but more because a global network of national organisations, devoted to research into atmospheric sciences, climate forecasting, ecosystems, energy-demand forecasting and new energy and information-gathering technologies, actively helped to create and disseminate concern. Basic environmental research serves to diagnose problems, but once action is agreed other forms of knowledge are needed. The research enterprise must therefore continuously invent new problems which it can then credibly claim to solve. To acquire policy relevance for climate-change research, ambiguity, a weak consensus and scientific controversy were as much an expression of real issues as they were a form of strategic behaviour. Once funded, scientific institutions demand freedom and prefer to withdraw from advocacy to an emphasis on uncertainty, ignorance and even indeterminacy. They seek to become neutral and value free. Such scientific advice has one advantage over most other tools of politics: it can legitimate U-turns on the basis of new evidence or persisting uncertainty. Science does not, therefore, make a reliable ally for environmentalists, and any international policy which defines itself in relation to 'rational and optimal' knowledge is pursuing a moving target that cannot be implemented. Scientific uncertainties invite delay not action. To the extent that science is always uncertain, it is useful to states that want to protect their sovereignty. International regimes are therefore particularly attractive to the research enterprise.[15] Here, action-oriented agreements are most easily resisted, while commitments to more research (or learning), via lowest-denominator agreements, are most attractive. This makes the research enterprise a potential ally for the development of regimes that remain very open to future politics, and allow for the growth and exchange of information, but avoid genuine global regulations. The consensual knowledge that academic policy advisors seek will rarely if ever be available in the complex area of global environmental impacts (Wynne 1992). It would be against the interest of research if it were.

The Parties to the FCCC will meet in 1995 in Berlin to consider whether they have made adequate commitments. Many governments are now considering their reply without additional scientific guidance. They will probably agree to do more research and collect more data. Responses beyond this are likely to be defined in a purely national context. Energy, information and the climate are far too important to be ignored for long in international relations, and the IPCC has successfully brought them to the attention of most governments. It allowed natural-science research and branches of economics both to define the global-change problem as a research issue and to suggest solutions, most of which would require further massive research (or subsidisation) efforts. The main allies at this early stage of problem definition have comprised the Northern environmental lobbies, some commercial interests and several international bureaucracies with strong research interests. Opponents have comprised a small number of scientists who did not want to be part of a 'government science' programme with strong energy-policy implications, as well as fossil-fuel and cheap-energy interests which promised to defeat 'new' fuels and technologies when an era of expensive energy ended in 1986. The oil companies, as the owners of gas, have emerged as the major winners – but this is another story. Global warming provided the justification for intervention on the side of potential losers, but the costs of this intervention have proved unpalatable to most governments.

In the end, the concept of the atmosphere as a global common needing joint protection proved of little help in analysing and explaining observed behaviour. No common interest could be identified beyond that which institutions could create between themselves. Research bodies and the global knowledge claims they make are self-serving and are best constrained, like other political actors, by open politics and the free flow of information. The climate-change story is therefore a hopeful one, since at the relatively anarchical international level, interests and values are expressed openly and the role of science in international relations is revealed more readily, perhaps, than it is at many national levels. It must remain the task of politics to transform available knowledge into policy in the context of many other ingredients. The question remains of whether the global epistemic community and the international environmental regimes it has created are indeed benign phenomena. Instead of being protectors of an asserted common property or resource, they may be just another manifestation of dominance and power politics – this at least is how they appear to be perceived at the global grass roots.

The study of the IPCC reported here suggests that for complex environmental issues there can be no common policy enterprise for mankind, only attempts to generate such an enterprise by certain actors with reference to global threats that cannot be proven. Such threats nevertheless possess considerable political and technical innovative potential. The assumption that leading members of the climate-change community subscribe 'to holistic ecological beliefs about the need for policy coordination subject to ecosystemic laws' (Haas, P. 1993: 9) is not justified in this case and would even be dangerous. Indeed, climate scientists have disagreed as much as anybody else about what to do. Humanity would be ill advised to accept any coherent plans put forward by climate-change experts for the management of entire ecosystems, or, in this case, of the entire atmosphere, biosphere, hydrosphere . . . indeed of virtually everything and everybody.

## NOTES

1 This paper is based on the project 'The formulation and impact of scientific advice on global climate change' (Y 320 25 3030) funded by the UK Economic and Social Research Council under its Global Environmental Change Initiative. Many people have commented on drafts of this paper, including IPCC participants, energy specialists and government officials, as well as research scientists and officials from British research councils. The UK Department of the Environment could have commented, but declined. David Victor, Jim Skea and Simon Shackley in particular have made most helpful comments. All assistance is gratefully acknowledged, but errors and misinterpretations remain entirely my own. What in retrospect may appear as intentional is perceived by some as coincidental. A full history cannot yet be written.

2 The IGBP was planned during the early 1980s by US research institutions and then disseminated globally for approval and implementation by the ICSU in response to the concern about climate change which had meanwhile been generated. In 1984, Roy Rapley, Head of Remote Sensing and Associate Director of the Department of Space and Climate Physics at the ULC's Mullard Space Laboratory, became its Executive Director.

3 About half of the lead authors in the IPCC science reports (WG I) came from the UK and USA; contributing authors and reviewers were selected by them. Policy-makers'

summaries were drafted by very small groups of senior science managers close to the UK government. Hartmut Grassl, Vice-Chairman of WG I from the Max Planck Institute for Meteorology, is the new Director of the WCRP at the invitation of the WMO, the ICSU and the Intergovernmental Oceanic Commission.

4  Apart from the critique presented here, there is a more fundamental objection. Pure environmental regimes, usually assumed by theorists, do not exist because of the many and varied impacts on costs of production, trade and competition. Trade or financial interests may therefore drive environmental 'regimes'.

5  This book is based on Aspen Institute workshops held in the USA and West Germany. Major participants were the US National Corporation for Atmospheric Physics (NCAR) based in Boulder and the Austrian International Institute for Applied Systems Analysis, where the climate threat was explored by two Germans, H. Flohn (climatologist, WMO) and W. Hafele (inventor of the breeder reactor) during the 1970s.

6  Opposition by social scientists in the EC Commission was overruled (CEC interview).

7  Organisations attending included the Joint Research Centre of the CEC, UNEP, the UNDP, the US Committee on Earth and Environmental Sciences and the Consortium for the International Earth Science Networks.

8  A 1992 German IGBP newsletter (*Global Change Prisma*) lists fifty-six satellite and four space-shuttle launches between 1992 and 1998 for remote sensing. The countries involved are the USA (NASA and NOAA), Japan, Russia, Germany, India, the UK and France – the major global-change research nations.

9  WGs II and III were merged in 1993 and a third group on cross-cutting (natural/socioeconomic) issues set up. This time, natural scientists have already planned joint meetings between WG I and the new WG III, thus by-passing governments.

10  It had previously been thought that aerosols would lead to another ice age. Luckily, the recent major volcanic eruption in the Philippines could be used to explain the less-than-predicted level of warming in 1992. The role of water vapour is not well understood, but would be affected by the unknown impacts of actual warming – as distinct from radiative forcing.

11  The Russians were quickly thrown out of WG I.

12  The Group of Experts on the Scientific Aspects of Marine Pollution (GESAMP) is much older and has over fifteen working groups. It has never attracted the same attention, but may have been more effective as a low-profile organisation.

13  W.J. McTegart was the Australian Vice-Chair of IPCC WG II until 1993, and I am most grateful for his assistance over several years. W.J. Zillman is Director of the Commonwealth Bureau of Meteorology. Both are thanked for their help.

14  Interpretation includes an expert assessment of predictions derived from general circulation models of the atmosphere, coupled to a consideration of oceans as energy-transfer mechanisms. These models developed from weather-forecasting and nuclear-winter (fall-out) research. Adapted for testing the effects of a changing atmospheric composition, they are best viewed as numerical experiments. The IPCC, however, called them the only available tool both for prediction and for the exploration of uncertainties. Only a handful of countries possess these models: the USA, Germany, the UK, Japan and France.

15  Others that may be considered for comparison are the acid-rain regime under the Geneva Convention and the control of marine pollution under the Law of the Sea Convention. Ozone is a different matter in that its agreement was one which advanced the interests of two chemical companies. Biodiversity also deserves to be studied.

## BIBLIOGRAPHY

Boehmer-Christiansen, S. A. (1993) 'Science policy, the IPCC and the Climate Convention: the codification of a global research agenda', *Energy and Environment* 4(4): 362–406.

—— (1994a) 'Global climate protection policy: the limits of scientific advice – Part I', *Global Environmental Change* 4(2): 140–59.

—— (1994b) 'Global climate protection policy: the limits of scientific advice – Part II', *Global Environmental Change* 4(3): 185–200.

—— (1994c) 'The operation and impact of the Intergovernmental Panel on Climate Change: results of a survey of participants and users', STEEP Discussion Paper No. 16, Brighton, June 1994: SPRU.

—— (1995) 'Britain's role in the politics of global warming', *Environmental Politics* 4(1) (forthcoming).

—— and Skea J.F. (1991) *Acid Politics*, London: Belhaven.

Bolin, B. (1977) *Energy and Climate*, Stockholm: Secretariat for Future Studies.

—— (1994) 'Science and policy-making', *AMBIO* 23(1): 25–9.

—— *et al.* (eds) (1988) *The Greenhouse Effect: Climatic Change and Ecosystems*, SCOPE 29, Chichester: Wiley & Sons.

Bretherton, F. (1994) 'Perspectives on policy', *AMBIO* 23(1): 96–7.

Bryson, R.A. (1972) 'Climatic modification by air pollution', in Polunin, N. (ed.) *The Environmental Future*, London: Macmillan, pp. 133–67.

Churchill, R. and Freestone, D. (1992) *International Law and Global Climate Change*, London: Graham & Trotman/Nijhoff.

Cole, S. (1992) *Making Science*, London and Cambridge: Harvard U.P.

Gee, D. (1994) 'Economic tax reform: shifting the tax burden from economic goods to environmental bads', *European Environment* 4(2): 8–11.

Greenpeace (undated) *Emerging Impacts of Climate Change*, Amsterdam: Greenpeace International.

Grubb, M. (1991) *Energy Policies and the Greenhouse Effect 2*, London: RIIA.

Haas, P. (1990) 'Obtaining international environmental protection through epistemic consensus', *Millenium: Journal of International Studies* 19(3): 347–64.

Haas, E.B. (1990) *When Knowledge is Power*, Berkeley: University of California Press.

—— (1993) 'Scientific communities and multiple paths to environmental management', paper given at the EMEC Conference 1993.

Hart, D. and Victor, D. (1993) 'Scientific elites and the making of US policy for climate change research 1957–1974', *Social Studies of Science* 23(4): 643–80.

Her Majesty's Treasury (1992) *The Economics of Man-made Climate Change*, London: HMSO.

Houghton, J.T., Jenkins, G.J. and Ephraums, J.J. (eds) (1990) *Climate Change: the IPCC Scientific Assessment*, Cambridge and New York: C.U.P.; published for the IPCC (updated 1992).

Information Unit on Climate Change (IUCC) *The United Nations Framework Convention on Climate Change* (UNFCCC), WHO/UNEP.

Interview with an IPCC WG I coordinator, Hadley Centre, UK Meteorological Office, Brackley, September 1992.

ICSU/IGBP (1992) *Reducing Uncertainties*, Stockholm: Royal Swedish Academy of Sciences.

IGBP (1994) *Global Change Newsletter 17*, March.

Jager, J. and Ferguson, H.L. (eds) (1991) *Climate Change: Science, Impacts, Policy: Proceedings of the Second World Climate Conference*, London: C.U.P., for the WMO.

Kellogg, W. W. and Schware, R. (1981) *Climate Change and Society: Consequences of Increasing Carbon Dioxide*, New York: Westview.

Lindzen, R. (1992) 'Global warming: the origin and nature of the alleged scientific consensus', *Energy and Environment*, special issue for the Proceedings of OPEC Seminar, Vienna, April 1992: 122–37.

McCracken, M. (1992) in Veggeberg, S. 'Global warming researchers say they need breathing room', *The Scientist* 6(2): 4.

McTegart, W.J. and Zillman, W.J. (1990) 'The International Panel on Climate Change', unpublished paper, Canberra.

Mansell, R. and Paltridge, S. (1993) 'The earth observation market: industrial dynamics and their impact on policy', *Space Policy* 9(4): 281–98.

Michaels, P.J. (1992) *Sound and Fury: the Science and Politics of Global Warming*, Washington, DC: Cato Institute.

Mukerji, C. (1989) *A Fragile Power: Scientists and the State*, Oxford: Princeton U.P.

Nilson, K. and Sunesson, S. (1993) 'Conflict or control: research utilisation strategies as power techniques', *Knowledge and Policy* 6(2): 23–36.

OECD Megascience Forum (1994) *Global Change of Planet Earth*, Paris: OECD Publications.

Pearce, F. (1994) 'Frankenstein syndrome hits climate treaty', *New Scientist*, 11 June 1994: 5.

Polunin, N. (ed.) (1972) *The Environmental Future*, London: Macmillan.

Price, M.F. (1992) 'The evolution of global environmental change: issues, research, programmes', *Impact of Science on Society* 166: 171–82.

Regens, J.L. (1993) 'Acid deposition', in National Academy of Engineering *Keeping Pace with Science and Technology*, Washington, DC: National Academy Press, pp. 165–88.

Royal Swedish Academy of Sciences (1994) 'Integrating earth system science', *Ambio* 23(1): whole issue.

Rubin, E. (1992) 'Keeping climate research relevant', *Issues in Science and Technology*, Winter: 47.

Skolnikoff, E.B. (1990) 'The policy gridlock on global warming', *Foreign Policy* 79 (Summer): 77–93.

Smithon, M. (1994) 'Climate and ocean', *Newsletter of Environmental Physics Group 9*, London: Institute of Physics.

Thompson, P. (ed.) (1991) *Global Warming: the Debate*, Chichester and New York: Wiley.

Tickell, C. (1986) *Climatic Change and World Affairs*, London: Harvard and University Press of America (first published 1977).

Tolba, M. (1982) *Development Without Destruction*, Dublin: Yycool.

Underdal, A. and Skodvin, T. (1994) 'The science–politics interface', paper prepared for the Annual Meeting of the International Studies Association, Washington, DC, March–April 1994, mimeo.

US National Research Council (1990) *Research Strategies for the US Global Change Research Program*, Washington, DC: National Academy Press.

Warrick, R.A. and Jones, P.D. (1988) 'The greenhouse effect: impacts and policies', *Forum for Applied Research and Public Policy* 3(3): 48–62.

Weart, S. (1992) 'From the nuclear frying pan into the global fire', *The Bulletin of Atomic Scientists* 48(5): 18–27.

Wigley, T.M.L. and Raper, S.C.B. (1992) 'Implications for climate and sea level of revised IPCC emission scenarios', *Nature* 357 (28 May 1992) (quotation from accompanying press release).

Winham, G.R. (1977) 'Negotiation as a management and process', *World Politics* 30(1): 96.

World Energy Council (WEC) (1993) *World Energy Council Journal*, July: 26.

World Meteorological Organisation (WMO) (1986) *Report of the International Conference on the Assessment of Carbon Dioxide and Other Greenhouse Gases in Climate Variations and Associated Impacts*, Villach, 9–15 October 1985, WMO Publication No. 661, Geneva: WMO.

—— (1992) *The World Climate Programme 1992–2001*, WMO Publication No. 762, Geneva: WMO.

Wynne, B. (1992) 'Global environmental change: human and policy dimensions', *Global Environmental Change* 2(2): 11–127.

Young, O. (1989) *International Cooperation: Building Regimes for Natural Resources and the Environment*, Ithaca, NY: Cornell U.P.

# 11 Environmental regimes

## Effectiveness and implementation review[1]

*Owen Greene*

Sustained international cooperation is important for tackling many transnational environmental problems. Research into the development and implementation of international environmental regimes is therefore important for everyone who is concerned with such problems, as well as to researchers interested in international institutions or processes of cooperation and conflict.

There are now hundreds of international environmental agreements, of which at least 120 are multilateral with contemporary relevance and some international legal substance (Sand 1992; UNEP 1993). However, less than twenty-five of these have received wide academic and public attention. There has also been a tendency to focus most attention on the agenda-setting and regime-formation stages of regime development. This is understandable, since these stages are typically most politically salient and accessible. But the implementation and effectiveness of established regimes matter too. Moreover, the principles, norms, rules and decision-making procedures of the regime normally continue to be negotiated and developed throughout its lifetime.

This chapter discusses factors affecting the effectiveness of environmental regimes, and the significance of institutional design. In particular, it explores the role both of implementation-review procedures and of systems for monitoring environmental performance. This is partly in order to illustrate the ways in which international institutional mechanisms can determine regime effectiveness. However, it is also to demonstrate the importance of monitoring and implementation review processes for the development, implementation and effectiveness of international environmental regimes.

The next section situates this discussion in the broader field of research both into the processes of global environmental change and into social responses to transnational environmental problems. It then briefly reviews the results of recent research on the development and implementation of international regimes. The section after this examines the factors determining regime effectiveness and levels of compliance with commitments, and encourages a concern with institutional design. The particular significance of implementation review and verification processes in this context is explored in the next section. Some key issues in institutional design are then identified. The significance of review procedures in helping institutions to adapt effectively to changing circumstances is highlighted, together with their role in managing the development and implementation of commitments in complex regimes, where effectiveness depends on changing the behaviour of a large number of actors, of many different types, operating in a wide variety of circumstances. To illustrate this argument, and to encourage hesitation before using the Montreal Protocol as a model for institutional design in these circumstances, the priorities for the further development of the climate-change convention are briefly discussed.

## STUDYING INTERNATIONAL ENVIRONMENTAL REGIMES

This chapter focuses on the role of international regimes in social responses to global environmental change. The classic definition of an international regime is that of a set of 'principles, norms, rules and decision-making procedures around which actor expectations converge in a given issue area' (Krasner 1983). This distinguishes it from an international organisation, and also from international conventions or structures that apply across a wide range of issue areas. It encompasses informal or politically agreed rules and procedures as well as legally binding ones. A regime is thus seen as an international social institution.

The notion of a regime was originally developed by 'institutionalists' who were concerned to demonstrate, against the claims of 'neorealists', that international institutions can matter in world politics (Rittberger 1993; Levy, Young and Zurn 1994). This broad point is now more or less accepted by most international relations scholars, and was probably never doubted by diplomats and others practically involved with international policy. Now, the key questions in this area of study are: why, when and how do international regimes form and develop; what determines their significance or effectiveness; and how can they shape or restructure transnational or domestic institutions and practices?

So-called 'regime theory' has been subjected to substantial criticism. In part this is because it is mainly used and developed within the neoliberal-institutionalist and neorealist perspectives in international relations. Thus, critics of these perspectives and of the research agendas they generate understandably include 'regimes' in their target lists. However, it is certainly true that the study of international regimes can lead only to a partial understanding of social responses to international problems. Communities respond to global environmental change at a number of levels. The many social, political and economic processes driving environmental change, and changing behaviour and social structures, extend far beyond the realm of 'international environmental politics'.

By focusing on the development and implementation of international agreements and their associated institutions, procedures and rules, students of international environmental regimes can miss a lot. Moreover, they are concentrating on processes in which governments, international organisations, 'experts', powerful domestic and transnational interest groups and organised environmental pressure groups play a privileged role. An excessive focus on international regimes could lead one falsely to assume that other communities are of marginal importance in global environmental change.

Nevertheless, having acknowledged this, I believe that the development and effectiveness of international environmental institutions remain an important area of study. Sustained international cooperation is useful or essential for tackling many transnational environmental problems. Agreements negotiated by states, and the development of institutions involving influential international and domestic actors, are key ways in which such cooperation can be organised and maintained. They provide an important framework for the interactions both between international and domestic actors and processes, and between 'knowledge', power and interests relevant to a particular issue area. Moreover, a regime provides a focus for the formulation and implementation of policies to tackle a particular set of transnational environmental problems.

Critics of 'regime analysis' further point out that the classic definition of a regime is somewhat vague, and that the components (norms, rules, etc.) it identifies are in practice hard to distinguish. Again, they have a point. The concept of a 'regime' remains essentially contested even amongst its supporters, and in practice it is defined and used in a range of different and inconsistent ways (Milner 1993).

It is obviously important to be as clear as possible on what we are talking about, particularly in discussions on 'regimes' *per se* or when conceptualising the constitutive structures and processes of world politics. However, if social scientists shied away from using essentially contested concepts, whole disciplines would collapse. In my view, a broad understanding of a regime as 'an international social institution with agreed-upon principles, norms, procedures and programmes that govern the activities and shape the expectations of actors in a specific issue area'[2] provides a good enough basis for getting on with studying actual regimes. A large number of researchers have proceeded on this basis in recent years, and have demonstrated this to be a productive approach generating reasonably robust and policy-relevant findings.

Empirical research on regimes over the last decade has refuted some of the early propositions about their character and formation. It has demonstrated that they come in a variety of different types. They can form and operate in a wide variety of circumstances, and in the absence of hegemonic powers.[3] Moreover, once established, they can survive and influence shifts in the distribution of power in international society, and can persist even if their obligations become inconvenient to one or more powerful states or if there is a deterioration in overall relations between their participants.[4] Thus, at least a number of regimes have been shown to be much more than epiphenomena: regimes can be robust and can have significant consequences.

Although states are typically the formal members of regimes, many case studies have demonstrated that non-state actors are often very important in the formation and development of international environmental regimes.[5] In relation to implementation processes and regime effectiveness, the links between international environmental institutions, states and non-state actors and processes appear to be particularly important and complex (though less research has been carried out on these). In other areas, such as arms control or trade, agreements mostly directly aim to regulate government action. The mechanisms by which governments can ensure domestic implementation are typically well developed and relatively direct. In contrast, implementing environmental commitments often involves the complex task of changing the practices of a wide range of non-state actors, semi-autonomous state industries or agencies, and local authorities.

In spite of attempts to identify one, it now seems clear that there is no single type of factor or process determining when, why and how regimes develop and what consequences they have. Power and interests certainly play a key role. However, so too do several other factors.

For example, understandings from the natural and social sciences typically play an important role in debates about the nature and scale of the environmental 'problems', their impacts and the formulation and implementation of policy responses. 'Knowledge' is clearly a key condition for the rational management of natural resources and the environment. Moreover, scientific and policy processes are in continual interaction, and they shape each other. Thus, scientists and environmental knowledge will be influenced by international environmental institutions. But scientific institutions, advisory bodies, 'epistemic communities' and individual scientists also typically play a major if not structural role in the development and implementation of such regimes.

Moreover, in addition to power, interests and 'knowledge', social learning, individual leadership and the international context can also be critical (Levy, Young and Zurn 1994). Combinations of all such factors, and of different types of actors, are usually significant for any given regime. Their relative importance changes as the regime develops through various stages: agenda-setting; institutional choice (the formulation, negotiation and agreement of the provisions of the regime); implementation; and further development. Moreover, the combinations involved are likely to be regime-specific and also, to a significant extent, historically contingent.[6]

Thus, our subsequent discussion should aim to identify and explore a range of possible mechanisms by which institutional design, and particularly implementation review, could relate to regime implementation and effectiveness, and should be cautious about generalising from a few well-known conventions.

## EFFECTIVENESS AND INSTITUTIONAL DESIGN

The definition of 'effectiveness' is itself contested. There are a range of possible definitions, and assessments of regime effectiveness can depend greatly on which criteria are used (Young 1994; Levy 1993). For example, an international institution could very successfully change the behaviour of relevant actors in line with its rules but nevertheless have little, or even an adverse, impact on the environmental problem itself. Alternatively, the environmental problem may be reduced, but with little contribution from the relevant international regime.

In this chapter, we are mainly concerned with effectiveness in terms of whether a regime contributes to the management or resolution of the environmental problem it was designed to address. However, since the causes of environmental change are often poorly understood, it can be relatively difficult to examine the effectiveness of a regime by using this criterion. Thus it is convenient in this and the subsequent section to focus mainly on a more directly observable behavioural understanding of effectiveness: how can a regime promote compliance and changes of behaviour in line with its norms and rules?

As is well known, the prospects for achieving the changes in behaviour which a regime seeks to promote depend substantially on factors that are *external* to the international institution itself. They will partly depend on the patterns of interests of the actors involved: there will always be some groups with an interest in opposing such changes, and others who would be positively affected. The distribution of coercive or structural power will be similarly significant: for example, pressure from a powerful state could be vital in securing or enforcing change. Non-coercive forms of influence, such as the existence of leaders, lobby groups or 'epistemic communities', have also been shown to be important (Haas 1992; Young and Osherenko 1993). Since those states and other actors which lack the capacity to implement the desired changes cannot comply with commitments even if they want to, the level and distribution of capacity amongst the regime's participants is also likely to be critical to its success.

The nature of the issue area is also important. The scientific or social complexity of the processes that the regime is aiming to manage or prevent will have an effect, as will the number and diversity of the actors involved. Moreover, international or public concern to 'do something about the problem' can be intensified by 'early warnings' or dramatic events. The unexpected appearance of the 'ozone hole' over Antarctica helped to galvanise support for phasing out CFCs. Other problems are less likely to become clearly transparent before it is too late to take effective preventive action. Evidence of anthropogenic climate change has, for example, only been accumulating gradually, tempting supporters of urgent action to try to link freak weather conditions with climate change in order to raise public concern.

Another potentially important characteristic of the issue area that is rarely emphasised is 'monitorability': the ability to monitor either the behaviour of relevant actors or processes, or the implementation of potential commitments. This depends on a combination of: the intrinsic characteristics of the relevant activities or materials; the state of both scientific understanding and monitoring technology; the existence of monitoring and data-collection infrastructures; and the social, economic and political characteristics of the societies or states concerned. Monitorability is an important determinant of the verifiability of (that is, the ability to verify compliance with) commitments, a factor which could in itself have a significant influence on the behaviour of significant actors. Perceptions of verifiability could affect the willingness of governments to negotiate or sign agreements. An awareness that others can monitor their environmental performance could affect the behaviour of governments and other actors. The ability to monitor and assess the performance of others could affect distributions of power and interests, and help with learning and capacity-building processes (Greene 1994).

All these 'external' factors could change behaviour in line with the rules of an environmental regime. However, an international regime cannot properly be said to be effective if it merely codifies changes that the relevant actors would have made anyway. Still less do high levels of compliance necessarily indicate effectiveness. Many regime commitments do not require changes of behaviour. Some are symbolic, or so ambiguously worded that compliance with them is virtually impossible to assess.

To be effective, a regime must make a difference. More precisely, its institutions, rules and procedures must alter external facts or processes (either directly or indirectly through their effects on the patterns of power, interest, influence, knowledge and capacity discussed above) in ways that change the behaviour of environmentally relevant actors. Thus, it is not enough to examine institutional design or external factors separately. The key issue is how they interact.

There are a range of factors that are internal to an international environmental institution that could be important in determining effectiveness. The nature and formulation of the rules and commitments of the regime, including the ways in which politically and legally binding provisions are combined and the mechanisms by which rules are developed or revised, can be important. For example, it has been shown that compliance with MARPOL rules to limit oil pollution from tankers became much better when they focused on technological regulations relating to tanker construction and port facilities instead of operational rules relating to the conduct of operators at sea (Mitchell 1994). The structure and role of the international secretariats or organisations associated with the regime can also be important. For example, a professional and relatively autonomous secretariat can play a significant leadership role and facilitate and provide resources for the effective operation and development of the regime. UNEP played a key role in the formation and early development of the regional seas and ozone conventions.

Mechanisms for resource transfers amongst participants can critically affect patterns of interest and capacity amongst participants. The ways in which scientific and technical knowledge-generation and advice are institutionalised can affect learning processes, the distribution of influence and the development of epistemic communities (Parson 1993; Haas 1992). Similarly, the design of consultative and dispute-resolution mechanisms can make a big difference to whether problems or concerns tend to be neglected or to escalate damagingly, or whether they are routinely tackled in a timely and constructive way. Finally, as discussed in more detail below, provisions for monitoring and reviewing the implementation and adequacy of commitments could significantly affect compliance, performance and the further development of environmental regimes.

The effectiveness of a regime depends on the extent to which a combination of these institutional characteristics and mechanisms are developed in such a way that they influence and interact with actors in a way that promotes desired changes in behaviour.

The best strategies for effective institutional development depend on the situation. For example, on the basis of a number of case studies, Haas, Keohane and Levy have suggested that the development and implementation of environmental commitments depend particularly on three factors: levels of concern (about the problem and about performance in implementing response measures); the development and maintenance of appropriate contracts and commitments; and the capacity to *implement* commitments (Haas, Keohane and Levy 1993). If one accepts this framework, then an effective regime should be designed so that its rules and mechanisms address whichever of these three factors appears to be lacking. If the main problem is a lack of concern amongst some or all actors, then the main area where a regime could be effective is to increase awareness both of the problem and of appropriate responses to it, and to encourage better performance – for example, by improving knowledge about performance, increasing domestic concern, embarrassing laggards and non-compliers, or facilitating the use of sanctions or rewards. If there are problems in all three areas, then it is a priority to develop institutions that are designed to tackle these problems on all fronts.

In order to achieve a better understanding of the ways in which regime effectiveness can be promoted, it is useful to identify and examine the mechanisms or pathways by which international institutional factors can influence both behaviour and implementation processes. These can broadly be divided into interest-based and learning-based mechanisms, and further divided according to whether they affect the behaviour of 'unitary' states or whether they affect domestic or non-state actors and processes.

In the next section, we examine in more detail the ways in which monitoring and implementation review processes could affect regime effectiveness. This is partly illustrative: in principle, a similar exercise would be appropriate for each of the other main components of international institutions. However, it also aims to demonstrate the potential importance of devoting careful attention to the relatively neglected issue of the development and design of implementation review mechanisms in environmental regimes.

## IMPLEMENTATION REVIEW MECHANISMS AND EFFECTIVENESS

Implementation review processes are the processes by which regime participants collect, exchange and review information relating to behaviour and performance. As such, implementation review is similar to verification. It includes monitoring, data collection and information exchange; data analysis; and assessments of the extent to which agreed measures are being implemented. However, it is not so focused on providing assurance against the risk of covert and deliberate cheating. Rather, it plays a broader variety of roles in promoting implementation and effectiveness.

Implementation review in environmental regimes typically involves a wide range of informal as well as formal processes. Individual governments or informal groups of states may engage in an independent monitoring and assessment of the other participants' environmental performance. There will also normally be a wide range of non-governmental monitoring and review activities involving all sorts of expert or interest groups. However, numerous international environmental agreements have also set up formal provisions or procedures for implementation review (Victor, Lanchbery and Greene 1994). These include provisions both for reports from governments and other recognised participants to be prepared, exchanged and audited, and for the environmental performance or compliance of regime members to be assessed. Finally, they may establish rights or procedures for independent inspections or monitoring systems.

In many cases, these mechanisms are relatively neglected. Reporting rates are often poor and reviews can be nominal (USGAO 1992; Victor, Lanchbery and Greene 1994). If they do operate, however, implementation review processes may result in additional monitoring and information collection in a form that is appropriate for reviewing national performance or compliance. They can increase overall transparency, and also affect patterns of access to relevant information. They can also provide an international framework within which regime members and other interested actors can discuss and assess national performance, and where governments are under at least some obligation to address findings or questions raised. The procedures will shape the access to, and participation in, the review process; and potentially provide a focal point both for the activities of concerned non-state actors and for institutional development.

The classic 'neorealist' way in which an implementation review mechanism can affect behaviour is that systems for verifying compliance could affect the calculations of costs and benefits made by individual states when they choose whether or not to join agreements or whether to comply. States may decide that it is not in their interests to accept or comply with commitments unless they are reasonably sure that treaty partners are also complying. Governments may be deterred from free-rider strategies by the threat of exposure. Similarly, countries that entered agreements reluctantly or under coercive external pressure may prefer covert non-compliance unless their environmental performance is made transparent to others. Moreover, the international review system can provide procedures that make it easier for treaty partners collectively to identify poor compliance and organise multilateral responses to it. In this way, the implementation review or verification system affects both the 'rules of the game' that self-interested states perceive themselves to be playing and the risks and potential payoffs involved in pursuing different strategies within it (Ausubel and Victor 1992; Greene 1993).

There are, however, a number of other mechanisms by which implementation review procedures could affect the implementation and effectiveness of environmental agreements.[7] Continuing for a moment with interest-based pathways involving self-interested unitary states, increasing transparency, information exchange and reviews could make it easier for states to achieve and maintain agreements which allow them to perform functions more efficiently through joint action. Centralising or coordinating monitoring and review activities can itself save time and money. This is an important mechanism if one believes, with Keohane (1984), that the main function of a regime is to achieve such benefits and to avoid the transaction costs that cooperating states would other- wise have to bear.

Monitoring and implementation review could affect the patterns of power and influence amongst states. In some circumstances, superior monitoring and assessment capabilities or access to information and review processes could be a significant source of influence. For example, multilateral monitoring and review systems could give weak member states access to information and a voice in international assessments. On the other hand, states with superior monitoring and assessment capacity may be better able to shape international assessments by working through international institutions. Furthermore, international organisations could be empowered: new monitoring or advisory organisations may be established, and existing ones could increase their resources and their influence as review systems are developed.

Monitoring and implementation review could also change states' behaviour by affecting learning processes. Their understandings of the environmental problems themselves could be changed. Moreover, states could learn more about their own interests, though it is not clear that this will necessarily improve regime effectiveness.

Just as important, monitoring and reviewing the environmental performance of other parties could help states to learn about their treaty partners. If governments know more about the circumstances and implementation experiences of other states, reactions to non-compliance are likely to be more sophisticated and less prone to undue suspicions of bad faith. Non-compliance could be due to a variety of factors, including: inadequate national capacity; obstruction on the part of powerful domestic or transnational interest groups; inappropriate implementation measures; or unachievable commitments. A better understanding of the reasons for poor performance could help other parties to respond in ways that promote regime effectiveness, by targeting assistance, being flexible about some non-compliance, adjusting targets or advising on more effective implementation policies.

Learning from the monitoring and reviewing of national implementation could thus help to target international assistance to increase national capacity. Moreover, by monitoring the implementation experiences of other countries, states may be better able to design effective domestic policies and measures of their own. Increased information and transparency could help governments to identify international best practice, or avoid the mistakes of others. International monitoring and information systems could also supplement inadequate national systems, thus improving the national capacity to implement policy.

As discussed above, states are not usually 'unitary' when it comes to developing and implementing environmental commitments. In any case, changing the behaviour of domestic and transnational actors is critical for the effectiveness of most environmental regimes. How could implementation review processes affect the behaviour of domestic actors?

First, such procedures could affect the cost–benefit calculations that powerful domestic interest groups or government bureaucracies make when calculating their interests. For example, trade ministries or powerful industrial groups could change their assessments of possible regulations or constraints if they knew that compliance in other states would be transparent, or if information gained as a result of international reporting procedures indicated that potential domestic costs could be offset by new trading opportunities. International monitoring and review mechanisms could also directly affect bureaucratic interests. Ministries involved in them could increase both resources and influence. Alternatively, they could reveal information to other branches of governments or interest groups about domestic practices that a ministry would prefer they did not have: knowledge is power in bureaucratic politics.

Furthermore, monitoring and implementation review procedures could change distributions of power and influence within a country. They could empower not only individual bureaucracies but also the entire state apparatus in relation to domestic society. International agreements could legitimise and provide resources for the development of systems that help the government to monitor and regulate new areas of domestic activity. Alternatively, non-governmental organisations (NGOs), special-interest groups or political parties may gain access to government information that was previously denied to them.

Moreover, in most environmental agreements, environmental NGOs and industrial associations have some standing or participation rights in the international review process. International implementation review meetings have provided an additional forum where such groups can exert pressure or embarrass their governments. They also facilitate the formation of transnational coalitions of like-minded national groups.

Implementation review procedures may be particularly significant for the empowerment of experts in established regimes. Scientists and other experts, particularly if they are outside the government, often find their influence reduced once the process of regime formation moves from agenda-setting to hard negotiations. To the extent that experts are important for monitoring and implementation review, international review procedures could increase their influence both in implementation processes and in the revision of commitments. In the International Whaling Convention (IWC), the Long-Range Transboundary Air Pollution agreement (LRTAP), the Convention on International Trade in Endangered Species of Flora and Fauna (CITES) and many other important environmental agreements, scientific and technical advisory groups have been established to assist with the review process, a process which gives them direct and privileged access to the Conference of the Parties.

Learning processes could also be important in this context. National senior scientists or technical advisors may be nominated by their government to participate in international panels. There they learn from international monitoring and information exchanges, and may also be inducted into the dominant 'epistemic community'. They may then provide an effective information channel to national- and local-government officials, industrial groups, and such like. Governments and other domestic groups are typically more willing to accept advice from an intergovernmental expert panel or from national experts than from foreigners.

Moreover, enhanced transparency may help domestic actors to learn from their counterparts elsewhere. International reporting and review systems could facilitate information exchange between those domestic groups whose behaviour is critical for implementation. For example, electric-power producers or regulators may be better able to formulate and share best practice relating to energy efficiency or gas emissions at power stations, or to design effective regulations or voluntary agreements between industry and government. By reading national reports or participating in review meetings, environmental activists may learn more about best environmental practice or campaigning tactics.

There are, thus, many potential pathways by which international monitoring and implementation review procedures could change the behaviour of states and domestic actors, and thus influence regime effectiveness. The importance and effect of each of these pathways will depend on many factors over which international policy-makers can have little direct influence. But it will also depend on institutional design, which is a matter which parties *can* control.

One key issue is where the information used in the international implementation review process comes from, and its usefulness and reliability. The process is undermined if there are no guidelines or systems for this, and if the information used is collected on an ad hoc basis. Numerous environmental agreements, including the Framework Convention on Climate Change (FCCC), LRTAP and the Montreal Protocol, require parties to provide regular reports on their own activities according to specific guidelines, so that national reports can be interpreted, assessed and compared with commitments. Such guidelines also often require states to establish new national data-collection and data-assessment systems, thereby generating information that would otherwise not be available.

There will often be a question mark over the reliability of reports provided by states about their own performance. Governments are normally reluctant to reveal embarrassing information, and they may be tempted to suppress or distort data that reveals inadequate compliance. Where such concerns are potentially significant, they can to some extent be addressed through institutional design.

A key part of the strategy is to formulate international commitments so that they are relatively verifiable, and so that the incentives or possibilities for providing inaccurate information are reduced (Greene 1994). Thus, governments are less able or willing to distort data if they also need it to manage core economic activities or government programmes, or if it is collected by relatively independent international or domestic bodies that are likely to resist government interference. Similarly, governments are more likely to stay honest if the information can be independently gathered or checked by other countries, international organisations or environmental NGOs, or if it relates to areas where there is already a high degree of transparency, or where there is a risk that 'whistleblowers' will expose false reports.

Moreover, international monitoring and review procedures can be established specifically to collect or validate data relating to national implementation. In LRTAP, the Cooperative Programme for Monitoring and Evaluation of the Long-Range Transmission of Air Pollutants in Europe (EMEP) maintains an international network for monitoring and assessing the chemical composition of rain, which can be used to deduce overall emissions of acid-causing substances from a particular country (Gehring 1994). The UN Food and Agriculture Organisation has long-established rights to collect data on land use and flora (which it does using its own systems), and most international agreements, plus most international conventions for the prevention of flora, come under its auspices. The International Convention on the Regulation of Whaling (ICW) has provisions for national reports on catches to be checked by foreign inspectors attached to factory ships or shore stations. Similarly, the 1980 Canberra Convention on Antarctic Marine Living Resources (CCAMLR) and the Convention on the Conservation of North Pacific Fur Seals permit international inspectors to board any vessel which they suspect to be in breach of the Convention, to make inspections and to confiscate any illegal catches (Lanchbery 1995).

A complementary approach is to design rules and review procedures that promote transparency in the ways in which national reports are prepared, or to establish systematic and expert reviews of these reports by international bodies that can compare them with relevant independent information and follow up with further questions or country visits to resolve any questions that may arise. This, for example, is the approach recently adopted in the Framework Convention on Climate Change (FCCC) for reviewing national reports on greenhouse-gas inventories (Greene and Lanchbery 1995; Victor and Salt 1994).

Each national submission in the FCCC contains substantial amounts of information involving complex and uncertain judgements, and would normally raise many technical questions. An effective review will therefore require substantial resources and expertise. This highlights another generally significant institutional factor: the extent to which the review involves a competent and well-resourced international technical review body. Unless the relevant facts about performance are entirely straightforward or transparent, a process whereby the assessment of national implementation is simply carried out by the Conference of the Parties without a prior systematic technical review is unlikely to promote learning, and is more likely to reflect pre-existing interests than to shape them.

The rules of access and participation, and the openness of the information-exchange and review process to all interested parties, are important. They obviously affect the ways in which learning processes and interest- or power-based mechanisms operate. Most contemporary environmental agreements normally allow interested non-members to participate as observers in reviews during the meetings of parties. However, their access to the detailed review of a party's implementation is normally more restricted. In the case of the Montreal Protocol, for example, for reasons of commercial confidentiality detailed data on imports, exports and the production of ozone-depleting substances in national reports may normally only be reviewed by the Ozone Secretariat and, if specific concerns about compliance are raised by other parties, by an Implementation Committee consisting of elected representatives of ten member states. Aggregate figures are circulated to all interested parties (including NGOs), together with a report from the Secretariat, and these form a basis for the review by the Meetings of the Parties.

Whether restrictions or open access is most likely to improve effectiveness depends on the particular circumstances. In general, openness is likely to promote learning and also the influence of 'outsiders', including environmentalists. However, confidentiality and restricted access may be important in order to elicit appropriate detailed information on implementation, or to make the review process less vulnerable to damaging disputes or misunderstandings. Openness could empower opponents of environmental protection as well as supporters.

There are numerous other potentially significant design features, such as the flexibility and level of formality of the process, the extent to which it is routine and systematic, the ways in which concerns about poor performance are raised and addressed, and the procedures for judging or resolving disputes about compliance.

However, perhaps the most important issue relates to the overall design. How do the implementation review procedures relate to the other institutional mechanisms within a regime, such as dispute resolution, responses to non-compliance, and reviews of commitments? In principle, the implementation review processes should be designed to reinforce each of these other mechanisms and vice versa. However, this is easier said than done. The next section briefly identifies some desirable overall design characteristics, and then discusses the potential role of verifiability, implementation review and procedures for developing commitments in the further stages of the climate-change convention.

## REVIEW AND OVERALL INSTITUTIONAL DESIGN

As emphasised above, an effective regime is one whose institutions, rules and procedures are well adapted to affect external factors and processes in such a way that the behaviour of relevant actors is changed in line with its objectives. These factors are specific to the situation and issue area involved. Moreover, institutions are established through a process of compromise amongst national and international policy-makers who have at best only a partial understanding of the external environment and of the most effective way of responding to it. Furthermore, the external situation is constantly changing. An institutional design that is extremely effective at one time will need continually to adapt and develop in order to remain useful.

This implies that a key characteristic of an effective regime is flexibility and the capacity to adapt its institutions, rules and procedures in a timely way in the light of its experience with implementation and as patterns of power, interest, influence, knowledge, capacity and concern develop.

Many international environmental conventions seem ill-equipped to achieve this. They have no provisions for regular meetings of the parties, and the procedures for review or for revising procedures and commitments are often unclear (Victor, Lanchbery and Greene 1994). For example, the 1940 Washington Convention on wildlife preservation in the Western hemisphere effectively has no review mechanisms and no provisions for meetings of the parties. Its Annex of endangered species is incomplete and almost permanently out of date: no species have been added since 1967.

In contrast, the parties to the 1946 International Whaling Convention (IWC) meet annually to review national reports of whale catches and the reports of expert groups set up to monitor whale populations or aspects of whaling activities. These expert groups can be set up or terminated by majority vote at any meeting of the parties. Commitments can easily be revised in the same way by amending the Schedule to the Convention. Similarly, CITES has several expert standing committees reviewing and advising the Conference of the Parties, which meets every two years. There are also provisions for additional Extraordinary meetings, which are occasionally held, and commitments are frequently and easily revised by altering the Appendices listing endangered species (Victor, Lanchbery and Greene 1994).

CITES and the ICW both share some of the essential flexible characteristics of 'framework conventions'. These are conventions which establish the basic principles, norms and procedures of a regime, including provisions both for regular reviews of implementation and of the adequacy of commitments and for the subsequent negotiation of protocols. The routine reviews facilitate learning and institutional development, and provide a forum for agenda-setting. Using these protocols, parties can develop or revise procedures and commitments as they see fit. The UNEP regional seas agreements (such as the 1976 Barcelona Convention for the Protection of the Mediterranean Sea Against Pollution) and the 1985 Vienna Convention for the Protection of the Ozone Layer are widely regarded as paradigms of this institutional approach. In contrast with the ICWs somewhat alarming potential for dramatic and sudden changes in rules, once the Montreal Protocol came into force, parties could only revise its main rules or commitments by separately negotiating and ratifying Amendments (as occurred in this case with the 1990 London Amendments and the 1992 Copenhagen Revisions).

Framework conventions are now widely regarded as the most appropriate model for the design of new conventions to tackle a wide range of global or regional environmental problems. For example, the main conventions emerging from the 1992 'Earth Summit' – the Framework Convention on Climate Change (FCCC), the Biodiversity Convention and the Desertification Convention – are all framework conventions.

For the reasons discussed above, this appears to be an effective overall approach to institutional design, leaving a great deal of flexibility to develop each regime's institutions, rules and procedures differently according to its particular situation and tasks. This latter point needs emphasis, because it should not be assumed that the institutional development of successful regimes such as the Montreal Protocol is a good model for the development of other conventions addressing different and often more complex issue areas.

The Framework Convention on Climate Change (FCCC), which came into force on 21 March 1994, is a case in point. The FCCC imposes few obligations on parties to it. The Convention allows each party to adopt whatever national programmes and commitments to limit greenhouse-gas (GHG) emissions it deems appropriate. However, the substance and implementation of these measures are to be regularly and internationally reviewed. All parties are obliged to provide detailed national inventories of greenhouse gases, together with a general description of steps taken or envisaged to implement the Convention. In addition, each developed country must provide: a detailed description of the policies and measures it has adopted to limit GHG emissions, projections of emissions in 2000 and a specific estimate of the effects of its policies and measures on net GHG emissions. These reports are to be regularly reviewed by the Conference of the Parties, with the assistance of two subsidiary bodies and expert review' panels.

At least until future protocols are negotiated, this 'pledge and review process will be central to the effectiveness of the Convention. By the end of 1994, the process had begun. All OECD states except Turkey and Mexico had made unilateral commitments to limit GHG emissions on which they should have made a start. Moreover, the first national reports submitted by developed-country parties were being subject to an initial review in preparation for the first Conference of the Parties in March 1995, pending more detailed scrutiny during the subsequent year.

Now that the FCCC is established, the question is how to further develop the regime to make it more effective. If one were to follow the Montreal Protocol paradigm for the development of a framework convention, attention would focus on starting a process of negotiating a series of increasingly stringent commitments to limit national GHG emissions.

In this context, a first priority would be to establish the stabilisation of developed parties' net GHG emissions at 1990 levels after the year 2000 as a legally binding obligation. Such a commitment would consolidate the already-declared unilateral commitments and encourage states to do more to ensure that they meet them. However, it is not clear that it is then a priority to press for more stringent targets and timetables. Encouraging other aspects of institutional development seems a higher priority, including establishing a well-developed implementation review process and promoting the effective formulation and implementation of national programmes to at least stabilise GHG emissions at 1990 levels. It is important to note that several OECD countries (and the EU) are still a long way from implementing policies that are likely to achieve this goal by 2000.

Moreover, it is important to be aware of the fact that the formulation of international commitments relating to national GHG emissions involves complex choices.

An effective protocol needs to set significant targets for limiting GHG emissions but also to allow states real flexibility about how they achieve them, not only to allow for efficiency and adaptability in view of countries' widely varying circumstances, but also to encourage states to focus on achieving their commitments rather than on developing tough negotiating strategies. To promote effective implementation, commitments should also be verifiable and subject to effective implementation review.

In principle, a protocol involving commitments relating specifically to a few important and relatively verifiable gases or sectors could go some way to meeting these requirements (Greene and Salt 1993). For example, limits on carbon-dioxide emissions from fossil-fuel burning (which probably account for more than half of any anthropogenic climate change) would be relatively verifiable, at least for developed states (Fischer, Katscheer and Di Primio 1990). Moreover, in most countries this is a sector large and diverse enough for the state to have a significant range of choices about how to implement commitments efficiently.

However, this approach appears to be unnegotiable for the foreseeable future. Several key states are insisting that any binding limits on net GHG emissions should be comprehensive: they should cover all of the main GHGs and sectors (apart from substances restricted by the Montreal Protocol). In any case, just because compliance with commitments to limit some types of emissions (such as methane from agriculture) is very hard to verify, it does not mean that we should abandon the attempt to establish obligations or incentives to limit such emissions.

However, any commitment expressed in terms of limits on parties' overall annual GHG emissions poses real challenges for the design of an effective regime. For example, how are national emissions of one GHG to be compared with those of another? The so-called 'global-warming potential' of some GHGs remains poorly understood and subject to change. Furthermore, if the national-emissions inventories for those gases and sectors that can be measured or monitored reasonably accurately were to be aggregated with those that are highly uncertain in this respect, the overall monitorability of any commitment relating to overall GHG emissions would prove to be poor, both for the government concerned and for the international community, and this would undermine any effective implementation review. If the implementing state itself cannot measure whether it is complying with its commitments, implementation is bound to suffer.

A promising strategy for tackling this problem is to build on the 'pledge and review' process that has already been established within the FCCC (Greene and Salt 1994). Thus, procedures could be established by which those parties legally obliged to limit their net annual GHG emissions should report on how they intend to achieve compliance. Each state would announce targets for each gas and sector, set so that their combined effect (calculated according to internationally agreed methods) would be sufficient to meet their obligation.

For some gases (such as carbon dioxide, as emitted from fossil-fuel burning) and some sectors, such a pledge would already be verifiable and amenable to implementation review. In others, this would not be the case, and the procedures for pledge and review would then require parties to further disaggregate their pledges. For example, a national pledge to reduce methane emissions from rice production by 10 per cent is relatively unverifiable. But a collection of national sub-commitments to achieve this – for example, by stabilising paddy areas; reducing inundation periods by 25 per cent; changing rice varieties; and carrying out programmes to reduce the use of organic fertilisers – *could* be amenable to effective implementation review.

This process would generate a verifiable set of political pledges and indicators of performance for each country according to its own preferences and circumstances but on the basis of a globally negotiated (but relatively unverifiable) overall legal commitment. These pledges would be defined by each country concerned, but in consultation with a review body and according to international guidelines. Such sub-commitments will often be closely related to a government's domestic targets and implementation programmes. This has the advantage that procedures for reviewing the implementation of commitments will not only be closely linked to the process of reviewing the adequacy and effectiveness of policies governments have adopted to meet these commitments, but may also be more effectively linked with programmes to assist with implementation.

Variants on this approach could also be useful for the development of other environmental regimes dealing with great complexity, and indeed both for promoting action relating to Agenda 21 and for increasing the effectiveness of the Commission on Sustainable Development. However, this would require specific study. As emphasised above, implementation review processes and other institutional characteristics of regimes can be a key factor in regime effectiveness, but their design should be sensitive to the particular context and adaptable in the light of experience and changing priorities.

## NOTES

1 This chapter draws on research done at Bradford University and funded by the ESRC Global Environmental Change Programme, and also on recent work done with colleagues in the project on the Implementation and Effectiveness of International Environmental Agreements at the International Institute for Applied Systems Analysis (IIASA). The author gratefully acknowledges the stimulation and support received. The views expressed are the author's own, and not necessarily those of the institutions.
2 This is very similar to the working definition and approach proposed by Levy, Young and Zurn 1994.
3 Hegemonic-stability theorists argued that this would not be the case, but the maintenance development of international trade and other regimes after the USA slipped from its hegemonic position in the 1970s provides counter-evidence.
4 The Anti-Ballistic Missile (ABM) Treaty provides an example of this – particularly in its survival and continued influence during the mid- to late 1980s when the US Administration found many of its provisions uncongenial.
5 See, for example: Elliott 1994; Princen and Finger 1994; Petersen 1992; Wapner 1991.
6 This may not always be the case. Future systematic empirical research comparing a range of different regimes may allow the development of some reliable and useful general findings on this and related issues.
7 The discussion in this section draws upon previous ESRC-funded work (for example, Greene 1993), and also has drawn substantially on recent work and discussions with colleagues in the IIASA project on the Implementation and Effectiveness of International Environmental Agreements, particularly with D. Victor and J. Lanchbery, Juan-Carlos Di Primio and Anna Korula (see, for example, Victor *et al.* 1994; Victor, Lanchbery and Green 1994).

## BIBLIOGRAPHY

Ausubel, J. and Victor, D. (1992) 'Verification of international environmental agreements', *Annual Review of Energy and the Environment 1992* 17: 1–43.

Elliott, L. (1994) *International Environmental Politics: Protecting the Antarctic*, London: Macmillan.

Fischer, W., Katscheer, W. and Di Primio, J.-C. (1990) 'A convention on greenhouse gases: towards the design of a verification system', *Berichte des Forschungzentrum Julich* 2390: whole volume.

Gehring, T. (1994) *Dynamic International Regimes: Institutions for International Environmental Governance*, Berlin: Peter Lang Press.

Greene, O. (1993) 'International environmental regimes: verification and implementation review', *Environmental Politics* 2(4): 156–73.

—— (1994) 'On verifiability, and how it could matter for international environmental agreements', *IIASA Working Paper WP-94-116*, Laxenburg: IIASA.

—— and Lanchbery, J. (1995) 'The Climate Change Convention: preparing for the First Conference of the Parties', in Poole, J. and Guthrie, R. (eds) *Verification 1995: Arms Control, Peacekeeping and the Environment*, London: Westview.

—— and Salt, J. (1993) 'Verification issues in the development of an effective climate change convention', *World Resources Review* 5(3): 271–85.

—— and Salt, J. (1994) 'Verification and implementation review of climate change commitments relating to methane emissions', in van Hamm, J. *et al.* (eds) *Non-CO$_2$ Greenhouse Gases*, Kingston upon Thames: Kluwer Academic Publishers.

Haas, P. (ed.) (1992) 'Knowledge, power, and international policy coordination', *International Organisation* (special issue) 46(1): 1–39.

—— Keohane, R. and Levy, M. (eds) (1993) *Institutions for the Earth*, Cambridge, Mass.: MIT Press.

Keohane, R. (1984) *After Hegemony: Cooperation and Discord in the World Political Economy*, Princeton, NJ: Princeton U.P.

Krasner, S. (1983) 'Structural causes and regime consequences: regimes and intervening variables', in Krasner, S. (ed.) (1993) *International Regimes*, London: Cornell U.P.

Lanchbery, J. (1995) 'Reviewing implementation of biodiversity agreements: an historical perspective', in Poole, J. and Guthrie, R. (eds) *Verification 1995: Arms Control, Peacekeeping and the Environment*, London: Westview.

Levy, M. (1993) 'Political science and the question of effectiveness of international environmental institutions', *International Challenges* 13(2): 17–35.

—— Young, O. and Zurn, M. (1994) 'The study of international regimes', *IIASA Working Paper WP-94-113*, Laxenburg: IIASA.

Milner, H. (1993) 'International regimes and world politics', *International Social Science Journal* 435(4): 491–7.

Mitchell, R. (1994) *Intentional Oil Pollution at Sea: Environmental Policy and Treaty Compliance*, London: MIT Press.

Parson, E. (1993) 'Protecting the ozone layer', in Haas, P., Keohane, R. and Levy, M. (eds) *Institutions for the Earth*, Cambridge, Mass.: MIT Press, pp. 27–74.

Petersen, M. (1992) 'Whales, cetologists, environmentalists and the international management of whaling', *International Organisation* 46: 147–86.

Princen, T. and Finger, M. (1994) *Environmental NGOs in World Politics*, London: Routledge.

Rittberger, V. (ed.) (1993) *Regime Theory and International Relations*, Oxford: Clarendon.

Sand, P. (1992) *The Effectiveness of International Environmental Agreements: Survey of Existing Legal Instruments*, Cambridge: Grotius Publications.

United Nations Environment Programme (1993) *Register of International Treaties and Other Agreements in the Field of the Environment 1993*, Nairobi: UNEP.

United States General Accounting Office (USGAO) (1992) *International Environment: International Agreements are Not Well Monitored*, GAO/RCED-92-43, Washington, DC: General Accounting Office.

Victor, D. and Salt, J. (1994) 'Managing climate change', *Environment* 36(10): 6–15, 25–32.

—— Greene, O., Lanchbery, J., Di Primio, J.-P. and Korula, A. (1994) 'Review mechanisms in the effective implementation of international environmental agreements', *IIASA Working Paper WP-94-114*, Laxenburg: IIASA.

—— Lanchbery, J. and Greene, O. (1994) 'An empirical study of review mechanisms in environmental regimes', *IIASA Working Paper WP-94-115*, Laxenburg: IIASA.

Wapner, P. (1991) 'Making States Biodegradable: Ecological Activism and World Politics', PhD dissertation, Princeton University.

Young, O. (1994) *International Governance: Protecting the Environment in a Stateless Society*, Ithaca, NY: Cornell U.P.

—— and Osherenko, G. (eds) (1993) *Polar Politics: Creating International Environmental Regimes*, Ithaca, NY: Cornell U.P.

# 12 Hegemonic ideology and the International Tropical Timber Organisation*

*David Humphreys*

> Our traditional societies always cared for the well-being of nature. Unfortunately for historical reasons they were forced to produce what they do not eat, and eat what they do not produce.
>
> (An African NGO's perspective, 12th Session of the International
> Tropical Timber Council, Cameroon, May 1992)

This chapter will argue that contention among actors in the international system arises from clashes of ideologies. Willetts, earlier in this volume, examines the environmental values advocated by actors. An ideology may be seen as an attempt to formulate the practical consequences of affirming a particular set of values. As Willetts has argued elsewhere, an ideology is 'a programmatic assertion of political values, which are held to be of universal validity for their proclaimed domain' (Willetts 1978: 244). An ideology has two broad features: first, there is a description of the processes by which social and political change occur; second, there is a normative prescription of how social and political change *should* occur. The normative component of ideologies will be the central concern of this paper. Adopting a neo-Gramscian approach, this paper will examine the ideological orientation of the International Tropical Timber Organisation (ITTO). Gramsci saw ideologies as 'political and social programmes and the concepts on which they are based' (Augelli and Murphy 1988: 15). Three competing ideologies will be considered: the current hegemonic ideology of neoliberalism and two counter-hegemonic ideologies, namely those of the New International Economic Order (NIEO) and ecologism.

## HEGEMONIC AND COUNTER-HEGEMONIC IDEOLOGIES

The currently hegemonic ideology of neoliberalism is articulated by core interests, but also attracts qualified support from co-opted peripheral interests. Here, hegemony is used in a neo-Gramscian sense, as opposed to Keohane's definition of hegemony as a 'preponderance of material resources' (Keohane 1984: 32). Robert Cox sees hegemony as 'a structure of values and understandings about the nature of [world] order that permeates a whole system of states and non-state entities' (Cox 1992: 140).

What is the nature of the hegemonic ideology? Ruggie sees the postwar economic system as a compromise between two demands. The first was the desire on the part of the postwar hegemon (here the Keohane definition of hegemony is used), namely the USA, to establish a multilateral free-trading system. The second was the demand for social and economic stability as expressed by a new collective balance in state–society relations in the industrialised world. Ruggie refers to this as the embedded liberalism compromise (Ruggie 1983) which can be read as one of ideological hegemony (Donnelly 1986: 638). Although American hegemony has declined (Keohane 1984), there has been a rise, on the other hand, in the economic power of the European Union (EU) and Japan, both of which accept the basic tenets of neoliberalism. Hence, despite the decline of the hegemonic power, the hegemonic ideology has persisted.

Three of the norms of neoliberalism will now be considered.[1] The first is the recognition that states have sovereignty over their resources. Principle 21 of the 1972 Stockholm Declaration on the Human Environment recognised that states have the sovereign right to exploit their natural resources, but married this with a responsibility to ensure that exploitation does not damage the environment of other states. Stockholm Principle 21 also stipulated that states have a responsibility to ensure that their activities do not damage 'areas beyond the limits of national jurisdiction', in other words the global commons, such as the atmosphere and the oceans. A second globally accepted norm is that trade should be free and open. Ruggie would see this norm constrained only by the demand for domestic social and economic stability. The norm of free trade has often been violated, although such violation has not detracted from its authority: norms are counter-factually valid, as '[n]o single counterfactual occurrence refutes a norm' (Kratochwil and Ruggie 1986: 767). Third, there is the norm of economic development. Governments from both North and South have promoted, encouraged and initiated modernising industrial development policies within their territorial domain, in part to achieve the domestic economic stability that Ruggie considers to be a feature of embedded liberalism.

One ideology that challenges neoliberalism is the above-mentioned one of the NIEO. The South's demands for a NIEO can be seen as counter-hegemonic (Cox 1983: 171; Lee 1995). In fact, Southern political elites have conceded a degree of acceptance to neoliberalism, whilst simultaneously, however, seeking to modify its norms. The sovereignty of states over their natural resources is accepted without question. However, while advocates of the NIEO accept the norm of free trade, they simultaneously seek to *overturn* it in certain respects. Trade should be free and open, but the market should be usurped with respect to, *inter alia*, financial-resource and technology transfers from North to South, external debt relief and the arrest of declining terms of trade. Advocates of the NIEO also uphold the norm of industrial development, but consider that such development should be firmly under the control of peripheral elites and not imposed by core institutions such as the World Bank, the International Monetary Fund and Northern-based transnational corporations and banks.

'The South' should clearly not be seen as an undifferentiated 'actor'. Different political elites within the South pursue different political agendas and objectives. It is also the case, as is argued by the structural theorists of the dependency school,[2] that certain Southern political elites have formed a collaborative relationship with their Northern counterparts. Nonetheless, it is equally the case that the vast majority of political elites within the South adhere to the NIEO as an ideology, and that they pursue the objectives of the NIEO within such fora as the Economic and Social Council (ECOSOC) of the UN, the Non-Aligned Movement and the Organisation of African Unity. The NIEO programme hinges on linkages, involving bargaining issues, asserted by the South between the supply of commodities to the North and the demand for a macro-level restructuring of the economic system. The oil crisis of 1973 may be seen as the brief peak of the South's commodity-related bargaining power. Thereafter the NIEO challenge waned as the South had comparatively little to offer the North in exchange for what was demanded (Renninger 1989: 249). However, environmental degradation, especially tropical-rainforest destruction, has given a new lease of life to the NIEO demands. The South has used the North's concerns about deforestation to attempt to strike a global bargain with the North. Throughout the forest negotiations for the United Nations Conference on Environment and Development (UNCED), the South advanced its NIEO claims, especially for financial-resource and technology transfers (Humphreys 1993). Some of these demands were included in UNCED's non-legally binding statement of forest principles which was concluded at Rio de Janeiro in June 1992.[3] The rise of forest conservation as an international issue has enhanced the value of tropical forests, which, in turn, has increased the South's bargaining leverage. The South's efforts to translate the North's concern on forests into the hard currency of economic gain has strengthened the counter-hegemonic challenge of the NIEO.

Advocates of the NIEO therefore seek to redefine the hegemonic ideology in terms of the perceived interests of the South. However, there are those who would consider that the NIEO ideology belongs not to a different economic system but to the same system as that of neoliberalism. Lummis, noting that one of the NIEO claims was that disparities in wealth between North and South are unjust, responds that

> The accusation of injustice cannot traditionally be made against inequalities between systems, but only within a system. The fact that the idea is intelligible today is evidence of the degree to which we accept that the world has been organised into a single economic system.
>
> (Lummis 1992: 44)

Clearly, any ideology seeking to replace, rather than redefine, the norms of neoliberalism would constitute a far more radical ideological challenge than that of the NIEO. Such an ideology may be expected to emanate from environmental concerns. A neo-Gramscian view would see global environmental degradation as an organic crisis. The political and economic elites of the present neoliberal economic system have, thus far, proved unable to tackle successfully the major symptoms or causes of environmental destruction. However, aware of the seriousness of the crisis, they have been prepared to co-opt environmental ideas and environmentalists in an effort to create a new coalition of political forces to deal with environmental degradation, but only in ways that do not threaten the ideological hegemony of neoliberalism.

Here it is useful to note the distinction made by Dobson between environmentalism and ecologism. Environmentalism merely seeks to control the effects on the environment of industrialisation and development. Ecologism, with its critique of consumption and production patterns, meets two of the requirements of a definition of ideology, namely 'a description of . . . "political reality" [and] a prescription for the future': ecologism is not 'simply embedded in other political ideologies – it is an ideology in its own right' (Dobson 1990: 3 and 130). In what ways may environmentalists and ecologists view the three norms of neoliberalism under consideration here?

In the case of forests, a bottom-up challenge to state sovereignty has emerged centred on the argument that local communities should partake in domestic and international policy-making, and that indigenous forest peoples should be granted title to their ancestral land. The ecologist opposes the notion that natural resources should be used by economic and political elites in line with national development policy; use of the word 'national' here serves to exclude the local. While environmentalism seeks concessions from the state on the participation of local communities, ecologism goes further and argues for a shift both in power distribution and in social relations.

Free trade, the second global norm, is also challenged by environmentalism. Environmental economists argue that the free market ignores social and environmental costs, which should be internalised into the price mechanism. However, the ecological view is that economics and free trade have been driving forces for environmental degradation. Lohmann argues that economics has evolved around a set of purposes 'providing a rational framework for a capitalist type of social organisation' (Lohmann 1991: 195). To Lohmann, nature has infinite value that cannot be internalised into a price mechanism or assigned a monetary value.

Environmentalists and ecologists differ once again on the norm of industrial development. The environmentalist seeks to ensure that environmental values prevail over developmental values so as to yield 'sustainable development'. However, the ecologist rejects developmentalism, and consequently dismisses the linkage of the environment with development (Sachs 1991). Environmental degradation is seen as an intrinsic feature, rather than an accidental condition, of modernising development. 'Sustainable development' is considered to be a rescue hypothesis for a discredited ideal.

Ideologies are not enclosed, hermetically sealed entities. Ideologies, including counter-hegemonic ideologies, should not be seen as independent variables. The dynamic interplay between ideologies defines international politics. Ideas from a counter-hegemonic ideology articulating the aspirations of a sizeable peripheral group may be absorbed into, and may redefine the norms of, the hegemonic ideology. The notion of 'sustainable development' can be seen as the modification of a hegemonic norm following the co-option of a counter-hegemonic idea.

'Sustainable development' fuses the neoliberal's emphasis on development with the ecologist's concern for sustainability. While still lacking clear definitional precision, the concept has gained widespread acceptance in international society since the mid-1980s. The decision at UNCED to create the Commission on Sustainable Development, an organ reporting to the ECOSOC of the UN, bears testimony to the degree to which the concept has been endorsed within the United Nations system.

In short, ecologism stresses the empowerment of local peoples, local modes of exchange free from the influence of the market, and opposition to top-down economic development. Figure 12.1 summarises the principal differences between environmentalism and ecologism on the three norms of neoliberalism under consideration here.

It is emphasised that a diverse spectrum of 'green' thought exists spanning environmentalism and ecologism, and that the distinction drawn here is an ideal-type one only: environmentalism and ecologism are two poles of a single continuum of thought. Environmentalism would not necessarily challenge neoliberalism; agents of this ideology would seek to co-opt the environmental challenge. Advocates of neoliberalism may thus safely become environmentalists, but to adopt an ecological world-view would be to compromise their original beliefs. The Club of Rome report, *The Limits to Growth* (Meadows *et al.* 1974), would fall into the environmentalist category as its authors took the

|  | *Environmentalism* | *Ecologism* |
|---|---|---|
| National sovereignty | Governments should integrate the views of local communities and indigenous peoples into the national policy-making process. | A shift in power relations from the national to the local level is necessary. The rights and basic needs of local communities and indigenous peoples should prevail over the perceived 'national interest' as determined by governments. |
| Free trade and the market | Environmental economics should internalise social and environmental costs. Market and non-market incentives should be used to promote environmentally friendly policies. | The environment has infinite value and cannot be internalised into a price mechanism or assigned a monetary figure. |
| Development | Environmental values should prevail over developmental values to yield 'sustainable development'. | 'Development' is a driving force of environmental degradation. 'Sustainable development' is seen as a rescue hypothesis. |

*Figure 12.1* Environmental and ecological views on the three norms of neoliberalism

ideology of the system as a given. Cox has criticised the systems-dynamics approach of the Club of Rome for accepting the system's currently dominant norms (Cox 1976: 181). However, ecologism, with its emphasis on a shift in power distribution, clearly challenges not only neoliberalism but also the ideology of the NIEO. Both neoliberalism and the NIEO see the state as a central actor. However, in emphasising the empowerment of the local, the ecologist eschews state centricity, and a realisation of the ecologist's world-view would necessitate not system maintenance, with the hegemonic ideology absorbing potentially counter-hegemonic ideas, but system transformation, driven by a new ideology.

The struggle of the ecologist begins in international civil society, in other words in that part of international society comprised of non-governmental voluntary-membership associations. Augelli and Murphy focus principally on intergovernmental agencies when considering international civil society in their neo-Gramscian analysis of US foreign policy during the 1980s. Such agencies are part of international civil society as they are private membership organisations (Augelli and Murphy 1988: 139). On this view, the ITTO should also be seen as a part of international civil society. However, one area of international civil society much neglected by many neo-Gramscian writers is that of Non-Governmental Organisations (NGOs). But in order to fully appreciate the work of intergovernmental organisations, it is necessary to consider the role of NGOs. Conservation NGOs[4] lobby intergovernmental organisations – such as the ITTO, where they have been granted observer status. The ideological position of NGOs will be considered below.

With his focus on the means of production, Gramsci, like other Marxist writers, exhibits a clear bias in favour of economic development, something which we have seen is anathema to the ecologist. The ultimate outcome of the ecologist's project would be not a single economic system but a multitude of different systems of social organisation; in its purest form it would constitute a very un-Gramscian notion of hegemony. The hegemony in question would not be that of a social class. The ecologist aspires to the hegemony of local knowledges and belief systems over the 'intellectual and ideological imperialism' of scientific rationalism (Banuri and Marglin 1993: 2), to the hegemony of decentralised systems of land use over centralised systems, and to the hegemony of localised methods of production independent of the influence of international capital.[5]

Gramsci considered that for any social group to achieve hegemony, it must engage in constructing, and leading, a coalition of social movements.[6] Here the question of political tactics arises; should ecologists attempt to achieve the hegemony of localised systems by working with core institutions, seeking to achieve incremental change, or should they work outside such institutions, engaging in pressure-group activity while maintaining the purity of their ideology? This question has preoccupied, and frequently divided, many of those involved in the green movement. Many of the more radical conservation NGOs are aware that one hazard of the former tactic is that of 'co-option', in which they legitimise the policies of the very institutions they seek to change.

Cox has argued that international institutions perform an ideological role, and that they may act as a mechanism through which universal norms are expressed (Cox 1983: 172). Alternatively, 'international institutions may also become vehicles for the articulation of a coherent counter-hegemonic set of values' (Cox 1980: 377). This paper will now assess the ideological orientation of the ITTO – or, more accurately, that of those actors who participate in the ITTO's work. Attention will first turn to the contents of the International Tropical Timber Agreement of 1983 – the 'ITTA 1983'.

## THE INTERNATIONAL TROPICAL TIMBER AGREEMENT, 1983

The ITTA 1983 emerged from a protracted series of negotiations held under the auspices of the United Nations Conference on Trade and Development (UNCTAD), and entered into force in April 1985. Since then the International Tropical Timber Agreement, 1994 ('ITTA 1994') has been negotiated, but at the time of writing it has yet to enter into force. The ITTA 1983, which had been due to expire on 31 March 1994, may now remain in force until such time as the ITTA 1994 receives the requisite number of ratifications.

The ITTA 1983 reflected the three global norms of neoliberalism. First, the sovereignty of the producing members over their forest resources is asserted.[7] Second, an objective of the Agreement is 'the expansion and diversification of international trade in tropical timber'.[8] And third, industrial development was explicitly endorsed; the Agreement was principally a commodity agreement that aimed at encouraging 'further processing of tropical timber in producing member countries with a view to promoting their industrialisation'.[9]

However, one clause of the ITTA 1983 had a clear ecological orientation, namely to encourage 'national policies aimed at sustainable utilization and conservation of tropical forests and their genetic resources, and at maintaining the ecological balance in the regions concerned'.[10] This objective rests uneasily with the 'expansion and diversification' of the timber trade, an objective entirely in keeping with the norm of free trade, but one which conservation NGOs have asserted is incompatible with a sustainable trade (Friends of the Earth/World Rainforest Movement 1992: 4).

As well as containing this internal contradiction, the ITTA 1983 also conflicted with clauses of the General Agreement on Tariffs and Trade, 1947 (GATT) in two ways.[11] Possibly the most important environmental case to go before a GATT panel, and one with particular ramifications for the international tropical-timber trade, was the 'dolphin–tuna' case between the USA and Mexico. In this case, the USA had banned imports of tuna fish caught by Mexican fishermen using nets that ensnared dolphins. The Mexicans complained to the GATT, and a GATT panel subsequently ruled that GATT Article XX(g) on the conservation of natural resources[12] could not be invoked by one party to ensure the protection of natural resources beyond its territorial boundaries.[13] Furthermore, under Article XX(g) the onus to prove a case lies with the party wishing to conserve the resource, not the party allegedly depleting it. As the World Wide

Fund for Nature (WWF) notes, 'This may be logical in the context of a free trade agreement, but does not further the objective of ensuring that any trade liberalisation resulting from the agreement is sustainable' (Arden-Clarke 1991: 17).

The second tension between the ITTA 1983 and the GATT concerned GATT clauses prohibiting discrimination between like products on the basis of their manufacture.[14] In effect, the GATT gives unsustainably produced timber the same status in the international market as sustainably produced timber; GATT signatories would be unable to use tariffs or quotas to favour timber from sustainable sources (Arden-Clarke 1990: 8). The WWF has recommended that the ITTO Secretariat seek a waiver from the GATT for any trade measures necessary to contribute to the sustainability of the tropical-timber trade, and has further recommended that the GATT be amended to allow discrimination between sustainably and unsustainably produced timber (Arden-Clarke 1990: 11). The Secretariat did not seek such a waiver,[15] however, and the GATT was not amended during the Uruguay Round to allow for trade discrimination against unsustainably produced products. Under neoliberalism, free trade is clearly of greater normative force than resource conservation.

## THE INTERNATIONAL TROPICAL TIMBER ORGANISATION

When the ITTA 1983 came into effect, there were twelve tropical-timber producer countries and fifteen consumer countries. By March 1994 membership had grown to twenty-three producers and twenty-seven consumers. The ITTA 1983 created the International Tropical Timber Organisation, the highest decision-making organ of which is the International Tropical Timber Council (ITTC). There are three permanent committees that meet alongside the ITTC, namely the Permanent Committee on Reforestation and Forest Management, the Permanent Committee on Forest Industry and the Permanent Committee on Economic Information and Market Intelligence. Voting rights within the ITTC and the permanent committees are divided equally between tropical-timber producer countries and tropical-timber consumer countries. The votes of consumer countries are determined by their share of global tropical-timber imports. Producer countries' votes are determined principally by their share of global tropical-timber exports, with some consideration also given to the forest areas involved. Indonesia, Brazil and Malaysia are the three countries holding the largest shares of votes for producer countries. Japan holds the most votes for the consumer countries, with the EU bloc second. However, with the exception of the votes for the headquarters site of the ITTO (Yokohama) and for the choice of Executive Director (a Malaysian), no vote has been taken at an ITTC session; the ITTA 1983 emphasises that the ITTC 'shall endeavour to take all decisions ... by consensus'.[16] However, an awareness of the different voting allocations of the member countries can influence how a consensus develops.

Representatives from NGOs and timber-trade organisations may attend ITTC sessions as observers,[17] and they may be invited to sit on national delegations in an advisory capacity. For example, a representative from the Timber Trade

Federation has sat on the UK delegation, while a representative from the Netherlands Timber Trade Association has sat on the Dutch delegation. Representatives from the WWF have served as forest-conservation advisers on the national delegations of Denmark, Malaysia and the UK. Other NGOs, either unable to gain a place, or unwilling to serve, on national delegations, but which have attended ITTC sessions as observers, include Friends of the Earth (FoE), Survival International, the Australian Conservation Foundation and the Rainforest Action Network (USA).

In 1990 the ITTO, with its Target 2000, adopted a target date by which time it is intended that the entire international trade in tropical timber should come from sustainable sources (ITTO 1990b: 7). This decision was adopted following a proposal by the Permanent Committee on Forest Industry. The main work of the three permanent committees comprises the vetting and approval of pre-projects and projects. Examples of projects, to name just a few, include the building of databases on the tropical-timber trade, research on incentives, reforestation projects and projects to improve the further processing capacity of producer countries. A pre-project is the preparatory phase of a project and is essentially concerned with background research and information collation. Not all projects go through a pre-project phase; this occurs only if exploratory research or preparatory activity is required. Proposals may be submitted only by ITTO members or by the Secretariat. In principle, inappropriate or poorly designed projects should not pass through the permanent committees. Pre-project and project proposals must fall within the remit of one of the three permanent committees. As Figure 12.2 details, two-thirds of ITTO project expenditure has centred on the work of the Permanent Committee on Reforestation and Forest Management. By 31 December 1992, the ITTO had also undertaken fifty-five approved pre-project studies.[18]

This section will assess the ideological bias of the ITTO throughout the lifespan of the ITTA 1983. Consideration will first be given to the norm of the

| Permanent committee | Approved projects | Total budget US$ m | ITTO budget US$ m |
|---|---|---|---|
| Reforestation and forest management | 96 | 99.9 | 71.2 |
| Forest industry | 60 | 39.5 | 25.7 |
| Economic information market intelligence | 23 | 10.4 | 9.6 |
| Total | 179 | 149.8 | 106.5 |

*Figure 12.2* Project work of the International Tropical Timber Organisation as at 31 December 1992

*Source*: UN document TD/TIMBER.2/3, 'Background, status and operation of the International Tropical Timber Agreement, 1983, and recent developments of relevance to the negotiation of a successor agreement', 26 February 1993, paras 46–7, pp. 9–10

sovereignty of states over their forest resources. The ITTO has produced three sets of guidelines that have been adopted by members at ITTC sessions. In May 1990 the ITTC adopted guidelines on the sustainable management of natural tropical forests (ITTO 1990a). The guidelines contain forty-one principles for sustainable forest management, and thirty-six recommended 'possible actions' that could be taken for these principles to be realised. The ITTO Executive Director recommended that the guidelines be modified 'into more specific guidelines which are compatible with regional and national forestry practices'.[19] The ITTC has also adopted guidelines both on biodiversity conservation (ITTO 1991) and on the sustainable management of planted forests (ITTO 1993).

It could be argued that the adoption of such guidelines by ITTO producers represents an erosion of some measure of sovereignty. However, producer governments have proved unwilling to enforce the ITTO guidelines at the country level, and to date not one country has used the guidelines as the basis for its own national guidelines. Furthermore, the poor level of national reporting has been a sustained topic of criticism for the NGOs, who have continually criticised member governments both for not demonstrating a greater commitment either to the ITTO's guidelines or to its Target 2000 objective, and for failing to follow through on ITTC decisions (Callister 1992: 7; Friends of the Earth/World Rainforest Movement 1992: 12–17).

A second NGO challenge to sovereignty comes from the claims on the part of indigenous peoples and NGOs that forest dwellers should be granted title to their customary lands, and that local communities should participate in decision-making. Indigenous peoples' groups are becoming increasingly well organised. One such group to have addressed the ITTO is the Coordinating Body for the Indigenous Peoples' Organisations of the Amazon Basin (COICA).[20] NGOs have forged a close working relationship with indigenous peoples' groups, and the former have lobbied the ITTC on behalf of the latter. At the ITTC's eleventh session, NGOs drafted a resolution which, if accepted, would have affirmed a commitment from ITTO members to respect the rights and secure the livelihoods of forest-dwelling peoples.[21] The draft was discussed informally outside the Council, where the European Community voiced support, but was not adopted due to producer opposition.[22] Despite the lobbying of the NGOs and indigenous peoples' groups, no ITTC decision has recognised land rights claimed by forest peoples. This, in effect, reinforces the norm of sovereignty; such claims can only be considered by the domestic legislative organs of the country concerned, and not by the ITTO.

Attention will now turn to the norm of free trade. The ITTO has debated the possible use of market interventions to promote a sustainable tropical-timber trade. In 1989 a proposal on labelling systems for the promotion of sustainably produced tropical timber[23] was tabled by the British delegation. The objective of the proposal was to provide a mechanism whereby timber from sustainably managed sources could be labelled as such in the producing country, thus enabling buyers in the consuming country to identify such timber. Prepared by FoE with some input from the Oxford Forestry Institute (OFI), the proposal met with opposition from Indonesia and Malaysia (Colchester 1990: 169), and the report of the Permanent Committee on Economic Information and Market Intelligence strongly implies that the proposal threatened the interests of the producer countries and the timber trade.[24] The British delegation subsequently redrafted the proposal during the course of the session without consulting FoE. In the new version,[25] every reference to labelling had been excised, and the proposal referred only to incentives for sustainable forest management. At this stage FoE withdrew their support for the proposal. The revised proposal was not debated but instead became the subject of further research.[26]

Following these developments, the British delegation engaged the OFI and the UK Timber Research and Development Association (TRADA), who drafted a proposal on financial and non-financial incentives for sustainable forest management. The proposal examined possible financial incentives, such as the funding of forest-management services by tax transfers, debt-for-nature swaps and grants, and non-financial incentives, including security of land tenure, certification schemes for good forest-management practice and the development of non-timber forest products. The OFI/TRADA report[27] was debated at the ITTC's tenth session in 1991 at a specially convened round table. In a comment that illustrates the ideological tensions within the ITTO, the round table Chairman considered there was a 'need to define an acceptable compromise between the environmental value of the forest and the economic value of trade in tropical timber'.[28] Seemingly reluctant to acknowledge that any tension existed between the ITTA 1983's objective both to expand the tropical-timber trade and, simultaneously, to conserve the resource, the ITTC passed a decision inviting members to enhance their ability to attain Target 2000 '*by investigating liberalized trade in tropical timber* within the framework of the multilateral trading system' (italics mine).[29]

The British delegation later engaged the London Environmental Economics Centre as consultants to study the economic linkages between the tropical-timber trade and sustainable forest management. Their report[30] considered how environmental and social costs could be internalised into the price mechanism. However, by March 1994, four years and eight ITTC sessions after the original FoE proposal, the ITTC had not passed a substantive decision on either labelling or incentives. The labelling/incentives debate illustrates how the ITTO's consensual decision-making procedures have blocked any form of market intervention, so that the norm of free trade has, *de facto*, been preserved. Any proposed initiative failing to attract the unanimous support of member countries is unlikely to be passed in an ITTC decision.

A further case illustrates how ecological challenges to free trade have been thwarted. In June 1992 the Austrian parliament passed legislation increasing the import tax on tropical-timber products and stipulating that all such products be labelled. At the ITTC's thirteenth session in 1992, an Austrian delegate stated that what mattered to the Austrian parliament was the growing desire of consumers to be informed on the contents of products.[31] The delegate asserted that the legislation was not discriminatory, nor motivated by protectionism, nor a restriction to trade. The measure was applauded by conservation NGOs at the ITTO[32] but met with opposition from producer countries. Following a protest to the GATT[33] by member governments of the Association of South-East Asian Nations, and complaints from Austrian industrialists concerned about the possibility of a trade war, the law was amended in December 1992 (Chase 1993: 760–3; Traynor 1993).[34]

The norm of free trade and the norm of conservation may be seen as emanating from differing ideologies, with the former belonging to neoliberalism and the latter belonging to ecologism. This is a form of normative incoherence which to Donnelly arises 'from inconsistencies between individual norms (either outright incompatibility or vagueness that allows for inconsistent interpretation) or from significant "logical" gaps in the overall structure of norms' (Donnelly 1986: 605). The findings of a study commissioned by the ITTO to research global forestry-management practices lend weight to the view that it is impossible simultaneously to expand the timber trade and to move that same trade towards sustainability. The study team concluded that 'The extent of tropical moist forests which is being deliberately managed at an operational scale for the sustainable production of timber is, on a world scale, negligible' (Poore *et al.* 1989: xiv). The report found that less than 1 per cent of the global tropical-timber trade, namely from Queensland, Australia, came from sustainable sources.

Consideration will now be given to the norm of development. Neither the producers nor the consumers have contested the economic exploitation of tropical forests for timber and for other forest products. Given this, and given also the conservation mandate of the ITTO, it is perhaps not surprising that the ITTO guidelines for the sustainable management of natural forests reflect inconsistencies between developmental and ecological objectives. 'Possible Action 33' notes that environmental impact studies should 'assess compatibility of logging practices with *declared secondary objectives* such as conservation and protection' (ITTO 1990a: 9; italics mine).

The most sustained critique of development has emerged from conservation NGOs and indigenous peoples' groups who have used their statements to the ITTC to challenge narrow definitions of sustainability. A COICA spokesman speaking to the ITTC in 1991 insisted that 'one cannot speak of sustainability without sustaining the livelihoods of those who live in the forests.'[35] Similar points have also been made by conservation NGOs. An ITTO Mission to Sarawak to investigate the sustainability of forest-management practices was criticised by the World Rainforest Movement for choosing a narrow interpretation of its terms of reference, investigating only the extraction of timber and 'thereby marginalising not only human considerations but also alternative forms of land use' (Colchester 1990: 171).

The rights to timber, as asserted by the timber traders and consumer and producer delegations, and the rights to land, as asserted by the alliance between indigenous peoples' groups and NGOs, have been one of the most acute points of conflict within the ITTO, with the former adopting an economistic view of sustainability, and the latter arguing that sustainability cannot ignore broader social concerns. While both the producers and consumers endorse the notion of 'sustainable development', it is the NGOs, with their stress on local communities and indigenous peoples, who are closest to the Brundtland ideal of 'sustainable development' which, with its emphasis on past and future generations, is essentially centred on the basic needs of people (Brundtland 1987: 43).

Consensual decision-making procedures, far from leading to agreement among the ITTO's membership, have served to mask disagreements, thus effectively reinforcing the hegemonic ideology. Donnelly may see the history of the ITTO as 'a diplomatic codification of unresolved conflicts' resulting from normative incoherence (Donnelly 1986: 605). Tropical forest conservation, while central to the ITTO's mandate, has not been allowed to challenge the sovereignty of producer members over their forests, to interfere with free trade or to prevent the exploitation of tropical forests for timber products.

Within the ITTO, the NGOs have provided a coherent challenge to neo-liberalism. It is more difficult to be certain on the precise strength of this challenge. This leads us back to the distinction made at the start of this paper; when does a challenge cease to be an environmentalist one, advocating adjustments to the hegemonic ideology, and when does it become the counter-hegemonic ideology of ecologism? The increasingly strident critiques provided by NGOs indicate that the challenge posed by NGOs is, overall, closer to the ecological end of the spectrum drawn above. In short, the NGOs have promoted a counter-hegemonic ideology. The ITTO membership has attempted to co-opt NGOs, and in doing so has been prepared to listen to their concerns. However, many NGOs are concerned that their attendance at ITTC sessions could legitimise the ITTO's poor conservation record. In 1992, the WWF withdrew its representatives from all ITTO national delegations,[36] and many other NGOs which originally attended ITTC sessions as observers have ceased to do so.[37]

## THE INTERNATIONAL TROPICAL TIMBER AGREEMENT, 1994

The UNCTAD negotiation conference for a successor agreement to the ITTA 1983 began in April 1993 and was scheduled to end in June of the same year. The scope of the successor agreement was the central point of contention throughout the negotiations. The consumers favoured a continuation of the tropical-timber-only format, as did those timber-trade organisations attending the ITTO. The producers, on the other hand, favoured an expansion of the scope of the successor agreement to include non-tropical-timbers. They were supported in this by the NGOs.

However, the producers and the NGOs favoured an expansion of scope for different reasons. While advocating expansion, the NGOs also argued for a contraction of the mandate of the successor agreement. Disillusioned with the poor conservation record of the ITTO, the NGOs favoured a reduced role for forest-conservation and timber-industry projects in a new organisation focusing primarily on trade-related issues, such as statistics, market transparency and pricing. The NGOs considered that the ITTO did not have the competence to deal meaningfully with forest conservation. However, as tropical and non-tropical timbers are substitutable for each other, they considered there was a need for a holistic view of the global trade in a new international timber-trade organisation (Callister 1992: 1–3; Friends of the Earth/World Rainforest Movement 1992: 3–5). The producers also favoured an expansion of scope, but unlike the NGOs they favoured a high project profile for a new international timber organisation. The producers further argued that the producers–consumers distinction should be replaced by a developing countries–developed countries distinction. The producers advanced some of the claims previously made in the NIEO debate and UNCED forest negotiations; in their view, the developed countries should undertake to supply the developing countries with financial and technological resources in order for the latter to attain sustainable forest management.[38] Hence, while the producers and the NGOs agreed on tactics, namely an expansion of the scope of a new agreement, their ideologies, and hence their strategies, differed profoundly. Forest conservation remained the overarching issue for the NGOs. However, the producers used the ITTO as another forum to advance the ideology of the NIEO.

A consensus on the text of a tropical-timber-only agreement, the ITTA 1994, was finally reached in January 1994. After four negotiating sessions, the producers agreed to a continuation of the tropical-timber-only scope in exchange for some concessions from the consumers. These were as follows. First, the consumer agreed to sign up to Target 2000 outside of the ITTO.[39] Second, and following the Austria labelling case, the producers succeeded in inserting a clause to the effect that nothing in the ITTA 1994 authorises 'the use of measures to restrict or ban international trade in . . . timber and timber products'.[40] This clause effectively strengthens the norm of free trade by prohibiting discrimination between unsustainably and sustainably produced timber. Third, the consumers were successful in inserting clauses both on 'the provision of new and additional financial resources' and on technology transfer 'on concessional and preferential terms and conditions'.[41]

This is the second time the South has succeeded in including these demands in an internationally negotiated forest-related document, with UNCED's non-legally binding statement of forest principles being the first. Furthermore, as well as containing NIEO-related counter-hegemonic clauses, the ITTA 1994 also contains evidence that NGO campaigning impacted upon the negotiations. The Agreement contains a reference to the need to give due regard to 'the interests of local communities dependent on forest resources'.[42] This is an issue on which NGOs have a long campaigning history, and the language of the clause is a modified version of the ecologist's counter-hegemonic demand for the empowerment of local communities at the expense of the state.

Ideological polarisation, or alternatively normative incoherence, is more pronounced in the ITTA 1994 than in its 1983 predecessor. The ITTA 1994 contains counter-hegemonic ideas from both the NIEO and ecologism, while simultaneously containing neoliberal ideas. Like the ITTA 1983, the ITTA 1994 also contains clauses on the expansion of the tropical-timber trade and the conservation of timber-producing forests.[43] The ITTA 1994 illustrates the tripolar ideological struggle that defines the contemporary international relations of global environmental change.

## THE ECOLOGICAL CHALLENGE TO THE HEGEMONIC IDEOLOGY

Ecologism challenges the Ruggie notion of embedded liberalism as a set of economic relations that is compatible with the requirements of domestic *social and economic stability*. Ecologism seeks to attain a set of international economic relations that is compatible with domestic and global *ecological stability*. The two are not necessarily incompatible. For example, domestic economic and social instability may lead to poverty, which is one of the prime causes of environmental degradation. Nonetheless, there are interfaces where economic stability and ecological stability are discordant, and it is at such interfaces that ideological tensions become manifest in domestic and international environmental policy-making.

Following on from Ruggie, we would expect a challenge to embedded liberalism to arise should ecologism execute a collective shift in state–society relations. In other words, ecological concerns become a major source of concern for domestic societies, including NGOs, so that the governments of these societies express a new collective concern in the international arena. However, a value shift on the part of those powerful economic actors that support and perpetuate neoliberalism, namely the USA, the EU and Japan, would be necessary. As Donnelly notes, there is a relationship between power hegemony and ideological hegemony: 'hegemonic power does ultimately require material power, and even hegemonic ideas have a limited ability to attract such power' (Donnelly 1986: 638).

The attempt by Austria to introduce a unilateral labelling system can be seen in this light. The comments, noted above, of the Austrian delegate at the ITTC's thirteenth session reveal that the legislation was passed as a result of consumer pressure or, as Ruggie may say, of a change in Austrian state–society relations. However, with economic actors, both inside and outside of Austria, not prepared to support the legislation, the Austrian parliament finally yielded to the hegemonic ideology.

If attempting to execute a collective shift in state–society relations is the first way in which NGOs will continue to challenge the hegemonic ideology, the second is at the international level. Conservation NGOs will continue to lobby intergovernmental organisations such as the ITTO with the intention of executing a value shift in such organisations, the ultimate objective being for such shifts to be effectively translated into policy changes at the country level. However, the ITTO experience to date suggests that such value shifts are difficult to engineer, and that even where guidelines are enunciated, they do not necessarily result in policy changes at the country level.

Disagreements in international society on environmental issues arise from competing ideologies, each of which seeks to attain or maintain a position as the hegemonic ideology. For the time being, the agents of neoliberalism have successfully staved off the challenges of the NIEO and ecologism. But these two ideologies will continue to gain force. First, the South, as the UNCED process and the negotiations for the ITTA 1994 have demonstrated, is prepared to use the North's environmental concerns, especially over tropical forests, to advance the case for a macro-level adjustment in global economic relations. And second, with many environmental problems worsening, the concerns of NGOs will continue to be transmitted to policy-making elites. Certainly, the case of the ITTO illustrates the need to consider further the role of NGOs in international relations. A purely state-centric analysis masks the real disagreements in international relations. By viewing conservation NGOs as the vehicles of a counter-hegemonic ideology, it is possible to expose some of the deep, and hidden, ideological disagreements that lie within international society as the result of environmental concerns.

## NOTES

* I am grateful to Mandy Bentham, Peter Hough and Kelley Lee for their helpful and constructive comments on an earlier version of this paper.
1 Norms have legitimacy only in reference to a specific ideological context. Other neoliberal norms include the free movement and convertibility of currencies, and the norm that those in a position of authority should not engage in corruption or profit from illicit activities.
2 See, for example, Frank 1967, Wallerstein 1979 and Wallerstein 1984.
3 UN document A/CONF.151/6/Rev.1, 'Non-legally binding authoritative statement of principles for a global consensus on the management, conservation and sustainable development of all types of forests', 13 June 1992.
4 'Conservation' is used here to refer to all NGOs with a political orientation along the environmental–ecological continuum. To refer to any given NGO as *either* environmental *or* ecological would be highly contentious given the ideal-type nature of the distinction.
5 Such views may be dismissed as romantic Utopianism, and it is certainly not easy to imagine how such a process can be achieved; most ecologists concede that there are no easy answers to this question.
6 Gramsci referred to this as a war of position. The alternative scenario for gaining hegemony, a war of movement (referred to by some neo-Gramscian writers as a war of manoeuvre), is in effect a revolution. (See Forgacs 1988: 225–30.) A war of movement is not considered a viable option for the vast majority of ecologists, and those ecologists who advocate revolutionary tactics have become isolated from mainstream green debate.
7 UN document TD/TIMBER/11/Rev.1, 'International Tropical Timber Agreement, 1983', Article 1, p. 8.
8 Ibid., Article 1(b).
9 Ibid., Article 1(d).
10 Ibid., Article 1(h).
11 Note that the recently negotiated General Agreement on Tariffs and Trade, 1994 consists of: the GATT 1947; all legal instruments that have entered into force under the GATT 1947 prior to the date of entry into force of the World Trade Organization Agreement, 1994; the instruments concluded during the Uruguay Round; and the Marrakesh Protocol to the GATT 1994. See Article 1 of the General Agreement on Tariffs and Trade, 1994, in GATT 1994: 23.
12 For Article XX(g), see GATT 1986: 38.

13  GATT document DS21/R, 'United States – Restrictions on Imports of Tuna: Report of the Panel', 3 September 1991.

14  GATT 1986: Article II, pp. 3–5; Article III, pp. 6–7; Article XI, pp. 17–18.

15  Luis V. Ople, Information Officer, GATT, personal communication (letter), 16 November 1993.

16  UN document TD/TIMBER/11/Rev.1, op. cit., Article 12, p. 11.

17  Any NGO interested in the ITTO's work that successfully presents its credentials at the start of an ITTC session is granted observer status: Lachlan Hunter of the ITTO Secretariat, personal communication to Peter Willetts, Yokohama, 23 March 1992.

18  UN document TD/TIMBER.2/3, 'Background, status and operation of the International Tropical Timber Agreement, 1983, and recent developments of relevance to the negotiation of a successor agreement', 26 February 1993, para. 48, p. 10. (This source does not provide a breakdown concerning the permanent committees responsible for these pre-projects.)

19  B.C.Y. Freezailah, ITTO Executive Director, 'Foreword' in ITTO 1990a.

20  The COICA, based in Lima, Peru, brings together 300 different Amazonian peoples united in eighty local federations and centralised in five national bodies.

21  Survival International internal document, 'Report on the XIth meeting of the ITTC, Yokohama, 28 November–4 December 1991.'

22  Francis Sullivan of the WWF–UK, personal communication (interview), Godalming, UK, 21 January 1993.

23  ITTO document PCM, PCF, PCI(V)/1, 'Pre-project proposal, labelling systems for the promotion of sustainably-produced tropical timber', 15 August 1989.

24  ITTO document PCM(V)/D.1, 'Report to the International Tropical Timber Council, Fifth Session of the Permanent Committee on Economic Information and Market Intelligence', 3 November 1989, p. 6.

25  ITTO document PCM, PCF, PCI(V)/1/Rev.2, 'Pre-project proposal, incentives in producer and consumer countries to promote sustainable development of tropical forests', 6 November 1989.

26  The author is grateful to Simon Counsell of Friends of the Earth for explaining this process to him – personal communication (interview), London, 16 February 1993.

27  ITTO document PCM, PCF, PCI(V)/1/Rev.3, 'Pre-project report on incentives in producers and consumer countries to promote sustainable development of tropical forests', February 1991.

28  ITTO document ITTC(X)/12, 'Interim report of the Expert Panel, Round Table on "The agenda for trade in tropical timber from sustainable managed forests by the year 2000", report by the Chairman of the Expert Panel', 3 June 1991, para. 8, p. 5.

29  ITTO document ITTC(X)/16, 'Decision 3(X), sustainable tropical forest management and trade in tropical timber', 6 June 1991, p. 1.

30  London Environmental Economics Centre, 'Draft final report: ITTO Activity PCM(IX)/4, the economic linkages between the international trade in tropical timber and the sustainable management of tropical forests', 16 October 1992.

31  'International Tropical Timber Council, XIII Session, 16–21 November 1992, Yokohama, statement by Austria', p. 1.

32  WWF International 'Timber labelling scheme seems inevitable', press release, 20 November 1992.

33  *GATT Focus*, November–December 1992, p. 4.

34  Here it is worth noting that no tropical-timber case has gone before a GATT panel, despite the contradictions between the ITTA 1983 and the GATT noted earlier. The Austria labelling case was resolved without recourse to a GATT panel.

35  'Position of the indigenous organisations represented by COICA at the tenth session of the International Tropical Timber Council', held at Quito, 4 June 1991; *ECO*, ITTO 10th Session, No. 5, p. 3. (*ECO* is a NGO newspaper produced at selected intergovernmental meetings, including ITTC sessions.)

36  Francis Sullivan, personal communication (interview), 21 January 1993. WWF representatives continue to attend ITTC sessions as observers.
37  An examination of ITTC lists of participants reveals that the Australian Conservation Foundation has not attended an ITTC session since 1990, and that Survival International, the Rainforest Action Network and COICA have not attended since 1991. FoE continues to attend as an observer.
38  The information on the positions of the producers and consumers is trawled from ITTO and UN documents, principally: ITTO documents PrepCom(I)/5, PrepCom(II)/2 and ITTC(XIV)/6; and UN documents TD/TIMBER.2/R.2 and TD/TIMBER.2/R.3.
39  UN document TD/TIMBER.2/L.6, 'Formal statement by the consumer members', 21 January 1994.
40  UN document TD/TIMBER.2/L.9, 'International Tropical Timber Agreement, 1994', Article 36, p. 30.
41  Ibid., Article 1, paras (g) and (m), pp. 6–7.
42  Ibid., Article 1, para. (j), p. 6.
43  Ibid., Article 1, paras (e) and (l), p. 6.

## BIBLIOGRAPHY

Arden-Clarke, C. (1990) *Conservation and Sustainable Management of Tropical Forests: the Role of ITTO and GATT*, Gland: World Wide Fund for Nature.
—— (1991) *The General Agreement on Tariffs and Trade, Environmental Protection and Sustainable Development*, Gland: World Wide Fund for Nature.
Augelli, E. and Murphy, C. (1988) *America's Quest for Supremacy and the Third World: a Gramscian Analysis*, London: Pinter.
Banuri, T. and Marglin, F.A. (1993) 'A systems-of-knowledge analysis of deforestation, participation and management', in Banuri, T. and Marglin, F.A. (eds) *Who Will Save the Forests? Knowledge, Power and Environmental Destruction*, London: Zed Books.
Brundtland, G. (1987) 'Report of the World Commission on Environment and Development', *Our Common Future*, Oxford: O.U.P.
Callister, D. (1992) *Renegotiation of the International Tropical Timber Agreement – Issues Paper, a Joint TRAFFIC/WWF Paper*, Cambridge: TRAFFIC International.
Chase, B.F. (1993) 'Tropical forests and trade policy: the legality of unilateral attempts to promote sustainable development under the GATT', *Third World Quarterly* 14(4): 749–74.
Colchester, M. (1990) 'The International Tropical Timber Organization: kill or cure for the rainforests?', *The Ecologist* 20(5): 166–73.
Cox, R.W. (1976) 'On thinking about future world order', *World Politics* 28: 175–96.
—— (1980) 'The crisis of world order and the problem of international organization in the 1980s', *International Journal* 35(2): 370–95.
—— (1981) 'Social forces, states and world orders: beyond international relations theory', *Millennium: Journal of International Studies* 10(2): 126–55.
—— (1983) 'Gramsci, hegemony and international relations: an essay in method', *Millennium: Journal of International Studies* 12(2): 162–75.
—— (1992) 'Towards a post-hegemonic conceptualization of world order: reflections on the relevancy of Ibn Khaldun', in Rosenau, J.N. and Czempiel, E.O. *Governance Without Government: Order and Change in World Politics*, Cambridge: C.U.P.
Dobson, A. (1990) *Green Political Thought*, London: HarperCollins.
Donnelly, J. (1986) 'International human rights: a regime analysis', *International Organization* 40(3): 599–642.
Forgacs, D. (ed.) (1988) *A Gramsci Reader: Selected Writings 1916–1935*, London: Lawrence & Wishart.
Frank, A.G. (1967) *Capitalism and Underdevelopment in Latin America: Historical Studies of Chile and Brazil*, New York: Monthly Review Press.

Friends of the Earth/World Rainforest Movement (1992) *The International Tropical Timber Agreement: Conserving the Forests or Chainsaw Charter?*, London: Friends of the Earth.

General Agreement on Tariffs and Trade (GATT) (1986) *The Text of The General Agreement on Tariffs and Trade*, Geneva: GATT.

—— (1994) 'The Uruguay Round, Trade Negotiations Committee: final act embodying the results of the Uruguay round of multilateral trade negotiations', document issued at Marrakesh, 15 April 1994.

Humphreys, D. (1993) 'The forests debate of the UNCED process', *Paradigms: the Kent Journal of International Relations* 7(1): 43–54.

International Tropical Timber Organisation (1990a) *Technical Series 5, ITTO Technical Guidelines for the Sustainable Management of Natural Tropical Forests*, Yokohama: ITTO.

—— (1990b) *ITTO Action Plan: Criteria and Priority Areas for Programme Development and Project Work*, Yokohama: ITTO.

—— (1991) 'ITTO guidelines on the conservation of biological diversity in tropical production forests', ITTO document ITTC(XI)/7/Rev.3, unpublished.

—— (1993) *Policy Development Series 4, ITTO Guidelines for the Establishment and Sustainable Management of Planted Tropical Forests*, Yokohama: ITTO.

Keohane, R.O. (1984) *After Hegemony: Cooperation and Discord in the World Political Economy*, Princeton, NJ: Princeton U.P.

Kratochwil, F. and Ruggie, J.G. (1986) 'International organization: a state of the art on an art of the state', *International Organization* 40(4): 753–75.

Lee, D.K. (1995) 'A Neo-Gramscian approach to international organisation: an expanded analysis of current reforms to UN development activities', in Linklater, A. and MacMillan, J. (eds) *Boundaries in Question: New Directions in International Relations*, London: Pinter.

Lohmann, L. (1991) 'Dismal green science', *The Ecologist* 21(5): 194–5.

Lummis, C.D. (1992) 'Equality', in Sachs, W. (ed.) *The Development Dictionary: a Guide to Knowledge as Power*, London: Zed Books.

Meadows, D.H. *et al.* (1974) *The Limits to Growth*, London: Pan.

Poore, D. *et al.* (1989) *No Timber Without Trees: Sustainability in the Tropical Forest*, London: Earthscan.

Renninger, J.P. (1989) 'The failure to launch global negotiations at the 11th Special Session of the General Assembly', in Kaufmann, J. (ed.) *Effective Negotiation: Case Studies in Conference Diplomacy*, Dordrecht: Martinus Nijhoff.

Ruggie, J.G. (1983) 'International regimes, transactions, and change: embedded liberalism in the postwar economic order', in Krasner, S.D. (ed.) *International Regimes*, Ithaca, NY: Cornell U.P.

Sachs, W. (1991) 'Environment and development: the story of a dangerous liaison', *The Ecologist* 21(6): 252–7.

Traynor, I. (1993) 'Another part of the forest', *The Guardian*, 16 April 1993.

Wallerstein, I. (1979) *The Capitalist World-Economy*, Cambridge: C.U.P.

—— (1984) *The Politics of the World-Economy: the States, the Movements and the Civilizations*, Cambridge: C.U.P.

Willetts, P. (1978) *The Non-Aligned Movement: the Origins of a Third World Alliance*, London: Pinter.

# Index